AN AMERICAN
YANKEE

In
King
Alfred's
Court

Dennis J. Turner

ISBN(ebook): 979-8-9942985-0-3
ISBN(Paperback): 979-8-9942985-1-0

Cover by Spike Gragard @TheBookWhisperer

Title Production by The BookWhisperer

This book is dedicated to: Geoffrey, Diana, Guy, Charles, John, and Susan.

ONE

First Impressions

Don't judge a book by its cover. Don't jump to conclusions. Don't judge a person until you have tried standing in their shoes.

My mother's oft-repeated words of wisdom resurfaced when I first peeked into Barrister Giles Adams-Smyth's office. It was in shambles. The coffee-stained, threadbare carpet might have been beige at one point in the distant past. From what I could see of the paper-strewn desk, it might have been rescued from the dump. The dusty shelves were strangely devoid of law books, but did contain what seemed to be an assortment of garage sale purchases. Usually, as an avid sailor, I liked seeing a ship model in a room, but this sloop-of-war's rigging was drooping like wet noodles. I had been told by the head clerk of Northgate Chambers to wait in Adams-Smyth's office until he arrived, so I cautiously sat on the only cushion of the leather couch that was not ripped and spilling its stuffing. As I scanned the room, I could not imagine a reputable U.S. attorney meeting with clients in such an office.

So, what was I doing there, a law professor from Dayton, Ohio? Perhaps "whim" would be the best description - or not. During the American Association of Law Schools conference in San Francisco, I struck up a casual conversation with a man who happened to be standing next to me during one of the countless mix-and-drink, or drink-and-mix, events that fill the Association of American Law Schools (AALS) meetings. His name was Michael Kennedy. He was an American trial attorney who was also a fully qualified British Barrister, and in his words, "Worked both sides of the pond." Michael described how he had navigated the challenging road to being admitted as a barrister in one of the four British Inns of Court. His journey began by becoming a "pupil" of a senior barrister who was a member of "Northgate Chambers" in Winchester, England. Was it the Pinot Gris, or me struggling to make conversation, or a whim? Whatever the motivation, I asked Michael, "Would it be possible for me to become a pupil of a barrister in England?" Michael immediately offered to send my resume to Northgate Chambers and see if any of the barristers would be willing to take me on as a pupil. I was sure nothing would come of Michael's offer and assumed it was a "pie crust promise", easily made and easily broken. Michael did as he promised, however, and much to my surprise, within two months, I received a letter from Barrister Giles Adams-Smyth offering me a pupillage.

I was gratified that Adams-Smyth considered me worthy of becoming his pupil, but I was having second thoughts. I felt like a poker player whose bluff had been called. Did I really want to uproot my family and move to England for a year? And another factor had to be included in my calculations. I had been diagnosed with a serious heart condition. Several of my coronary arteries were partially blocked, and my doctor was urging a new procedural treatment for my condition called "bypass" surgery. The mechanics of the operation did not concern me so much as the 15% chance that I might die on the operating table. I did not like the odds. So, my whim evolved into an opportunity to escape and avoid having to decide whether to undergo the bypass operation. The Dean of my law school removed the last hurdle to my accepting the pupillage by granting me a year's sabbatical, and now I was awaiting the appearance of Giles Adams-Smyth.

Giles was late, which I soon learned was usually the case. I had time to consider what I had gotten myself into for the next year. Was I indentured to a down-at-the-heels barrister who did not earn enough to have a decently furnished office? In my experience, the most poverty-stricken American attorney would take food from his children's mouths to ensure he had an office furnished to showcase his success as a lawyer. Giles's office was a testament to failure. I was tempted to sneak out, but Mom's advice kept me slumped on the couch.

Giles swooped into the room, which is the only way to describe his entry. He was almost as tall as I, wearing a dark gray pinstripe suit. He was thin with a mostly unnoticeable paunch. His face was aquiline, punctuated by a hawkish nose, centering his faded blue eyes. It was his hair, however, that dominated his appearance. He had a full head of cheek-length blond, perhaps slightly highlighted hair, like a lion's mane. Giles clearly considered it a distinguishing feature. Rather than use his hand to brush the long locks out of his eyes, he would give a quick toss of his head, flipping the wayward wisps back into place. How long had it taken Giles to master that skill? Did he ever have to repeat the head toss, spoiling the performance? It would be like a magician needing to reach into the hat twice to pull out the rabbit.

We shook hands, neither too firm nor too soft, then he dropped into his chair, clearly sizing me up. I must have passed the first test because Giles immediately launched into an itinerary of what I would be doing for the next few weeks.

If Giles were a less-than-successful barrister, there was no hint of it in his demeanor, which oozed charm and brimmed with self-confidence that bordered on arrogance. I wondered how I was going to cope with Giles's ego for twelve months. Was I expected to play Sancho Panza to Giles? I was supposed to be his pupil, but did that mean I was destined to be his lackey? Could I resist my predilection to stick pins into inflated egos?

Giles tossed me a couple of books to read on honing advocacy skills. Was I going to be tested on a homework assignment? Giles was treating me like a student who knew nothing about trying a case. If he had read my resume, Giles should have known that I had been an assistant county prosecutor, a magistrate judge, and a law professor who had taught ten or more trial practice courses and had coached dozens of mock trial teams. Did Giles assume that most American trial attorneys were only marginally competent and were not conditioned to breathe the rarified air of the barrister world? My ego was raising my hackles when Mom's advice, "Don't jump to conclusions," cooled my irritation.

Without taking a breath, Giles jumped to an entirely new topic. He asked me how I planned to get to the law courts in places like Portsmouth, Chichester, and Bournemouth. I had obviously not read the small print in the unwritten pupillage arrangement. I had assumed all the cases would be in the Crown Court of Winchester. Instead, Giles had cases scheduled all over Hampshire. I was taken aback, but I was trying to exude confidence when I said, "I'll take trains." Giles looked skeptical and responded, "You can use one of my cars." I was nervous before, but this offer oddly troubled me. Why was Giles being so chummy? We had met only 15 minutes before. There must be strings attached. I was not sure I could abide Giles's arrogant company. So, could taking what had been his ex-wife's car create more social ties that I would later regret? Would it make me indebted to Giles, creating a 21st-century version of serfdom? I also knew something about driving on British roads. The vision of me trying to navigate England's motorways, highways, lanes, and city streets while driving on the "wrong" side of the road in a borrowed car was a scary prospect. I declined the offer.

I thought the offer of his ex-wife's car was generous, but the next offer by Giles was munificent. He invited me and my family to spend a long weekend with him at his château in Normandy, France. My image of Giles as a needy barrister was replaced by an image of him greeting guests at the door of his château in a red velvet smoking jacket, sporting a white silk scarf loosely hanging from his neck. I skeptically considered his invitation as the equivalent of "Let's do lunch sometime." I assumed visiting Normandy with Giles was never going to happen, so I readily accepted with an appropriate level of excitement in my voice.

The interview ended just as abruptly as it had begun. Giles stood up, extended another brief handshake, and rushed out of the office in the same grand manner he had entered. I was left standing in his tacky office, wondering what had just happened. The only clear thing in my mind was that Giles must have accepted me as his pupil. But the nature of the relationship was nebulous at best. I had a weird and unnerving feeling that I was about to become a small planet captured by the gravitational pull of a much larger planet, and soon I would be a satellite circling planet Giles. I pondered my potential orbiting fate. If I had any chance of resisting Giles's force field, I had better escape immediately before the laws of physics made escape impossible.

My possible escape route narrowed the next day when Giles treated me to lunch at the Wickham Arms, which, according to him, was voted one of the best pubs in England for food. After scrutinizing the wine list, Giles selected a bottle of Bordeaux to complement our Shepherd's Pies. I deferred to Giles's wine selection, a deference that became a habit, and I was never disappointed with his choice. Giles was still in an offering mood and offered his mother's help next. He said she would be happy to give us an insider's tour of Winchester Cathedral, built by order of William the Conqueror in 1079, and one of the largest cathedrals in the world.

I tried to limit my wine intake to avoid befuddlement, but Giles, being the gracious host, would not permit my glass to drop below half full. Even with the socializing effect of the wine, I could not tell if Giles and I were "hitting it off." We spoke the same language and had many traditions in common, yet there was a substantial cultural gap. Giles was not U.S. Midwestern-friendly.

Although the common mantra is that the British class system no longer exists, that's mostly wishful thinking. British culture does not discourage members of the upper class from acting as if they are members of the upper class and deserve to be there. In America, members of the upper class try not to flaunt it too much. So, the owner of the most famous and expensive restaurant in town will describe himself as "just a hamburger flipper." It may be total hypocrisy, but the rich, untitled aristocrats in America pretend everyone is equal under the skin. In England, if you attended an expensive prep school, graduated from Oxford or Cambridge, and speak with the Oxbridge accent, you need not pose as the common man. You are not ostracized for acting slightly arrogant and adopting a condescending tone to those of lesser social status. Typical of Giles, he deviated from the norm. After finishing prep school, Giles hitchhiked from New York to San Francisco in his prep school blazer, communing with common folk. His adventures in America, though, did not appear to enhance his opinion of Americans. Giles's mitigating trait, and one that many Brits displayed, is the disarming ability to make fun of themselves, suggesting that they do not take themselves so seriously. The implicit suggestion is that neither should you, but not so much that you would look on them as just ordinary folk.

Our conversation over lunch reinforced my belief that Giles did not consider me to be a member of the same social class and certainly not his equal. He posed no questions about the American criminal justice system and was uninterested when I dared to opine about the differences I saw in the two systems. The British legal system was the gold standard, so there was nothing to discuss.

Giles told me there was a "Con" scheduled next week with a client, and I should sit in. I was speculating if it was my duty as a pupil to sit on the ripped couch cushion so the client could take the good cushion. I asked if the Con, which I assumed was shorthand for conference, would be in his office. Giles looked confused and said, "Oh, I never meet with a client or a solicitor in my office. We will meet in the Chambers conference room. I try to spend as little time as possible in my office." I later learned that barristers earn most of their fees when they are in the courtroom. Barristers who spend days in their offices are considered failures. To paraphrase, Mom was right again: *one shouldn't judge a barrister by his office.*

By the time dessert and the obligatory coffee were served, I was perhaps unwillingly pulled more and more into Giles's orbit, unable to escape his gravitational pull. Giles was not going to change, so if I was to avoid a miserable year, it was my attitude that needed to change, and none of my mother's adages came to mind. Three somewhat contradictory factors fed my apprehension. Giles was wasting no time assigning me chores. Ideally, sabbaticals are intended to provide professors with downtime to recoup their energy levels—a kind of vacation. I could foresee my restorative time ebbing away. Then there was my insecurity. I was an American academic hoping to stay afloat in the British legal system. Displaying my ignorance was a perilous prospect. Plus, there would be all the opportunities to inadvertently show American tactlessness. Finally, there was the problem of ego. Not Giles's—that was not likely to change, but my own ego. Could it endure regular bruising from Giles without me striking back? Was I capable of sitting respectfully at Giles's feet, acting grateful for the wisdom he would deign to share with me?

I walked down to the fast-flowing local river, the Itchen, to reflect on my attitude. Giles was like the river, rushing along, never hesitating, with twigs, branches, and leaves caught in its current. Even the mallard ducks could not resist the flow. Their attempts to paddle upstream left them swimming in place. I was like the Mallards. I had three choices. I could escape the Giles torrent by taking the first opportunity I had to pull myself up on shore and break away from the rushing water. I could resist Giles's formidable current and hope I had the energy to at least stay in place. Or, I could just surrender to the flow and resolve to accept wherever it carries me. I chose to drift.

Just surrendering, however, seemed cowardly. Would my capitulation continue to haunt? So, I needed a rationalization to justify my weak-kneed response. When I teach students trial skills,

I am constantly asking them, "What is your goal?" I want them to focus on what they hope to achieve through their direct or cross-examinations. What was my goal? Why was I in England doing a pupillage with Giles? The facile answer was clear and uncomplicated, easy to mouth when asked, "Why are you in England?" The response became a mantra. "I want to learn as much as I can about the British criminal justice system and the roles played by judges, solicitors, and barristers." The messy reason was that I was trying to ignore the precipice I was standing on with my clogged coronary arteries. I wanted to be distracted. Giving in to my concerns would create roadblocks for me to reach either of my goals. Learning requires labor. Burying one's head in the sand requires someone to pile up the sand, so I should be grateful to Giles for assigning me many tasks.

As for my other anxieties, knowledge and personal growth often arise from failure, and failure combined with embarrassment often begets the most lasting wisdom. Allowing the possibility of a bruised ego to derail both the growth of learning and the distraction, I thought, would be foolish.

TWO

Settling In

Fortunately, Giles did not have anything for me to do for a couple of days when he was going to "collect" me for a trip to the Chichester courts. So, my wife, Susan, and our eleven-year-old daughter, Nancy, had time to unpack, learn the idiosyncrasies of our townhouse, and explore Winchester. If Disney wanted to recreate a picture-perfect medieval town, it would turn out very much like Winchester. There was the wide flagstone-paved High Street guarded by a statue of King Alfred the Great with an upraised sword. King Alfred chose Winchester as his capital in the late 9th century, and the city remained the capital until the Norman Invasion of 1066. A maze of narrow, twisting lanes and alleyways connected to the High Street, where I half expected to bump into Oliver Twist or the Artful Dodger around every corner. Dominating the town was the thousand-year-old Winchester Cathedral with its soaring bell tower. It is one of the largest churches in the world, with a nave so long that a bride trailing a lengthy gown might need to stop halfway to catch her breath before reaching the high altar. Our townhouse looked out over the cathedral, and we soon became accustomed to using the bells to tell the time. On Wednesday evenings, we were entertained by the bell ringers practicing their peals. Jane Austin's tomb was in the north apse of the cathedral, and the house where she died was just around the corner from our townhouse.

Our preconceptions of the British being a bit stand-offish were dispelled on our second day in Winchester. A neighbor, Ann Bennett, a woman in her sixties, knocked on our door, introduced herself, and invited us over to tea. The tea was a "proper tea," with no tea bags floating in the cups. Instead, boiling water was poured over loose tea in a pre-warmed teapot and steeped for four minutes. The tea was then poured into delicate cups through a tiny sieve, filtering out most of the loose tea leaves. The pouring of the tea was followed by a cart full of "sweets and savories," which were assorted pastries, biscuits, and slices of fresh Harvester bread, eliminating any desire for dinner.

Ann had more in store for us the next day. She offered an exploratory drive around Hampshire. She suggested we wear our wellies because "it may be a bit muddy." Uh-oh, another cultural divide. We correctly assumed Ann meant boots.

The first stop was Winchester Hill. Although called a hill, it looked like a small mountain to us flatlanders from Ohio. Ann chose a footpath, and we followed behind. Muddy it was. Flakes of snow added to the ambiance, according to Ann. If it had been just my family, we would have decided to come back on a nicer day. But we were determined not to be wimpy Americans who could not keep pace with a sixty-five-year-old woman who survived the Blitz in WWII. I might have also wanted to test the condition of my heart. If I made the climb without dying, then perhaps my heart was not as iffy as my doctor claimed.

The climb was worth it. On the summit were the remains of an Iron Age hillfort, and almost all of Hampshire lay at our feet. Winchester Cathedral was clearly visible 12 miles away. I could not help imagining the thoughts of the fur-clad, Iron Age people clustered behind the low dirt walls, watching the Roman legions approach with their armor flashing in the sun. The legionaries' ranks would be approaching in even, solid lines, perfectly in step, horns blaring and drums beating. An irresistible force. It would be like how the Polish cavalry must have felt when they saw lines of oncoming German tanks in World War II.

The trip back down the hill was just as challenging as the hike up. It was literally "the slippery slope." We had to watch each step carefully to avoid the especially tricky spots. No matter how much care we took, it did not keep us from accumulating mud on our boots. Susan told Ann we would remove our boots before getting in her cute GM Vauxhall. Ann quickly nixed that plan— "A little good English soil never hurt anyone." Another lesson. Brits who lived through the Blitz learned to accept life's petty annoyances for what they were—petty annoyances. Not worth worrying about.

Ann's coping ability was even more apparent for the remainder of our frolic in the countryside. Ann wanted to show us the real Hampshire, which meant literally getting off the beaten path. Ann negotiated the A and B roads with remarkable speed and agility. Ann did not have a route planned, but she had a definite navigational strategy. If she were driving on a paved road, spotted a narrower paved road, and then, despite having no idea where it might lead, she took the road less traveled. Her eventual goal was to explore the narrowest unpaved lanes she could find. She called them "two trackers," two narrow tire ruts with grass down the middle. To Ann's delight, she found just what she was looking for: two parallel, muddy paths wending their way through woodlands and farm fields.

I was sure we would ultimately end up at a dead end and be stuck trying to turn the car around, but I kept my wimpy American concerns to myself. When we finally emerged from our hedged-lined lane, we did, in fact, encounter a roadblock. A farmer was moving his sheep across the two-tracker. Was Ann annoyed? Not in the least. She exclaimed, "Oh, what fun." And she was right. It was a matter of perspective—and of enjoying the moment. It was not a delay, just another turn in our meandering journey. We were watching an event that was unique in our experience: a farmer shepherding a large herd of sheep from one grazing field to another. It came with a bonus. We were mesmerized watching the farmer's collie do most of the work. She would scurry back and forth around the herd in a half circle, keeping the sheep all together, occasionally nipping at the back legs of the laggards. The farmer whistled, and then the collie would force the herd in a different direction.

When the sheep had crossed the two-rut road, it was time to return to Winchester. Ann did not ask the farmer for directions on how to get back to the main road. Another piece of Mom's advice came to mind: *There is no excuse for being lost as long as you have a mouth.* Ann did not mind being lost. She enjoyed it and liked solving the puzzle of determining where she was and how to get home. We pressed on. Eventually, we came to a gravel road, which led to a paved road that, in turn, led to an A road with signs pointing to Winchester.

Finally, on the direct route to Winchester, we arrived at another of England's many roundabouts. These traffic devices eliminate the need for traffic lights at intersections. Drivers turn left, merge onto the circle, and loop around clockwise until they get to the exit for their desired road. If the drivers happen to overshoot the exit, then they simply do another loop and try again. Ann maneuvered her car onto the circle only to discover that the exit she wanted was blocked and the road was closed. I thought surely this thwarting of her planned route would annoy Ann. I would be muttering some four-letter words. Ann's reaction? "Oh, what fun!" How lucky we were to have a next-door neighbor like Ann.

My last excursion before starting my pupillage obligations with Giles did not involve a detour but was a bit of a frolic. I took the train to Southampton, 12 miles south of Winchester, to purchase part of the school uniform Nancy was required to wear at La Sainte Teresa Academy in Romsey. I enjoyed riding British trains. I can relax and appreciate the scenery, read, daydream, or doze off. I did notice that, unlike Americans, British train riders avoided engaging in conversation with other riders, even riders they may see every day during their commutes. A good morning greeting seemed to be a breach of etiquette. In fact, the train passengers made a noticeable effort to pretend the other passengers were invisible. On my return trip from Southampton, there was a nearly naked example of passenger invisibility. A man boarded the train wearing nothing but a pair of pants and sandals, sporting a coiffure like a haystack. The temperature was zero degrees Celsius, bolstered by a brisk ten-knot breeze. I thought he might be a figment of my imagination because not one passenger in the car looked up as this half-naked man ambled past them. It was literally a case of sangfroid.

THREE

The Road To Chichester

The next morning, Giles "collected" me for a trip to Chichester. He was late, of course. I stood on the curb, wondering if I had misunderstood and whether I was supposed to meet him at Chambers. Needless to say, I was willing to take the blame—in other words, plead guilty to a crime I did not commit. Was that a foreshadowing of what happened in the Chichester Court? Apologies proved unnecessary. Giles offered none when he pulled up in his Citroën sedan.

It is often said that men, as opposed to women, are dreadful at multitasking. Giles was clearly an exception to that rule. As soon as we weaved our way through Winchester traffic and hit the M-4 motorway, Giles accelerated to 85 mph. I tried to appear calm by not saying anything and disguising my peeks at the speedometer. With one hand on the wheel and his other hand holding a mobile phone, Giles rocketed down the M4. When he was not talking on the phone, he had me read the latest filings in the Chichester case. The plan was that the defendant, Bart Cook, would plead guilty to burglary, and it would all be over in half an hour. A recent letter sent to Gilles by Bart Cook, however, confirmed that he still intended to plead guilty, but claimed he had only been waiting in the car while his brother broke into the house. Bart said in the letter that he was unaware of what his brother was doing. This was a patent lie, according to Giles, because the two brothers had been burgling houses as a team for years. Giles blew his stack and accelerated even more. I did not understand his fury because the defendant was still going to plead guilty to burglary.

To say I was not worried about getting to Chichester would be a lie. I was, however, strangely comforted by an ironic thought. Susan had prohibited me from ever riding with the Dean of the law school because he was such a terrible driver, and here I was facing death on the M4 while supposedly on a relaxing sabbatical.

Once off the M4, Giles adeptly navigated around partially flooded streets where shops had piled sandbags to block water from seeping across their thresholds. Another preconception shattered. Major English cities can be submerged in floodwaters. Giles splashed to the curb in front of the jail/courthouse and parked right next to the sign declaring "No Parking." Giles blithely retrieved a premade sign from the back seat, which declared, "BARRISTER WITH CLIENT," and set it on the dashboard.

We descended into the depths of the 18th-century jail to a small interview room. I was disappointed not to see manacles hanging from the walls. Inside, the two brothers—Calvin and our client Bart Cook—were waiting for us. Giles did not bother to shake their hands or explain who I was. Handshakes are part of my professional DNA, so I shook their hands and introduced myself. Dispensing with any pleasantries, Giles, using his I-am-quite-irritated-with-you tone, asked Bart, "Which version of your story is true? The one in which you teamed up with your brother to burgle houses, or the one in your recent letter claiming you only sat in the car and were unaware your brother was robbing houses?"

Bart stuck with the story he told in the letter. I did not understand the problem. In America, defendants often plead guilty to crimes they may not have committed, typically as part of a plea bargain with the prosecutor. And it was clear from all the circumstantial evidence that the client was aiding and abetting his brother's burglary. Giles wasn't having it. He told Bart that he would not be pleading guilty today and that he could no longer represent him in the future. If the atmosphere was tense before, it was now explosive. Calvin began shouting at Giles, and Giles snapped back, "Shut up." Suddenly, the tiny interview room shrank even further, and I realized we were toe-to-toe with two angry, well-built thugs. Giles was not fazed and escalated the rhetoric further after Calvin accused him of only being in it for the money. Giles was now angry. His professionalism was challenged. He moved even closer to Calvin and shouted that he had only earned 45 pounds and had wasted his entire morning, and if he had allowed Bart to plead guilty, he would have earned triple that amount.

Giles left no time for a rejoinder from Bart or Calvin and sailed out of the interview room with me following in his wake, carrying his robe and his wig case. I fretted that Giles was going to be in a foul mood the rest of the day, but I could not have been more mistaken. Within a minute, he had regained his composure, assuming he had truly lost it. He waltzed into the barrister's robing room like he didn't have a care in the world, greeting the other barristers and trading rapid-fire gibes and quips. It was like a football locker-room except that they were playing for opposing teams and were donning their wigs and robes instead of cleats and shoulder pads.

A client might expect total loyalty from his barrister, but client loyalty must be balanced with a barrister's duty to the "Barrister Club" and to the court. Pressing a client's cause too much might run afoul of the barrister's obligation to do nothing, which could diminish the appearance of barrister solidarity or the prestige of the court. In fact, Giles considered it a weakness for him to adopt the client's cause as his own. It would cloud his objectivity. Odd though it may seem, Giles was less concerned with winning or losing than with how well he played the game. The goal was to play well and fairly, and the verdict of unpredictable juries was largely irrelevant. Barristers and the legal profession win by litigating in a way that does not mar the integrity of the profession.

Barristers are a "Band of brothers" who are bound together by the unique, shared experience of litigating cases before judges and juries.

One aspect of that shared experience is the barrister's robing ritual. First, there is a detachable, priest—like shirt collar starched to a cardboard stiffness. The collar has two-pointed butterfly wings protruding from the front, poised for take-off. It was amusing to watch the barristers wrestling to insert the collar studs through the collar into their shirts. Second, there are two white, oblong, slightly starched barrister bands, about five inches long. They are tied at the neck and droop down like the afterthoughts of a cravat. Next is a black gown with open sleeves, much like the gowns worn at college graduations. Junior barrister gowns are made of 'stuff,' a coarse fabric which contrasts with the gowns worn by barristers who have been elevated to Queen's Counsel (QC). They are privileged to wear a silk gown and are often referred to as 'Silks.' The term might have been originally coined as an insult, but time has eroded its sting. Finally, the crowning touch, the placement of the wig. It resembles a toupee with elaborate curls and is made of horsehair. Down the back are two petite pigtails sometimes adorned with tiny bows. I noticed Giles surreptitiously using a bobby pin to keep his wig in place on top of his full head of hair.

Why this elaborate plumage? I came to England with an American prejudice against wigs, and I agreed with Thomas Jefferson, who said, "Discard the monstrous wigs which make the English judges look like rats peeping through bunches of oakum." "Tradition!" is the inevitable response. If tradition were such a powerful driver of courtroom fashion, barristers would still be wearing knee breeches and parading around in buckled shoes. The barrister's finery gives the barrister both notoriety and obscurity. When on display anywhere outside the courtroom, they are impossible to ignore. Gliding down a courthouse hallway with their robes aflutter, no one will confuse them with the somber-suited solicitor. Once inside a courtroom, however, that same plumage provides a cloak of obscurity and anonymity. I cannot say that all barristers look alike, but I can say they all share a similar appearance.

The costume hides a barrister's less flattering features—like a protruding paunch or a shiny pate—while also muting the more appealing ones, like a trim figure, a nice ass, and flowing locks. Lady Justice may be blindfolded, but jurors are not. Attractive advocates have a distinct advantage in the courtroom. I recalled the sinking feeling I had when an Adonis-like opponent walked into the courtroom and some of the women in the jury pool emitted an audible gasp. Giles had that kind of star quality, but it was diminished by the drab, shapeless robe and dowdy wig. The wig also inhibited his hair-flipping trick.

When Giles was properly attired, we walked into the courtroom, a three-story affair resembling a king's throne room. The bewigged judge was perched behind a bench raised so high that it was impossible to hand any document to the judge without first handing it to an usher in the well of the court. The usher would then pass the document up to the court clerk, positioned one level above, who would hand the document up to the judge.

Giles made a ceremonial slight bow to the judge, acknowledging respect for judicial authority without a hint of obsequiousness. Although bowing to anyone was contrary to American customs, I followed his lead.

Our case was called, and Giles explained to Judge Edwards that the defendant would not enter a plea and, furthermore, that he was withdrawing as counsel. Ordinarily, judges are not pleased to have their tightly scheduled dockets cavalierly disrupted by lawyers making procedural requests that interfere with a smooth-running docket. American judges are especially annoyed when lawyers attempt to remove themselves from a case and require the defendant to hire a new attorney, causing considerable delay in the proceedings. Judge Edwards only looked bored, thanked Giles, and told his clerk to set another day for entering a plea.

We returned to the robing room, where Giles shed his

plumage and handed me his robe and wig box for me to carry to his un-ticketed Citroën waiting for us in the no-parking zone.

The journey back to Winchester was no slower than the trip to Chichester, except that the windows were wide open and Giles's CD was blasting out a Mahler symphony. I hate Mahler. I shouted my questions about what had just happened, and he shouted his answers back. I asked him, "What was the big deal about the defendant pleading guilty to a crime he may not have committed in the hope of getting a reduced sentence? In America, that scenario is acted out in courtrooms every day."

Giles said, "David, he lied to me."

"So what?" I responded, "American clients routinely lie to their lawyers." Giles was clearly taken aback by the unprofessional behavior of American attorneys, who casually tolerate a client's falsehoods. Giles proceeded to explain to me the "vouching business". In England, barristers vouch for the truthfulness of their witnesses, including clients, when they speak to the court, even if not under oath. Barristers represent to the court that they are persuaded that their witnesses believe their testimony to be the truth. A barrister may correctly and wisely surmise that their witnesses' version of the facts may be at odds with the actual events; nevertheless, if barristers genuinely think their clients are telling the truth as they see it, then allowing clients to tell their version of the facts to the court is entirely ethical. The ethical dilemma for Giles in this case, however, was that the defendant provided two conflicting accounts of how the robbery occurred. Both descriptions could not be true. Simply, Giles was lied to. He could not accept that the latest tale was one the client truly believed was true. It was obvious to Giles that the defendant would tell whatever version of events that would help his case. Giles could not vouch for the client's honesty to the judge.

At this early point in our relationship, I was not eager to challenge Giles's pronouncements. I was certainly not going to try drowning out the roar of the wind through the open windows and the brass of a Mahler symphony, while blasting along the M-4 at the now reduced speed of 80 mph.

Later, in a more conducive atmosphere, aided by a glass of wine, I posed my questions to Giles. "How was pleading guilty lying to the judge?" I contended that Bart might have believed he did not know what his brother was up to, sneaking into strangers' homes. But a jury—or a judge—hearing his explanation would probably not have believed a word of it, and convicted him anyway. That guilty verdict was more likely since Bart had a prior robbery conviction for waiting in the car while his brother burgled homes. I posed a hypothetical question to Giles.

"If an accused believes that he is likely to be found guilty as charged by the jury, even if he believes there are facts which, if true, might support a claim of innocence, shouldn't the accused have the right to plead guilty in the hope of mitigating his possible sentence?"

My argument fell flat. As far as Giles was concerned, Bart lied to him, and he was marked with a scarlet 'L' for liar. Giles could not, in good conscience, call and vouch for someone as a witness whom he believed was a liar.

People do not always tell the truth. Their version of events may bear little resemblance to reality. Should that disqualify them from having a lawyer? Giles's seemingly rigid attitude was more nuanced than it first appeared. I learned early on that Giles might assert definitive positions on topics only to moderate his beliefs in the face of reasonable counter-arguments. Rather than being annoyed by my challenging his pronouncements, he welcomed my opposition, more evidence of his self-confidence. He was content to adjust his beliefs in the face of contrary evidence. His self-worth was not based on needing to be 'right' all the time. It arose from his ability to analyze the facts objectively and assess their accuracy, even if they undermined his preconceived assumptions. My reasoning on this issue did not induce Giles to modify his views. Bart had provided two contradictory versions of the same event. One version had to be a lie. Giles could not vouch to the court that whatever version Bart would tell was true. Furthermore, even if Giles accepted Bart's latest version of events as true, then Bart would not be guilty of the crime with which he was charged, and his pleading guilty would be a lie. Either way, Giles would be helping Bart lie to the court.

The next question I tactfully asked was about the ease with which Giles was allowed by the judge to extract his client painlessly, like a bad tooth. In the U.S., judges are not keen on attorneys abandoning clients once the attorney-client relationship has been established. Disliking one's client was not sufficient grounds for a judge to allow an attorney to drop out of a case. A client is free to dismiss his or her attorney for any reason. An attorney, however, will have to present a persuasive argument to end their representation. Saying, "Your honor, I do not believe everything my client is telling me," might elicit a knowing smile from the judge, but would not be sufficient grounds for abandoning a client. In the U.S., to justify withdrawing from a case, an attorney must allege that the client is insisting on carrying out a crime or is acting in a morally repugnant way. Of course, saying to the judge who will ultimately sentence your client that your client's in-court statements may be lies is also throwing your client under the bus.

So, I asked Giles why the judge allowed him to jettison his client so easily with little more than a wink and a nod. Giles answered my question with a question, a tactic that became quite familiar to me. He asked whether in America, people accused of a crime hired attorneys to represent them. Hedging, like any good lawyer, I agreed that it was what happened in many cases. And, Giles continued, "If the lawyer decides that the client is going to be a pain in the ass and the relationship was destined to be fraught with regular conflict, can the lawyer reject the client?" Again, I had to agree, since in my own practice I had often not accepted as a client a person whom I thought would be a pain in the ass. Giles gave me an annoying, condescending smile and said, "I do not have that luxury, David."

He then told me how barristers acquire clients who have been charged with a crime. An accused cannot engage a barrister directly. In fact, not only would it be unethical for barristers to advertise their services, but they also cannot be listed in the British equivalent of the Yellow Pages. The accused must first hire a solicitor, who then considers possible barristers to represent the accused in court. A solicitor usually has a few favorite barristers, but the solicitor cannot approach those barristers directly. A solicitor must contact the Clerk[1] in the Chambers where the barrister has an office. The solicitor might ask about the availability of a specific barrister on the court appearance date, or the Clerk may suggest a barrister in Chambers who would be available for the court appearance. If the solicitor agrees to engage a barrister, and that barrister's diary is open on that date, without consulting the barrister, the Clerk commits the barrister to the case and negotiates the barrister's fee.

Giles said, "Barristers operate under the cab rank rule." Having been to many airports where I wanted to hire a cab, I was familiar with the phrase. Outside the airport arrivals gate, the available cabs line up. The driver of the first cab in line has no choice but to take the person who is first in the passenger line. That person may look like he spent the night in a homeless shelter and may want to take the cab to a location the cabbie would rather avoid, but the cabbie cannot say, "No, thank you."

According to Giles, the cab rank rule also applies to solicitors hiring barristers. If the barrister's schedule, kept by the Chamber's Clerk, indicates the barrister is available on the scheduled court date, the barrister cannot refuse to represent the client.

Furthermore, Giles added, a barrister may not actually meet

---

1. It is often said that the Clerk, pronounced "CLARK," is the CEO a Chambers. The Head Clerk is the "Rainmaker" for Chambers who secures work for the barristers by marketing Chambers and building relationships with Solicitors. The Clerk is largely in control of the Diaries of all the barristers in Chambers and negotiates and collects barrister fees. The Clerk is also responsible for budgeting and financial planning along with accounting and bookkeeping, plus training junior clerks. In return, the Clerk receives a percentage of all fees collected.

face-to-face with a client until the first hearing date in court. Even then, the conversation may be limited to an exchange of pleasantries in the hallway outside the courtroom. There is no opportunity for the barrister to be 'warm and fuzzy.' The barrister has no interest in trying to build a client's trust, which many American attorneys believe is essential for an attorney-client relationship. Giles was dismissive of the idea that it was necessary for a barrister to win a client's trust. To Giles, a barrister, by definition, could be trusted to advocate for the client to the best of his ability, and in his mind, his best was superior to most other barristers. If one of his clients, for some strange reason, did not trust him, then that was the client's problem, not his. Giles would not condescend to try to change the client's mind.

Not surprisingly, personality conflicts between clients and barristers were not uncommon. That kind of toxic relationship would not be beneficial to the client's case. As Giles pointed out to me, the relationship with the Chichester client was more than toxic. They almost came to fisticuffs. Judges were aware that sometimes clients and barristers were incompatible and allowed barristers to abandon their clients with little more than a wink and a nod.

Not for the first time, or the last, I had to concede the logic of Giles's argument. He enjoyed the role of teacher, and yet he did not play the role of the sage on the stage. I sensed he liked me challenging him, so I became less reluctant to question his analysis, strategies, and tactics in cases. Giles was exceedingly self-confident, approaching the point of arrogance, but his confidence was seasoned with enough modesty to listen to and even adopt another person's ideas, but only if he believed them to be better. A less confident person tenaciously hangs on to his opinions even when faced with strong contrary evidence. Another Giles lesson, "Conceding an argument when you are wrong not only makes you wiser, it enhances your self-confidence."

FOUR

In The Winchester Court

Three weeks into my pupillage, on a Thursday afternoon, like Christmas presents, two neat stacks of file folders, addressed to Giles, arrived at Chambers, both tied up with red ribbons and topped off with a bow. They were the case files for criminal cases scheduled to be tried in the next two weeks, the first one starting the following Monday. Giles knew nothing about the cases except that the Clerk had agreed with a solicitor that Giles would represent the defendants in the trials. Giles had no choice under the cab rank rule. The case that had been on Giles's schedule for the next two weeks was postponed, so unless Giles had penciled in a vacation for those two weeks, he was on the hook. Of course, Giles was not some reluctant fish that needed an enticing lure to bite. Both he and Northgate Chambers would be well compensated. It is a fact of life that if a barrister is not in a courtroom trying cases, no fees are coming into the Chamber's coffers.

I was stunned by the prospect of trying two serious felony cases in two weeks, cases we knew nothing about. Giles appeared unfazed. Last-minute case assignments were not uncommon for barristers "doing crime." He proposed that over the weekend, he would concentrate on the first case. For my part, I should digest the material in the brief packet for the second trial and draft a summary, outlining the issues, the essential facts, and who the key witnesses would likely be. The case beginning in four days was a child abuse case, and the next case, my case, was a rape case. If I still had any lingering worries that Giles considered me a gofer with a Juris Doctor degree, they vanished when I carried that beribboned pile of folders home.

The child abuse trial did not begin until 11:30 a.m. on Monday, so I spent some time chatting with a few of the court personnel. I explained why I was visiting the Winchester Courts. A court bailiff then suggested I go into Court 1, where Justice Marshall would be doing a summing-up to the jury in a manslaughter case. She added that Justice Marshall was a visiting High Court Judge and was considered one of the best. I was not sure what a summing-up of a case by the judge entailed. I assumed it was similar to an American judge instructing the jury on what the law required parties to prove and how much evidence is required for the parties to meet that burden.

Court 1 was the largest courtroom in the Winchester Courthouse and the first one I had an opportunity to visit. When I walked into the courtroom, I was the only person in a very large space. The jury box was immediately apparent, with fourteen chairs, and was isolated on the right side of the courtroom. The judge's bench towered over the courtroom. I thought it curious that there was no witness chair adjoining the judicial bench. There was a kind of booth positioned on the left side of the room where a witness had to stand while testifying. The distance of the witness box from the jury necessitated the use of a microphone by the witness. I speculated how having to stand during one's testimony might affect the quality of a witness's testimony. Nervous, shaky legs would be noticed by the jury. A vigorous, challenging cross-examination might literally make a witness weak at the knees. But where should I sit? I chose what looked like a public gallery on the same level as the judge's bench on the opposite side of the courtroom. After taking a seat, however, I began to have doubts. Why were there only four chairs, and why was there glass between the chairs and the rest of the courtroom? The penny dropped. I was sitting in the prisoner/defendant dock. It would have been amusing and embarrassing if the defendant and his two guards had chosen that moment to enter the dock. I scampered to the only seating area remaining in the courtroom, which was for the public. I was the sole person in the public gallery, except for a newspaper reporter who stayed there just long enough for me to tell him that the only thing happening was Judge Marshall's summation in the case. He said, "It was not worth his time," and left.

After the jury and the barristers were seated, Judge Marshall entered in his scarlet robe and long wig. There was bowing all around, which I assumed meant I should bow too. The judge immediately began to sum up the facts of the case for the jury. The barristers had already delivered their final arguments the previous Friday. As an American lawyer, the process of a judge summarizing the facts for the jury was completely foreign and improper. In theory, American judges are permitted to "comment" on the evidence. The reality, however, is that if they do wander down the comment road, they are much more likely to be reversed by the Court of Appeals. The appeals court would assume that if an American jury got the slightest hint of how the presiding judge thought the case should be decided, the jurors would follow the judge's lead like a pack of lemmings, undermining the jury's fundamental role of being the final arbiter of a defendant's guilt or innocence.

Judge Marshall took no chances that the jury might miss the hints he was dropping about the verdict he thought proper. He launched into a summary of the facts, stopping just short of telling the jury it should acquit the defendant. Because Judge

Marshall was putting his judicial thumb on the scale in favor of the accused, it was not likely he would ever be reversed by an appeals court since the Crown had no right to appeal a jury verdict of not guilty.

Judge Marshall began by reminding the jury of the glowing testimony of the character witnesses called by the defense. They described the defendant as a paragon of virtue. Judge Marshall also pointed out that the Crown Prosecutor did not introduce any contrary evidence to the litany of praise. Then, in a clever tactic to make his summation appear neutral and balanced, he instructed the jury, "Of course, you cannot decide this case on the basis of sympathy." Like a good sailor, he tacked again to ensure the jury knew which way the judicial wind was blowing. "On the other hand, the defendant's sterling character could be taken into consideration in assessing the credibility of the defendant's testimony and whether a person like the defendant would throw the first punch."

During a short recess, a loo break perhaps, Judge Marshall's usher approached me and asked, "Justice Marshall wanted me to ask who you are, and why are you here?" I wondered if I was in violation of some unwritten British code of conduct. The usher seemed satisfied with my answer, and the court reconvened.

Justice Marshall did not want to leave a jury verdict too much to chance, so he provided a "hook" for the jury on which they could hang a "not-guilty" verdict. He explained that if they believed a punch was thrown, the Crown had the burden to make them "sure" the punch was not thrown in self-defense. That was a high burden for the prosecuting barrister, but it was an especially high hurdle when the one witness who literally had a ringside view of the fight was dead. I had little doubt in my mind that the jurors would acquit the defendant, but only after they had had their free lunch.

As I was leaving the courtroom, the court usher approached me with an offer I could not refuse. He invited me to have lunch with Justice Marshall in his chambers on Friday. I was stunned.

To be asked to share soup and a sandwich with a High Court Judge, who also sits in the House of Lords, was like receiving an invitation from a Supreme Court Justice to drop by his judicial chambers for a light meal. I eagerly accepted.

In another courtroom, the child abuse case began at 11:30, and I was intrigued by the trial process from the outset. A twelve-person jury was impaneled and introduced. Judge Griffin asked our client, Ben O'Neill, if he had an objection to any of the jurors. Curiously, the judge did not ask Giles. Unless Ben happened to know one of the jurors, there was no reason to excuse a juror from sitting in judgment in the case. Neither barrister had a right to *voir dire*[1] the jurors and ask them if there was something in their past that would disqualify them from being fair and impartial jurors. Each juror was sworn in separately while holding a Bible. Judge Griffen did ask if the juror knew the defendant or the barristers, and asked Ben if he had any reason to dismiss the juror. If the juror happened to be Ben's drinking mate, would Ben have mentioned it? Unlike jury selection in the U.S., barristers had no peremptory challenges, which would allow the barristers to excuse a juror for no reason other than the barrister having an intuitive sense that a specific juror might harbor a bias against someone or

---

1. Voir Dire examination means "To speak the Truth." It is theoretically designed to provide prosecuting and defense counsel the opportunity to question potential jurors about their backgrounds, biases, prejudices and if they have any connection to the case being tried with the goal of impaneling an impartial jury. The reality is less idealistic. Attorneys use the opportunity of voir dire so shmooze potential jurors, ingratiating themselves if possible. Another less idealistic goal is for a lawyer to identify potential jurors who might be biased in favor of his or her client's case and maneuver to keep them on the jury.

something in the case. Consequently, the first twelve jurors who entered the jury box were the twelve jurors ultimately impaneled.

The next surprise occurred during the opening statement phase, or more precisely, what did not occur during that phase. After the prosecuting barrister, Collin Slater, finished his restrained opening speech explaining to the jury the essence of the Crown's case, I looked at Giles. He just sat there. Was his silence part of his strategy, building a bit of anticipatory suspense in jurors? Apparently not. Judge Griffin directed Prosecutor Slater to call his first witness. Did Giles waive his opening speech? Was he daft? No American attorney would ever waive the opportunity to address the jury before any witnesses were called. Study after study confirmed that many jurors were already predisposed to one side or the other after hearing opening statements. If defense counsel does not tell the jury about the defendant's side of the case at the outset of the evidence, it is like a batter who comes to the plate with one strike against him. No, Giles was not crazy. In England, the defense counsel must wait until the conclusion of the Crown's case before giving an opening statement.

The first witness for the Crown was Detective Sergeant Barnes, who investigated the case. Detective Barnes set the stage for the testimony of the key prosecution witness, the mother of the allegedly abused child, Jessica O'Neill. Giles's desultory cross-examination of the detective was not inspiring. He was going through the motions, asking just enough questions to introduce his voice and his persona to the jury.

Jessica O'Neill testified next. Giles's cross-examination was devastating. He gently took Jessica through a litany of prior statements she had made and when she had made them. Every one of those prior statements that Giles introduced supported Ben's version of events—that he had never struck his stepdaughter, Robyn. The use of prior inconsistent statements is a fundamental tactic used by cross-examiners, a skill my Trial Practice students had to demonstrate repeatedly. Once the witness concedes the inconsistency, however, it is often dangerous to ask follow-up questions, as this may offer an opportunity for the witness to explain or mitigate the inconsistency. Ever the risk taker, Giles spent the next half-hour reviewing those same statements and getting the witness to admit she had lied when she had told multiple people that Ben had **not** struck the child. I squirmed in my chair when Giles violated another cardinal rule with the next question. "So now, under oath, you told my learned friend during his examination that Ben regularly struck Robyn. You are now saying that is the truth?" She readily agreed to that. The trap was set, and Giles sprung it. He induced Jessica to admit that all her prior statements about O'Neill not striking her daughter had occurred before June 25th.

Furthermore, Jessica had to agree that all the statements she made alleging Ben had regularly struck her daughter were made after June 25th. Prosecutor Slater looked uneasy. He knew what was coming next.

"Isn't it true, madam, on June 25th your husband, Ben O'Neill, walked out on you, calling you a fat, flabby whore?" When Jessica answered "Yes." Giles flashed his can-you-believe-that look to the jury and sat down. I whispered to Giles, "Jessica knows how General Custer felt." The prosecutor did not attempt to rehabilitate Jessica on the redirect examination. She was damaged goods.

Later in the afternoon, Giles, the solicitor, and I were reviewing the testimony of Jessica. Giles threw out a question. "If Jessica was going to lie, why didn't she go nuclear and allege Ben had sexually abused Robyn?" Two years earlier, Social Services had investigated the family about possible sexual abuse, but nothing came of it. Giles said that if Jessica alleged Ben had sexually abused Robyn, the jury would be prejudiced against Ben even if there was no evidence to support Jessica's accusation. I asked if I could offer a possible explanation. I reminded Giles that when Social Services was doing its investigation of possible sexual abuse of Robyn, Jessica—the wife and mother—was also implicated as a possible aider and abettor of the abuse. If she accused Ben of sexual abuse in our case, she would be opening the door to questions about her role in the sexual abuse investigation by Social Services. Giles practically jumped out of his chair and complimented me on my excellent analysis.

Prosecutor Slater rested his case-in-chief, and Giles's opening speech was scheduled for the next day. On our way out of the courthouse, I quipped about how I was feeling sorry for Collin Slater, who had to prosecute a case with such a cast of characters for witnesses.

Giles's opening speech the next day did not disappoint. I was 'chuffed'[2] that his opening line was inspired by the casual comment I made about feeling sorry for the prosecuting barrister. The thought crossed my mind that perhaps I should be charging Giles royalties for using my material. Giles began with, "Ladies and Gentlemen, you may be feeling some sympathy for my honorable colleague, the Crown Prosecutor, who must base his case on the pitiful witnesses he had to call. But you cannot allow sympathy for the prosecutor to sway your judgment."

It was time for our case-in-chief, and one potential witness was Aiden Hutchinson, Jessica's uncle. Giles asked me to read Aiden's witness statement and advise him whether we should call him as a witness. I read Aiden's statement, and in light of our defense theory, I concluded that on balance, the positives

---

2. Very pleased

outweighed the negatives. We then discussed the "safe" questions we could ask Aiden. A safe question is one that elicits a useful piece of information but does not open the door to painful and dangerous cross-examination questions. Giles rapidly wrote down the possible questions in his illegible script.

The problem was that it would be unethical under British criminal procedure for Giles to review the list of questions with Aiden. That would be prepping the witness, which is forbidden. Giles proposed a workaround. His plan had all the ingredients of a farce. Giles handed me the list of questions and directed me to find an interview room, where I would go over the list of questions with Aiden to hear how he would answer them. I asked, "Why me? Wouldn't it be better if you heard the answers yourself rather than relying on my summary of what they were?"

He said, "It would be unethical for me to discuss with Aiden the questions I planned to ask him when he took the stand." In the U.S., we call that rehearsal "woodshedding" or "sandpapering." We would regard it as practically malpractice not to prep witnesses shortly before their testimony, since both the attorney and the witness need to be on the same page, so to speak.

I collared Aiden in the hallway and escorted him toward an available interview room. I began asking Aiden about his work, where he lived, if he had a family, and if he had ever testified before, chatting like we had just met at a pub. It was my way of establishing rapport with a witness and building a sense of trust. In America, it is one of the basic trial skills taught in law schools. Apparently, it is not the barristers' way. They are not interested in building rapport. When I was halfway through the list of questions, Giles poked his head in the door and did not seem pleased with my progress. Giles swooped into the room, sat down, and acted like Aiden was invisible, not introducing himself or greeting him in any way. A delicate ballet commenced, in which Giles was able to question a witness while dancing around an ethical violation of preparing a witness. Giles would direct me to ask Aiden a question from the list, Aiden would answer, and I would repeat the answer to Giles. Giles did get Aiden's answers to his questions, but he did not get the important information cached in Aiden's memory. That tidbit of evidence was volunteered by Aiden during my casual, open-ended questioning. Giles's questions were focused on the relationship between Robyn and Ben. My questions led Aiden to mention that he had seen Jessica smacking Robyn on several occasions. When I told Giles about Aiden's comments about Jessica and Robyn, he immediately added them to the questions he would ask Aiden during his direct examination.

For the most part, our case-in-chief went smoothly. Its strength was based on the weakness of the prosecution's case. Nevertheless, Giles still had to put Ben, our client, in the witness box, a move that was always a risky proposition. Ben did okay with only one wrinkle. He tried to *gild the lily*, a bogus tactic witnesses often adopt. They try to make good testimony look better by adding exaggerated testimonial flourishes. It often backfires. A cross-examiner can focus on the exaggerations, chip off the phony gilt, and undermine the credibility of the witness. Ben tried to portray himself as a kind, gentle stepfather, with the "milk of human kindness by the quart in every vein," never raising his hand or his voice to a troubled six-year-old stepdaughter.

Fortunately, Prosecutor Slater made no attempt to tarnish the defendant's lily. Evidence rules also prevented him from asking Ben about a slew of theft-by-deception charges Ben was facing and to which he planned to plead guilty.

Slater's cross-examination of Ben was not without a bit of farcical humor, which damaged the prosecutor's credibility. In the middle of his questioning of Ben, Slater pulled out of his pocket an enormous, bright red bandana worthy of a rodeo star and noisily blew his nose.

The final speeches and Judge Griffin's summation were anticlimactic; everyone in the courtroom, including the prosecutor, knew what the jury would decide. I predicted the jury would return a not-guilty verdict in an hour. I was wrong. They returned a verdict of not guilty in less time than I thought it would take to pick a foreperson.

The real excitement occurred later in the barristers' robing room. Giles was convinced someone had "pinched" his wig. To an unsophisticated Ohioan like me, such a caper seemed more like a cause for humor. Why would anyone want a bunch of knotted horsehair? The mystery was solved a few minutes later when a barrister rushed into the robbing room and confessed to taking Giles's wig, thinking it was his.

Ben was greatly relieved by the verdict. Although the sentence for child endangerment was shorter than what he was facing for the theft-by-deception charges, Ben had been adamant about not pleading guilty to child endangerment. His steadfast resolve had convinced me early in the case that he was innocent. He was more than willing to accept the stigma of being labeled a thief, but not a child abuser.

FIVE

Largesse

The next afternoon, I met Giles at the Crown Courts to talk about upcoming cases. As we were walking down the hall, a security guard and a bailiff said, "Hello, Professor Turner." Giles looked surprised, or as much as Giles lets himself look surprised, and said, "I see you have quickly become well known around here." There was a lesson in that—for Giles, but I was not about to impart it. People respond well when someone, even a complete stranger, takes an interest in their lives. Their cloak of invisibility is removed, and they are recognized as real individuals with their own stories to tell. All I had done was provide the opportunity for bailiffs and security guards to share a little bit about their lives, and they remembered me.

Giles said he was working late, so I invited him to take "potluck" and have dinner with us. He asked if he was supposed to bring a dish to share. Not for the first or last time, Giles pointed out that I had used the wrong word. I had thought that taking "potluck" meant being invited to dine with a family on the spur of the moment and having to eat whatever was on the menu for that evening, or whatever was simmering in the pot. Giles explained that the term had been in use for hundreds of years and meant being invited to dine, but it also obligated a person to bring a dish to share. I apologized and said he was not obliged to bring anything, and I had no idea what Susan was planning to cook that night. Giles was delighted with the offer to take potluck.

It was not wise for me to bring a guest to dinner without checking with Susan first, especially a guest who is known to be a connoisseur of fine cuisine. Fortunately, our neighbor had given Susan a wild-caught Scottish smoked salmon that morning. Susan had also made her vegetarian chili, which was accompanied by fresh-baked Harvester multi-grain bread. Giles was delighted with the meal. He had brought the wine, so it was necessarily good stuff.

Soon after arriving, Giles looked around our sitting room and said, "This will not do." He said our walls needed some legitimate artwork, our floor lamps were tired, and our couch looked lonely without a decent coffee table. When Giles sat down for dinner, he declared our dining room chairs totally inadequate for comfort and that he would loan us four decent chairs. Since two of our chairs were wobbly, Susan readily accepted Giles's offer.

Early on during the dinner, Giles focused his attention on Susan. He was not flirting with Susan but engaging her in a way that made her feel special. With her raven hair, willowy figure, and iridescent green eyes, men often flirted with Susan, but she had cultivated an invulnerability to such obvious masculine ploys. Giles's tactic was brilliant and explained why women were so attracted to him. He avoided compliments about a woman's looks and concentrated on discovering the depths of her entire persona. Giles's strategy was not calculated to smooth his way into a woman's bed. Giles was genuinely interested in gaining an insight into a woman's character. It worked with Susan, and I was a bit jealous. Susan was normally a quiet and reticent person. Still, Giles managed to break down her instinctive barriers, and she gave a full summary of her life with little need for prompting questions. It was clear to Susan that Giles was eager to hear her story. Susan talked about growing up in Springfield, Massachusetts, and going off to Trinity College, an all-girls school in

Washington, D.C., and majoring in biology. Giles asked how she met me.

"It was a blind date for the Trinity Junior Prom. I was wearing a black spaghetti-strap sheath dress, and David was in a black tuxedo with a gaudy plaid bowtie and cummerbund. I hated the tie and cummerbund but said nothing at the time. A few months later, I suggested he deep-six the plaid and get a black tie and black cummerbund."

When Giles heard this, he knew he had found common ground with Susan, namely, me being sartorially challenged. Susan regaled Giles with how, until she sorted me out, I mixed blacks with blues, wore polyester suits, combined checked sport coats with paisley ties, and perhaps the worst getup was wearing long boxer shorts that were longer than my tennis shorts. With Giles's encouragement, Susan told how she had enlisted the help of a faculty secretary to assess my clothes at the beginning of the day and, if necessary, suggest a change of tie or a shirt. Susan said she knew she was making progress when the faculty secretary told her that I "no longer looked like a doofus," and my students' teaching evaluations included comments such as "Shirts better, suits the same."

At that point, Giles had the decency to cease his and Susan's combined assault on my wardrobe and bring Nancy into the conversation. He asked her how she liked her school and if she was enjoying her time in England. I sensed Nancy regarded those questions as typical patronizing questions adults ask pre-teens. She responded with predictable, terse answers. Giles realized he was not making any progress in fostering a conversation with Nancy, so he shifted to another topic. He asked Nancy if she participated in any sports, to which she answered, "Yes, I like to sail." Giles was still struggling, and he took an unexpected tack. He asked Nancy if she had read any Arthur Ransome books. Nancy's face changed from teenage ennui to a devotee's enthusiasm. Nancy told Giles she had read all of Ransome's books, and Giles said he, too, had read most of them when he was growing up, and he particularly enjoyed the sailing adventures. The next ten minutes were spent by Giles and Nancy discussing their favorite Ransome books and characters; Nancy preferred *Swallows and Amazons,* and Giles liked *Peter Duck.* The bond Giles had hoped for was being forged. He also encouraged Nancy to describe racing a small boat like her Sunfish. Nancy was becoming another Giles convert.

Giles was unprepared, however, when Nancy solicited his opinion on a hypothetical legal issue involving the hearsay rule. Nancy asked Giles to assume a defendant, Peter, was charged with burglary, and part of the evidence against him was a comment made in a pub to a mate, Clay, which was overheard by the bartender. According to Tom, the bartender, Peter told Clay, "People are so careless. I didn't have to break into the Smith house because the owners had left their door unlocked." Nancy followed up with a leading question to Giles: "That out-of-court statement by Peter is hearsay, correct?"

Giles agreed, "Yes, it is hearsay."

Nancy then asked, "Will Tom be able to testify in court about what Peter told Clay?"

Again, Giles agreed, "Yes."

Without missing a beat, Nancy asserted, "But you just said it was hearsay."

I then recognized the trap Nancy had set for Giles. It was like the trap I used on members of my mock trial team when Nancy was sitting in on the team's practice sessions. Giles took the bait. "What Peter said to Clay is an admission of an opposing party and is an exception to the hearsay rule.

Nancy sprang the trap. "I do not think what Peter told Clay is hearsay at all, and there is no need to create an exception to justify its admissibility." Giles was intrigued and asked Nancy to explain. First, Nancy asked Giles, "Isn't it true that the purpose behind the hearsay rule is to protect the right to cross-examine witnesses and test the accuracy of their memories and perceptions and disclose to the jury facts that suggest a witness is being less than truthful?"

Giles had to agree with Nancy's premise. Nancy concluded, "Therefore, since the out-of-court statement was made by Peter, there is no need for Peter to cross-examine himself to test his memory, perception, or his truthfulness. Peter is the best person to know the accuracy of his memory and perception of his conversation at the pub. Peter would certainly know whether he was lying when he told Clay about the unlocked door. No need to cross-examine, not hearsay."

I expected Giles to accept Nancy's challenge and contest her analysis of the issue. Instead, he said, "I think you are right." Giles once again demonstrated his shrewd insight into human psyches, even that of a pre-pubescence girl. He conceded the battle, knowing that by doing so, he would prevail in his campaign to convert Nancy into another admirer.

When it was time for dessert and coffee, Giles said that I had to do something about my suits. He felt they were clearly not fitted by a tailor. The material was obviously a blend, and it did not enhance my professional appearance. He asked if I had ever purchased a bespoke suit. The question was difficult to answer because I had no idea what a bespoke suit was. Giles was delighted to enlighten me. It literally means "to give an order for it to be made." That was no help, so Giles described the process of making a bespoke suit. First, you consult with a tailor to select the fabric, the lining, and the style. Then, the tailor makes detailed measurements of every part of your body. Based on those measurements, the tailor chalks out a pattern on the fabric and cuts the pattern out with shears. The pieces are assembled and loosely basted together with white thread. You then return to the shop weeks later, put on the suit, and the tailor re-measures, making new adjustments and drawing more chalk lines. Only then does the tailor do the final stitching and pull out all the white basting thread. More weeks pass, and you return to the tailor for the final—perhaps—fitting. Tweaks may be required. So-called permanent stitching is gingerly removed, and the suit is hopefully stitched for the final time. Although weeks later, when you try on the suit, the tailor may still require a few more alterations.

After hearing Giles's description of a bespoke suit, I could definitely say that I had never owned one, all my suits being off the rack. To Giles, this was like admitting to wearing flour sacks, so he insisted that I needed to purchase a bespoke Savile Row suit. I was an unsophisticated Midwesterner, but I had heard of Savile Row, the place where British royalty shopped, and thousands of pounds could be spent on a single sport coat. I told Giles he would just have to endure the embarrassment of a poorly dressed pupil.

Like the skilled barrister making his case to a jury, Giles had been setting me up for his pitch. He told me that he knew how I could obtain a bespoke Savile Row suit for a mere pittance. He said that was how he had been clothing himself in Savile Road suits for years. Giles explained that there was a tailor located just off Savile Row by the name of Nelson & Pitts. They had carved out a unique niche for themselves and sold slightly used suits, including suits from the best Savile Row tailors, at huge discount prices. Nelson and Pitts had worked out an arrangement with most of the undertakers in the London metro area. They bought suits that were used to clothe male corpses lying in their coffins. Families of the deceased always supplied the best suits worn, or sometimes never worn, by the deceased.

In most cases, the families declined the undertaker's offer to return the suits. Since it would be a tremendous waste for such fine suits to rot in the ground or be turned into ashes, Nelson & Pitt resold those Savile Row suits for a comparable trifle. For a small additional fee, the tailors at Nelson and Pitt will alter the slightly used suits to fit the bodies of the new owners. The only wrinkle, so to speak, was that the new owner not be too squeamish about wearing a suit that had been last worn by a corpse. Giles estimated I could buy a Savile Row suit for between £500 and £1000. I am not sure if I was deterred by the thought of wearing a dead man's suit, but the price was still $800 more than the cost of my best suit. So, I told Giles, "But I, that am not shaped for sportive tricks, nor made to court an amorous looking glass and would not do justice to a Savile Row suit."

Without missing a beat, Giles replied, "David, if I remember correctly, Richard III came to an unseemly end." Point taken. Giles knew his Shakespeare.

Giles followed through on his offer the next day when he invited us to a five-story Georgian townhouse he was in the process of restoring. Susan and I climbed up to the fifth floor, where we entered a veritable Aladdin's Cave brimming with antique furniture and artwork. Original paintings and prints were stacked against one wall like cordwood. Giles urged us to take whatever appealed to us, since we would be the ones who would be looking at it every day. Not wanting to appear greedy and remembering Aladdin was limited to three wishes, we only picked three framed pieces: an 1870 map of Winchester, a still life oil painting of flowers, and a charming female nude in ink. Giles was more definitive about the other items we should take. He chose two floor lamps and a square, Georgian, floral-painted mahogany coffee table.

Then there was the matter of replacing our inadequate dining room chairs. Giles insisted that we borrow four hand-carved Jacobean chairs, made of black English oak, from the 17th century. I protested that they were a chair too far and I would be nervous using them lest we damage them in some way. Giles chuckled and said, "Pick up that chair, David." I could barely lift it. "Do you think you could do anything to hurt that chair?"

I was glad we had taken the chairs. Sitting in them made eating my morning oatmeal feel like a royal banquet. Was this another Giles lesson—showing us the value of functional beauty and the joy people can get from incorporating beautiful things into their daily lives?

SIX
Lunch With A Judge

On Friday, I returned to the Winchester Courts for my lunch with Justice Marshall. After I passed through the security checkpoint, I was met by Justice Marshall's usher, who said, "Good afternoon, Professor. I have been instructed by His Lordship to escort you to his chambers."

An escort was necessary. Due to the court's security regime, it would have been impossible for me to find the judge's chambers, or even the floor of the courthouse where his and the chambers of all the other Crown Court Justices were located. Technically, it was on the third floor of the building. To the ordinary visitor to the court, however, the floor did not exist. It was neither included in the building directory nor appeared on the building schematic in the lobby. The public elevator's control buttons went from the 2nd to the 4th floor. Access to the 3rd floor was not concealed behind a fake bookcase, but the stairwell and elevator accessing the 3rd floor were protected by two steel doors, guarded by an armed officer. The usher told me all the precautions to protect the judges were installed for the trials of the Irish Republican Army bombers. Winchester was chosen as the site for all their trials because it was outside of London and had one of the most secure courthouses in England. It also had cells for twenty prisoners in the cellar from which the prisoners could be conducted directly to the courtrooms by a secure passageway, thus avoiding the risk of transporting the prisoners in conspicuous police vans through public streets.

Our elevator had only a 3rd floor button, and it opened onto a wide hallway with ten judges' chambers on each side. At the east end of the hallway, in front of a floor-to-ceiling window overlooking the town, was a long, carved wooden table surrounded by thirty chairs. The usher said the judges often hosted dinners there.

The usher led me to Judge Marshall's chambers, rapped once on the door before opening it, and, standing aside, he allowed me to enter. I like dogs, but I was startled when a Labrador Retriever sprang up from the corner to check me out. I must have passed muster since he immediately returned to his corner when Justice Marshall said, "Sit." Are dogs more prone to obey the commands of a High Court Justice? The usual pleasantries were exchanged, with Justice Marshall and me throwing in a respectful bow. Justice Marshall chuckled and said, "That must be hard for Americans," and said I could call him "Charles." A cook from the courthouse kitchen arrived with soup and sandwiches. I hate having soup on such occasions. Soup and I do not mix. It is either slurp or spill, neither of which is socially acceptable.

I finished my soup without any social faux pas, and the usher cleared away the dishes. Charles, anticipating my question, said, "You probably want to hear about our wigs; most Americans do."

I said, "I did want to ask about judges summing up the facts at the close of a jury trial, but now that you mention it, do wigs serve any useful purpose?" Charles explained, "In England, something that has acquired the patina of a tradition is by definition useful. Our traditions generate a seamless web between the past and the present, so we are loath to discard them unless there is a good reason to do so. However," he continued, "wigs do have some practical purpose: they level the playing field between barristers."

If both barristers are required to wear wigs, then both look slightly ridiculous. An attractive female barrister loses her edge trying to keep a wig in place on top of her coiffure. A handsome male barrister just looks commonplace.

Charles said another important aspect of wigs was that they served as disguises for judges. They provided a bit of anonymity to judges who were increasingly coming under vitriolic attacks from pundits and politicians. Charles had presided over a notorious case which proved his point. The defendants, a man and his wife, were charged with the torture and murder of fourteen young women. The media covered the case, and reporters were in court every day. Charles presided, wearing his long, shoulder-length wig and scarlet robe. Charles said he could walk by those same reporters in the morning and no one would recognize him as the judge in the case. No one attempted to shove a microphone in his face. I had to agree that perhaps wigs did serve a purpose.

A big question for me was why, under British law, judges were required to sum up the evidence at the end of a trial. That summation is the last words a jury hears before retiring to reach a verdict. I was skeptical that any judge would be incapable of forming an opinion about the guilt or innocence of a defendant and would be unable to keep that opinion from seeping into the summary of facts. This, in turn, could easily influence the jury's verdict. I was expecting Charles to launch a vigorous defense of the value of summing up the facts. Instead, he offered a more nuanced response. He said it was possible to craft a neutral summation, but that in the real world, judges sometimes used the summary of the facts to tilt the balance toward a verdict the judge preferred. Charles said he favored a light touch, which could "aid" the jury in its decision-making but still not trigger an appeal that would lead to a reversal of the verdict. He also added that he believed British jurors could be a cantankerous lot, and if jurors felt the judge was telling them how to decide a case, they would rebel and do the direct opposite.

I asked for an example of how such a delicate balance could be achieved. Charles told me to assume there was a witness, for either prosecution or the defense, whom he did not think was credible. Yet, he was worried the jury might not recognize the credibility gap. A neutral summation could be delivered in a normal, flat monotone. "You may believe Mr. Smith when he says he saw a knife in the defendant's hand." However, if Charles believed Smith's credibility was questionable, he could use essentially the same words and convey his opinion that there was good reason to doubt Smith's testimony. "Now, you *maaaaaay* believe Mr. Smith when he says he saw a knife in the defendant's hand." I noticed that when Charles demonstrated this technique, he could highlight his skeptical-sounding pronunciation by raising one of his bushy eyebrows, as if forming a big question mark lying on its side.

I explained to the judge that in the U.S., if a judge made such a statement, or attempted any kind of analysis of the evidence, or hinted about the credibility of a witness, there would likely be a reversal by the Court of Appeals. If the judge's instructions to the jury contained the merest hint of favoring one side or the other, the case would soon return to the judge's docket. It was clear from Charles' expression that he had serious doubts about the efficacy of a legal system that so rigorously muzzled a trial judge. It was a puzzlement to him. Charles thought all the wisdom and experience of a judge in analyzing evidence and assessing the credibility of witnesses, which had been acquired during years on the bench, not to mention the required 20 years of practice as a barrister, would be wasted.

"Surely," he said, "a judge is well qualified to help the jury in making better decisions." When I explained, however, that most judges in America, including judges on State Supreme Courts, are elected, Charles nodded and said, "Now I understand."

Before our lunch ended, I had to ask Charles about the pageantry that comes with the office. He did admit it might seem excessive, but then again, tradition is meant to demonstrate British respect and compliance with the rule of law. Charles described the elaborate ceremony welcoming a visiting High

Court Justice, who would preside over the Winchester Court in cases involving serious felonies. First, the High Sheriff greets the High Court Justice outside the main door to the Cathedral and welcomes the Justice to Winchester. The Sheriff is in full regalia, wearing a resplendent uniform bedecked with ribbons, medals, and medallions, sporting a sword and a tri-cornered hat with a black cockade. The Sheriff is flanked by two rows of military cadets standing at attention, each holding a six-foot-long busine.[1]

When the Justice and the Sheriff move toward the Cathedral, their entry to the Cathedral is heralded by a blast from the trumpets. Inside the Cathedral, all bewigged and robed barristers and Crown Court judges are gathered. Following a brief service, during which a Te Deum is sung by the Cathedral's boys' choir, everyone walks to the Great Hall, built in the 13th century, where a banquet awaits them. Charles said an additional perk was that his accommodations in Winchester were superb. He was housed in a large townhouse in the Cathedral Close, with a first-rate cook, butler, and chauffeur who ferried Charles around in a limousine.

The appearance of my usher escort signified that lunch break was over. I shook Charles' hand and thanked him for his hospitality. Charles' dog ambled over and gave me a farewell sniff while I patted its large head.

---

1. A busine is a type of long, straight metal trumpet, also called a herald's trumpet.

SEVEN

One trial down and one to go. The attempted rape case began the next Monday. Over the weekend, Giles read my summary of the case and the stack of files in the brief packet. Meanwhile, Susan, Nancy, and I took two enjoyable trips to London on the train.

I was not as sanguine about the attempted rape case as I was about the child abuse case. Family relationships involving an attentive favorite uncle and an attractive teenage niece, often morphing into something more intimate, were all too common. The likelihood of that happening is enhanced when the teenage girl flirts with a relative she finds attractive. The fact, however, that the niece may have been flirtatious, and the intimacy was consensual, was not a viable defense against an attempted rape charge involving a minor. Nevertheless, Noah Watts was adamant in his denials. Giles never told me what his inclination was regarding the client's guilt or innocence after reading the brief.

Monday began at a typically Giles frantic pace, which by the end of the day left everyone trying to keep up with him "knack-ered."[1] Kate Perry, our solicitor, told me Giles was always like that. Kate should know; she preferred hiring Giles for criminal cases if

---

1. Like old, exhausted horses which are often sent to a glue factory.

his calendar was open. Outside the courtroom, Kate said his private life also ran at the same blistering pace, and spending 24 hours with Giles required expending forty-eight hours of energy. He crammed too much into a fleeting period of time, doing some things on the spur of the moment and procrastinating on things that should have been done before the last minute. If Giles's work pattern was one of the lessons I was supposed to learn as his pupil, I was doomed to fail. I told Giles that while he seemed to enjoy flying by the seat of his pants, I needed to have everything planned out in advance.

Giles scoffed, asserting that if I wanted to be a good trial lawyer, I would need to show spontaneity and be adept at improvisation. On the first day of the attempted rape trial, Giles's point was driven home. The Crown Prosecution Service had been slow in providing the phone records of the complainant, Felicity Thompson. The records had been requested a month before. Giles was handed fifty pages of phone records at the start of the trial, and he needed to use the records during a cross-examination that afternoon. Before he could prepare for a cross-examination, he had to consult with Noah, Kate, and me about the calls between Noah and Felicity Thompson. Judge Walsh, though, was eager to move the case along and was not amenable to calling a recess. He gave Giles 45 minutes to consult with Noah. It was a chaotic forty-five minutes. Giles peppered Noah, Kate, and me about the various dates and times of the phone calls and asked Noah what he could remember about the calls. One of us would respond, and Giles would make tiny illegible notes in the margins. He appeared hopelessly adrift. Near the end of the allotted time, Giles asked us to leave the room for a couple of minutes while he collected his thoughts. Three minutes later, he coolly strode into court with no hint that only a few minutes before, he had been scrambling to make sense out of a plethora of phone calls.

Somehow, Giles had organized in his mind that hodgepodge of margin notes and other scribbles into a superb, three-hour cross-examination. His grasp of the facts was formidable, dispelling any notion I had just a few minutes before that he was adrift without a rudder.

Felicity Thompson testified during her direct examination that Noah had been her favorite uncle and was like a father to her for years after her own father died. She said that during that time, Noah had never touched her, but on July 15, 1993, he made indecent advances, touching her in inappropriate places and attempting to rape her. Cross-examining Felicity required a delicate balancing act. Our theory of the case avoided turning Felicity into the villain of the story, as such a tactic could backfire with the jury. Juries start out sympathetic to victims like Felicity. If the cross-examiner plans to beat up on an alleged rape victim, the barrister had better be damn sure the jury will think the complainant deserved the verbal abuse. Not wanting to take that risk, Giles took the tack that Felicity was a mixed-up and confused teenager who had a crush on her favorite uncle, Noah, and she only accused him of making improper advances toward her after Noah refused to take her on a trip that he and his wife, Penny, were planning to take to Spain.

Giles gently led Felicity through a series of questions. The questions did not suggest she had done anything wrong. Neither did he employ a technique I had seen him use on other witnesses. Giles would ask a witness a question dripping with skepticism, clearly conveying the message. "Now I am going to ask you a question. You know your answer will be a lie, and I know your answer will be a lie, but I am going to ask the question anyway."

On the surface, Giles's questions seemed benign, with nothing in his manner to suggest he did not believe every word. I could see that Felicity was getting comfortable; her hands stopped gripping the rail around the witness box, and she began to slouch. Giles did not want to make her turn defensive and stir up a bout of teenage petulance. Felicity was more than willing to admit she liked her Uncle Noah, and she took every opportunity to spend time with him. "Noah was fun to be around." Giles then took Felicity through her phone records. She acknowledged calling

Uncle Noah every day up until August 3rd, which was more than two weeks after the date of the alleged rape. On August 4th, Felicity begged Uncle Noah and his wife to let her go with them to Spain, but they told her, "No." Felicity conceded that the refusal made her angry.

Felicity testified she did not tell anyone about the attempted rape, including her mother, Molly Thompson, until two months later, when she told two of her friends, Rose Booth and Corey Holland. Felicity nodded her head when Giles suggested she had not planned to tell anyone other than her friends about what her uncle had done to her. Felicity said she was surprised when the principal of her school, Kimberly Atkinson, called her into her office and asked about the alleged assault. Felicity told Giles she knew it must have been Rose and Corey who had told the principal about what she had said. Felicity did not anticipate where Giles was leading her and said she repeated the same story to the principal that she had told her friends. Ms. Atkinson then called Felicity's mother. When Molly Thompson arrived at the principal's office, Felicity repeated the now much-told story to her mother.

Giles asked, "Were you surprised, Felicity, when the police arrived?"

"Yes."

"You never intended to involve the police, right?"

"No."

"Do you mean it was never your intention to tell the police about what you say happened?"

"Yes."

Felicity repeated almost verbatim to the police the same story she had told four other times.

I knew where Giles was going with his line of questioning. He again was taking a big risk, allowing a witness to repeat her story over and over. He was going to argue that Felicity enmeshed herself in a web of lies. She had to tell a second lie to the principal to avoid being caught in a lie to her friends. The third lie to her mother was needed to appear truthful to the principal. The fourth lie to the police was necessary to avoid confessing to all her previous lies. Once charges were brought against her uncle, what could this poor teenage girl do but repeat the lie for the fifth time in court?

Giles's cross-examination of Felicity lasted nearly three hours, and it was all an intricate prelude to his final question. Up to that point, Felicity may have thought Giles was more a helpful friend than a foe. Thus, the stage was set for Giles's abrupt transformation from the benign, unthreatening barrister to an aggressive, unbelieving cross-examiner. His final question dripped with skepticism and implied that no one was going to believe the lie Felicity would tell in answer to the next question.

"You told this jury that you were terribly disappointed when your favorite Uncle Noah, who you called several times a day, a person you loved, refused to take you to Spain. And yet you say that your anger with Uncle Noah had nothing to do with you telling your friends he had tried to take advantage of you. True?"

"Yes."

Giles finished the question, not looking at Felicity, but at the jury with an expression displaying total disbelief.

We were pleased with how the case was unfolding and unwinding for the prosecution. After the first day of testimony, Giles, Kate, Noah, and I were brainstorming about the strategy for the rest of the week. We lawyers in the room were having a grand time tossing out ideas and batting them around. A few were idiotic, provoking sharp retorts and laughter. For a moment, I felt a little ghoulish. We lawyers get an adrenaline rush from strategizing how to play the game and sharpening our tactics. I wondered how Noah was feeling about our levity. His life was at risk if the game was lost. If we lawyers lose the game, our lives change very little. My sober moment passed; I was having fun.

By the end of the first day of trial, my original impression of the case had changed dramatically. I was convinced Noah was innocent. I also liked him, and I liked his family. I clearly had not absorbed one of Giles's lessons—keep the client at a distance. I chatted with Noah, his wife Penny, and his mother during breaks in the trial. Felicity's allegations and the trial were a nightmare for the entire extended family. The family had been a close-knit one, including grandparents, aunts, uncles, cousins, and in-laws. Now, the family was in pieces, and, regardless of the trial's outcome, would likely never be the same. I became a sympathetic listener to other members of Noah's family. They trusted me. It was the opposite of the professional distance Giles advised me to maintain. Giles learned about my descent from being a barrister to being a hand-holding social worker when he mentioned to the family that the next day, Kate, the solicitor, would not be there. They immediately asked, "But will David be here?" Giles knew then I was too entangled in their lives and emotions to ever pull free—and I would have to endure the emotional consequences of a guilty verdict.

The next day of the trial was less hectic, but Giles was still operating at a high energy level. The same could not be said of Prosecutor Alex Butler. He did not show much enthusiasm on his side of the case. In America, I am accustomed to prosecuting attorneys assuming the role of righteous defenders of society, protectors of law-abiding citizens. It is a part they are forced to play. Prosecutors are elected by the people. Voters will not re-elect prosecutors who do not win a large majority of their cases. Plus, they must display the requisite vengeful ardor for putting lawbreakers in prison. In England, barristers who are members of the criminal bar may prosecute one week and defend the following week. As Crown prosecutors, they do not see themselves as avenging angels, but as helpful guides to a jury, conducting the jurors through the thicket of documents and testimony so they can reach a just decision. Emotional rhetoric urging the jury to convict a defendant to safeguard the community is perceived as unprofessional, and, worse still, it may result in a reprimand from the judge. Of course, considering what had transpired in the trial, there was not much Alex Butler could be excited about. His lack of enthusiasm was no excuse, though, for asking such ill-formed questions that witnesses were unable to decipher and often had to ask him to rephrase his questions.

Giles's cross-examination of Felicity's mother could have been a minefield in which any question, no matter how benign, might trigger an explosion of anger, or worse, sobbing. It soon became clear, however, that there would be no emotional displays from Molly Thompson. In fact, her answers implied she may have had doubts about Felicity's story. Molly was willing to accept facts proposed by Giles that undermined her daughter's testimony, and she made no attempt to put a favorable spin on them. Ms. Thompson supported her daughter, but she was not going to lie for Felicity intentionally.

What happened next would never have occurred in an American courtroom. However, I was later told it was common in a British one. Prosecutor Butler called two of Felicity's teachers, Ms. Barnes and Ms. Grant, as witnesses and only asked them their names, occupations, and how they knew Felicity. Butler then turned the witnesses over to Giles for cross-examination. If Giles himself had called them as witnesses during his case-in-chief, he would have been restricted to using non-leading questions and constrained in how far he could go in attacking their credibility. Developing the parts of their testimony that were favorable to Noah could have been challenging if the teachers believed Felicity's claims. Using leading questions, Giles had the advantage of putting the words he wanted the witnesses to say into the witnesses' mouths and having them answer "Yes" or "No." I was not sure why Giles wanted Ms. Barnes to testify. He only asked her a few questions about Felicity's behavior in school and ended his questioning.

Judge Walsh called a brief recess before Ms. Grant's testimony. During the break, I told Giles I had a bad feeling about Ms. Grant and that her testimony might be more hurtful than helpful. It demonstrated how much I had risen in Giles's esteem that he agreed with me without argument. When Giles returned to the courtroom, he put on a bit of a charade. Giles could not simply excuse the witness without asking any questions. Judges are cranky with barristers who waste the court's time calling irrelevant witnesses. So, Giles asked a few safe questions using a tone and manner that gave the impression he was introducing salient testimony and then excused Ms. Grant.

My assumption that I was considered by Giles to be a co-equal litigation partner collapsed the following day when I was demoted to the role of gofer. During the 15-minute recess, Butler told Giles he could not find the audiotape of Noah's statement to the police. Butler wanted to play the tape for the jury as part of his case-in-chief. Under the Rules of Evidence, such statements are not hearsay; in fact, anything a defendant says is not considered hearsay. I thought Giles would commiserate with opposing counsel, shedding crocodile tears, and say to Butler, "Oh, that's too bad," while thinking, "Oh, that's great, a huge hole had just opened up in the Crown's case." Instead, Giles said, "No problem, I have a copy of the tape back in Chambers and David will run there, collect the tape and be back here in less than 10 minutes." I was less troubled by being relegated to an errand boy than I was disturbed by the possible ethical issues raised by Giles's offer of the tape to the prosecution, an issue I planned to raise later.

I jogged three blocks to Chambers and came back with time to spare, and handed the tape to Butler. I was breathing hard and had chest pains. I was worried, but I was okay after about five minutes. Butler played the entire recording to the jury. Little of it hurt our case. That may have been the reason Giles was so generous about offering it to the prosecution. It was a clever tactical move.

That evening, while Giles, solicitor Kate, and I sipped our after-trial glasses of wine at the Green Man, I raised my ethical issue. I began by asserting what I believed to be the obligation of attorneys and barristers defending in a criminal case: to represent the interests of the defendant zealously. I did not understand how helping Butler prove his case against Noah could be characterized as maintaining a zealous defense. Neither could I imagine any defense counsel in America offering such help, even if asked. Giles patiently explained that a barrister also had an ethical duty to maintain the integrity of the judicial system and of the professional relationship among barristers who had been admitted to the Bar.

That sounded to me like the "Good ole boys barrister network, you scratch my back now, and I will scratch your back sometime in the future." The fact that barristers switch back and forth between prosecuting defendants and defending them reinforces the mutual back-scratching culture. Giles was happy to save a fellow barrister from the embarrassment of having lost a piece of evidence, knowing that in the future he may need a similar favor from an opposing barrister.

Giles quickly rejected my crass, self-serving characterization of the custom and substituted a more principled rationale, a tactic he often used in the courtroom. He said that the comity among members of the Bar was an essential element in maintaining the integrity of the criminal justice system. The purpose of the criminal judicial process was to achieve a fair and just result as much as was humanly possible. That goal would be unreachable if it became the customary practice for barristers to take advantage of other barristers' innocent mistakes or employ tricks that may not be clearly unethical but skew a jury's fact-finding process. Relevant evidence the jury should consider would be kept from them for no legitimate reason. In Noah's case, his statement to the police was properly obtained, relevant, and admissible. Only Butler's piece of bad luck would have kept the jury from hearing Noah's statement. Giles concluded with, "Justice should not be determined by the roll of the dice. Zealously representing a client does not require engaging in unseemly behavior, and winning a tainted verdict does not justify diminishing the torch of justice."

I was not sure Giles was just honing his rhetorical skills, but there was truth in what he said. Wouldn't the course of justice run more smoothly, with fairer results, if the advocate culture incorporated the Golden Rule: treat others as you would like others to treat you? I speculated whether barrister-like civility would appeal to American juries, or whether they expect trials to resemble *Shootout at the OK Corral*?

I could not resist teasing Giles about his sending me trotting off six blocks to fetch the audiotape of the defendant's interview with the police. "Giles, were you trying to kill me when you volunteered me to jog nearly a half mile in less than 10 minutes?"

Giles refused the bait, but Kate asked, "What do you mean?"

I explained how I was so out of breath and had chest pains. "I could have died, playing your errand boy."

Demonstrating his sangfroid, or just a lack of empathy, Giles replied, "You are fortunate to have a heart condition, if you have one, rather than a lingering, deteriorating disease. You are likely to recover from a heart attack, or you die." Then, without missing a beat, the generous side of Giles's personality emerged. He insisted I should see a doctor, his personal doctor, and he would make an appointment for me.

Kate interrupted Giles. "Enough of this cheerful conversation, I must get home, and you, Giles, must open the defense case tomorrow." Giles graciously offered to drive Kate home.

Before Giles began his opening speech, Judge Walsh lodged another dagger in Prosecutor Butler's chest. Judge Walsh must have had doubts about Felicity's testimony. Judge Walsh told us he was going to include in his instructions to the jury that they should be wary of unsupported claims like Felicity's because they are easily made and hard to refute, even if untrue. The judge would essentially be implying to the jury that he had doubts about Felicity's version of events. Such a judicial undermining of a witness's credibility would have American appeals court judges foaming at the mouth. Once again, I found myself feeling sorry for the prosecution, and it was only going to get worse.

The advantage of requiring defense counsel to forgo their opening speeches until the end of the prosecution's case gives the defense counsel the opportunity to attack the strength of the Crown's case. It is more of a final argument than an opening speech. Instead of being limited to telling the jury "What the evidence will show," Giles and the jury knew all the evidence the prosecution had introduced. So, it allowed Giles to launch a full-scale attack on the substantive strength of the prosecution's evidence and the credibility of the Crown's witnesses. Giles spent most of his opening remarks on Felicity's believability, or lack thereof. Yet, he did not depict her as a bold-faced liar. He remained true to his theme. Felicity was a mixed-up teenager who was striking out at her favorite uncle for reasons that seemed legitimate to a teenage mind. Felicity only told her story to her friends to get attention, but as Giles pointed out, the initial lie spun out of control, trapping Felicity in her own self-spun web of lies.

It is common for defense counsel to decline calling the defendant as a witness and subjecting the defendant to a potentially devastating cross-examination, which unearths damaging facts, strengthens the prosecution's case, or destroys the defendant's credibility. There was less risk of that happening in our case. Noah had given an extensive interview to the police, which, thanks to my speed afoot, Butler had read into evidence. What worried me, though, was what Noah hoped for at the end of the trial. Noah wanted more than a not-guilty verdict; he wanted vindication, a declaration that he was the innocent victim. Noah's life, whatever the verdict might be, had been wrecked, his family split apart, his community reputation in tatters, with people believing he was a rapist regardless of the verdict. Would the prosecutor's aggressive, accusing questions trigger an outburst of Noah's temper?

My concern about Noah's anger disappeared when I saw how nervous he was as the time for his testimony crept closer. Giles told him that he would calm down after the first few questions and that the trick was to look directly into Giles's eyes and talk to him. Whatever nervousness Noah did have quickly dissipated, and his answers to Giles's questions proceeded smoothly, like two friends having a conversation over a couple of beers. Alex Butler's cross-examination technique did little to upset Noah's equanimity. It was more like an out-of-control bulldozer than a cross-examination with finesse. Butler would repeat the main allegations against Noah, who would respond with strong denials. For example, Butler would growl, "You fondled your niece's breasts, didn't you?" To which Noah would look him in the eye and respond, "I certainly did not, sir!"

It was such a contrast to Giles's cross-examinations. Giles weaved a web of circumstantial facts the witnesses could not deny, facts which reinforced the story Giles wanted the jury to believe. It was only after the web was spun that Giles directly challenged witnesses, forcing them to deny the truth of their previous answers. Giles's questions may have appeared haphazard. They were not. Their intent and purpose were hidden from the witnesses until Giles sprang the trap.

I thought the case was going so well, I suggested to Giles that we not call a school friend of Felicity's to testify. In my opinion, the benefit of her testimony did not outweigh the risks. Kate pushed back against my advice. As the solicitor, she had done a lot of work finding and cultivating the witness and did not want it to all go for naught. Giles seemed especially reluctant to hurt Kate's feelings, but in the end, he took my advice.

The case was going so well that I described our win as a "slam dunk," which I naturally had to explain to Giles. However, I still worried that overconfidence could lead to carelessness, and one can never be sure what a jury will do.

Reviewing the case, I focused on the seven charges brought against Noah and what the likely instructions Judge Walsh might give to the jury. Would they confuse the jurors and induce them to find Noah guilty of one of the lesser charges as a compromise? I proposed a jury instruction that could eliminate that possibility. Giles took my idea and made a splendid application to the court. On the face of it, the instruction he was requesting seemed favorable to the prosecution. The reality, however, was that it bolstered the defense.

"If you are sure the complainant is substantially telling the truth, then you should convict the defendant on all seven charges. If you are not sure the complainant is telling the truth, then you should acquit the defendant on all charges."

Surprisingly, Butler agreed with Giles's proposed jury instruction. I whispered to Giles that Butler did not realize he had just stepped into a bear trap. The instruction increased the likelihood of an acquittal because Felicity had been caught numerous times admitting she had lied. A domino effect was in play. If the jurors concluded that Felicity had lied about one of the charges and acquitted Noah on that charge, then the instruction directed them to acquit Noah on all charges. The instruction focused the entire case on whether Felicity was a truthful person. Butler would be forced to admit that Felicity had lied on several occasions and repeated a few fibs in court. I tried to imagine Butler's closing speech. Could he say with a straight face, "Ladies and gentlemen, we know that the complainant lied numerous times, but the Crown urges you to convict the defendant and send him to prison because I can assure you that when she told you the defendant assaulted her, she was telling the truth."

The prosecution's case deteriorated further during the testimony of Felicity's grandmother, Florence Reed. She testified for the defense. Grandma Reed told the jury that Noah was an exemplary uncle to Felicity, filling in for Felicity's deceased father. Grandma added that Felicity was not always truthful and lied from time to time. Butler should not have tangled with Grandma during his cross-examination. He only had one approach for cross-examining a witness. Butler would pose a question in a grand magisterial style while flashing a severe expression, pretending he had just asked a devastating question that barely qualified as trivial. He adopted the same harsh, imperious manner with all witnesses he cross-examined. That might work with witnesses who are easily bullied and intimidated, but it was suicidal to use it on a sweet 70-year-old grandma who was obviously distraught by having to question the veracity of a granddaughter she loved. At the end of the cross-examination, it was Butler's blood that was spread around the courtroom.

A verdict of not guilty seemed assured, although one can never be certain what a jury might do, and this jury had a Joker wildcard on it. Juror number five thought he was a natural-born barrister. Throughout the trial, he kept handing the usher questions he wanted to ask the witnesses. The usher would pass the questions on to Juge Walsh, who, to my complete amazement, without consulting with the barristers, would read the questions proposed by the juror to the witnesses. Many of the questions were plainly ridiculous, and others were meant to elicit inadmissible evidence. It was a "no-win" scenario for Giles. If he objected to the question in open court and the question was ruled out of order, he risked alienating members of the jury who might conclude Giles was hiding something. Giles would be making an enemy of at least one member of the jury. If Judge Walsh asked the witness the juror's question, the jury might attach more meaning to the answer than it deserved. Wincing by Giles and me was out. We were obliged to sit in our chairs and assume a completely blasé expression, suggesting the question was so innocuous we couldn't care less about the witnesses' answers. I later told Giles that in America, such behavior by a judge would guarantee the appeals court would reverse any verdict.

That evening with the three of us nursing a bottle of Claret, Giles declared he was "chockablock with joy" about the case. I was not eager to tarnish Giles's good spirits, but I could not help asking how he could be feeling so chuffed when the jury had yet not rendered a verdict.

He responded: "David, would you wager your happiness on whether the slot machine you are playing comes up three cherries, or not? A jury is like a slot machine. If you let that group of twelve often confused people dictate your feeling of self-worth, you are destined to have a depressing life as a barrister."

Giles was euphoric because he knew he had won the match. He knew he had outplayed the Crown Prosecutor, and the prosecutor knew he had been outplayed. Finally, Judge Walsh knew the Crown Prosecutor had been outplayed. Giles's reputation among members of the Bar was safe.

I had to admit our defense was almost flawless. The theme we chose, portraying Felicity as a deluded teenage girl who should be pitied, was spot-on. Giles's tactic of focusing on Felicity's credibility without labeling her as a bold-faced liar was deftly executed. Finally, Giles had prevailed in the skirmish over the jury instructions. Why was I not feeling the same euphoria? The answer to that question did not occur to me until later that evening.

In part, Giles was right. Why would I allow jury verdicts, which are as unpredictable as slot machines, to measure my performance as an advocate? If I demonstrated skilled professional work, and other members of the profession agreed, then a jury finding my client guilty should not undermine my self-confidence. After all, my client may very well have been guilty and deserved punishment.

I concluded my lack of joy arose because I had violated one of Giles's cardinal rules. I did not keep a professional distance between Noah and me, and worse, I had become close to his family. I liked his wife, sister, and mother-in-law. I became a believer in Noah's innocence. I knew what a tragedy it would be to his family if the jury found Noah guilty. The family trusted me. They relied on me to rescue them from the yawning abyss. It was Giles who presented Noah's case in court, but it was I who held their hands, analyzed the evidence, explained our trial tactics, and assured them the omens were favorable. So, it would be me, and not Giles, who would have to look in their distraught, tearful faces and feel guilt-ridden. The elation from a well-tried case would not ease my remorse and prevent me from torturing myself about what we could have done differently to change the outcome.

This was a Giles lesson I was incapable of putting into practice. Building a sense of trust with a client was at the heart of my approach to the attorney-client relationship. Demonstrating empathy to the client was a necessary element in establishing trust. Giles would consider it a flaw, and it probably was, but I would find it difficult to defend a client for whom I felt a complete lack of empathy. The downside, of course, is the distress I feel if the client is convicted and led off to prison. Remorse is piled onto my sorrow when the client blames me for the conviction. In a moment, I would be transformed from hero to goat. In addition to my personal foibles, the American system of justice hinders an attorney from keeping aloof from a client. There is no solicitor to serve as an intermediary between the client and the attorney. An American attorney assumes both roles: a trusted, hand-holding friend outside the courtroom, and a detached, unsentimental, objective litigator in court.

On the final day of the trial, with only closing arguments and Judge Walsh's instructions to the jury, followed by jury deliberation, I was tempted not to attend. The prospect of spending time with Noah and his family while the jury decided Noah's fate was disheartening. I would have to strike a balance between cautious optimism and preparing them for the worst. Then, if the verdict was guilty, it would be me they would look to for comforting words, which do not exist. In England, a losing barrister cannot resort to the soothing phrase, "We will appeal." Unlike in America, there is no automatic right to an appeal of a guilty verdict. My sense of duty and affection for the family trumped my cowardice, and I took my usual seat next to Giles.

My gloom lifted when I heard the judge's summing-up to the jury. I had to respect Prosecutor Butler's stoicism as Judge Walsh pounded the final nail in his coffin.

"Ladies and Gentlemen, you must be careful in cases like these to accept the testimony of a person like the complainant when there is no supporting evidence to her allegations. Furthermore, as a matter of law, there is no supporting evidence in this case."

Coffin shut; prosecutor buried. The only thing left would be for the jury to fill in the grave with dirt. The judge had just instructed the jurors to acquit the defendant. I nudged Giles and said, "The jury will be back in two hours or less."

While the jury was deliberating, we could not leave the courthouse, so Giles brought a stack of newspapers for us to read. I spent some of my time with Noah and his family. Naturally, they were so stressed and eager for me to reassure them. I felt confident that the verdict would be "not guilty," yet I also wanted to prepare them for the worst. Giles had told me he had trouble reading the jury, which was unusual. A couple of the younger members appeared disengaged during his summing-up and were not making eye contact. He also admitted to being concerned about a guilty verdict. He had won tougher cases in the past, and if he lost this one, it would tarnish his reputation.

In exactly two hours, the jury returned. I took it as a positive sign that one of the women jurors smiled at me, or at Giles, as she entered the jury box. My optimism grew when I realized she had been selected as the forewoman for the panel. Giles grew more confident from the fact that she was not holding any paper in her hand. There were seven charges, and if there were a mixture of guilty and not guilty verdicts, she would need some kind of score-card to make sure she reported them correctly. No notes meant the verdict was the same for all seven charges, which increased the likelihood that the verdict was not guilty. A great weight was lifted from my shoulders when the forewoman told the judge they had found the defendant not guilty on the first charge. I knew then there would be no guilty verdicts on the other six charges, which the forewoman quickly confirmed. Noah was immediately discharged from custody and reunited with his family.

There was a surge of joy filling the corridor. Hugs were freely distributed, which included Kate and me. This was the upside side of fostering a relationship with a client and his family. I could feel their wave of happiness wash over me. Giles only exchanged handshakes with Noah. I am sure it did not bother Giles that he was not embraced. To the family, he was the hired gunfighter engaged to protect Noah and the family against an imminent threat—"Have wig, will travel." When the danger was over and the family safe, he had earned his fee and then moved on to fight for someone else who could pay him. He was respected by Noah's family but not loved.

My happiness for the family was diminished by the realization that there were scars to a close family relationship that would never completely heal. Felicity was a confused teenager who lost everything to satisfy a momentary desire for revenge. Once she told the first lie, she could not back down. I hoped she would get effective counseling. Grandmother Reed confided in me that she was worried her daughter, Molly, would resent her testifying for the defense and forbid her from seeing her two grandchildren.

That night at the Green Man pub, Giles sprang for the champagne while Kate and I talked about the ups and downs of the case. When Giles ambled over to the bar to chat with a fellow barrister, and I was fortified by several glasses of champagne, I asked Kate if she and Giles were ever in a relationship. Whether it was the champagne or Kate's natural candidness, she replied, "Oh, we had our fling after his divorce. It started when we were celebrating a win, and I gave him a rather passionate kiss. But I would never enter a serious relationship with Giles." Paraphrasing Shakespeare, she said, "Giles is too costly to wear every day. I ended our dalliance when I told him I could not accompany him on a trip to Italy. Two days later, he was advertising in the paper for a female traveling companion."

Giles ended his conversation at the bar, so Kate had little time to elaborate except to say that Giles was a delightful companion in short bursts. When he was with a woman, he was totally focused on making her happy. But when Giles was absent, a woman was little more than one of the names in his black phone book. Out of sight, out of mind. Kate accepted those conditions. It allowed Giles and her to remain friends and colleagues.

When Giles returned from the bar, he announced, "David, we are going to Normandy this weekend." The barrister he had been chatting with was one of the timeshare holders of a château Giles owned in Ravenoville, called Manor Magnifique. The barrister told Giles that although it was his two weeks to stay at the château, he would not be staying there that weekend. Once more, I was caught up in the Giles whirlwind, and with no hesitation, I said, "Great!"

By the next day, Giles had made all the arrangements, including booking a cabin on the overnight ferry from Portsmouth to Cherbourg. As an afterthought, he said, "By the way, David, you have an appointment with Dr. Hudson tomorrow at 2:00 pm."

EIGHT
The Normandy Invasion

Giles is happiest when he can cram two days of activity into one. Obviously, packing and preparing to take a spur-of-the-moment trip to France was not hectic enough. He also arranged for Susan, Nancy, and me to have dinner with him and Dana Cooper at the Hotel du Vin on Friday evening before the ferry sailed.

On Friday afternoon, I also had to squeeze in a visit to Dr. Hudson. It caused less of a time crunch for me than I anticipated. Unlike most doctor visits, I was immediately ushered into an examination room. In contrast, other patients who filled the waiting room gave me the side-eye. I suppose I should have felt some guilt for jumping the queue, which is a major faux pas in England. I learned that lesson during my first week in Winchester. I was waiting for a bus, and I wedged myself near the curb where I hoped the driver would stop and open the door. If I guessed right, I would be ahead of the scrum, pushing to enter the bus. Much to my surprise, an elderly woman administered two sharp raps on my shoulder with her umbrella. The protest I planned to deliver died in my throat once I was confronted with a scowling, care-worn face with a clipped British accent informing me, "There is a queue."

Dr. Hudson's nurse asked me about my medical history and

the symptoms I was experiencing. Dr. Hudson took my blood pressure, checked my temperature, and listened to my heart and lungs with his stethoscope. A technician ran an EKG test. The squiggly lines on the printout meant nothing to me, but they must have indicated something to Dr. Hudson. He said he was not happy with the EKG. He would not offer a diagnosis, however, until more tests were run. On my way out of the office, I stopped at the reception desk to pay my bill. The receptionist had a puzzled look when I asked, "What do I owe?" I was equally baffled by her answer. "Nothing." She explained that the National Health Insurance covered all the costs, even for someone who was a visitor to the country. When I offered to pay £100 as a thank you for seeing me so quickly, her perplexity changed to a worried look. She told me that such a thing was just not done and was not permitted under National Health Insurance. As an afterthought, she said that accepting such a donation would also cause troublesome logistical problems. They had no internal accounting system in place to record and deal with the extra income. Not a bad healthcare system.

That evening at the Hotel du Vin, I sensed Dana and Giles were in a serious relationship. Dana had dark brown, almost black hair and eyes of the same hue. She was of medium height, and I estimated she was a few years younger than Giles. She was simply yet stylishly dressed in a tailored suit, and she knew the art of using just the right amount of make-up. Dana was unpretentiously elegant, a fact confirmed after a few minutes of conversation, when she employed her self-effacing wit and charm to make us three Americans feel comfortable. Although Dana was a professional actor, her kind and welcoming demeanor seemed to be part of her natural persona. We found common ground immediately, thanks to my love of the theatre and her passion for acting on the stage. Dana earned her spurs with the Royal Shakespeare Theatre Company in Stratford-on-Avon, playing roles alongside Ian McKellen, Judi Dench, Derek Jacobi, and Alec Guinness. Dana had also appeared in London West End productions, with an occasional stint on the BBC detective series, *Inspector Morse.*

Dana and I also had a common penchant for jabbing pins into Giles's overlarge ego. We enjoyed playing as a tag-team, taking turns launching pointed barbs in Giles's direction. It was like we were scripted. In a way, we were. I usually took my cue from one of Dana's sharpened witticisms. I thought Dana and Giles were a perfect match. The time flew by, but there was still flying to do. Dana was not going to Normandy, but Giles, Susan, Nancy, and I had to catch the overnight ferry from Portsmouth to Cherbourg. We winged down the M-3 and were practically the last car to drive onto the ferry, which probably was part of Giles's plan, making us well-placed to be one of the first cars exiting in Cherbourg.

While Giles was making the final arrangements with the car, we took our key to our cabin. When I opened the door and turned on the light, I jumped back, thinking I had somehow entered another person's cabin. There was a woman who was sleeping on the floor between the two berths on each side of the compartment. She sat up and, in a relaxed voice, said, "Hello," as if she were expecting us. She was. Giles had told her about us sharing the cabin with her, but had neglected to tell us about her. Introductions among bunkmates were in order. She told us her name was Francine and that she was a friend of Giles. She knew a lot about us, including our names and the pupillage arrangement I had with Giles. Relations warmed up quickly when she said, "Giles told me you were brilliant."

Only a few preliminary questions were needed to get a synopsis of Francine's life. She was fifty-one and had decided, when she turned fifty, to completely change her lifestyle. Francine's career as a teacher of grammar school kids for thirty years was apparently not adventurous enough. Francine was determined to do all those things she had wanted to do for most of her life. Thus far, she had backpacked in both Nepal and the Andes Mountains of Bolivia, toured China, skydived, and gotten her pilot's license. After a couple of days with Giles, she was going to Switzerland to learn to ski. In the summer, she planned to try scuba diving. Francine was not bragging or trying to make an impression, which she did. She listed her adventures like they were the kind of things any 50-year-old retired schoolteacher would do when she walked away from the classroom. I may have insulted Francine when I volunteered Nancy to exchange her berth for the space on the floor. Francine said that compared to some of the places she had been forced to sleep, the floor was quite comfortable.

Except for Giles, we all slept well, lulled by the gentle rocking of the boat and the low throb of the engines like a mother's lullaby. Giles used his berth light to spend a couple of hours reading the brief for the case we were to start on Monday.

The ferry arrived in Cherbourg at 7:00 AM, French time. Giles had roused us a half-hour before landing to make sure we were in the car when the ferry docked. Francine did not ride with us but left with the foot passengers. Cherbourg was disappointing, but as Americans, we were hardly justified in criticizing its lack of old-world ambiance. The American Eighth Air Force razed Cherbourg in World War II. Cherbourg may have lost its medieval architecture, but it has compensated for its loss with a plethora of hypermarkets, like American supermarkets on steroids. They were magnets to the Brits who could travel to Cherbourg, load up their cars with high-fashion clothes, cosmetics, jewelry, high-tech equipment, food, and alcohol, take them home in their original packaging, and save 20% on what the same items would cost in England. The return on their investment exceeds the fare for the ferry.

Giles was determined to recoup the cost of the ferry. He drove straight from the dock to Intermarché Super. I knew I was not in a Kroger anymore when an attractive young woman in a miniskirt handed each of us a warm croissant as a welcome gift. I confess that I acted like an ugly American by circling back, reentering the store, and accepting another croissant. Giles commandeered three shopping trolleys, and we trailed him around the Intermarché like three little ducklings. The first stop was at the wine department, where Giles bought thirty bottles of wine. He took his time to select them, no "plonk" for Giles. We then filled the trolleys with ten varieties of cheese from a display of a hundred varieties. We managed to buy some food for our meals, like chicken packed in goose grease. Finally, the rest of the space in the trolleys was filled with mounds of large chocolate bars. We made a brief stop in the women's department to buy a chic blouse for Dana, after holding it up to Susan and determining it was the right size. At the checkout counter, the bill was over £2000. With that much being spent, I felt justified in asking the young mini-skirted lass for another croissant.

When we pulled into the courtyard of the Maison Magnifique, I half expected a liveried footman to step out of the château and take our luggage; it was that grand. Any lingering doubts I had about Giles's economic success as a barrister evaporated with the morning sun reflecting off the façade of this large villa. The next question that popped into my mind was how even a successful barrister could buy this mansion. The Maison Magnifique was built in 1750, constructed of yellow stone, and boasted twenty rooms, as well as an indoor swimming pool. The ceiling and roof were supported by one-foot-square oak beams. The kitchen would delight the finest chef with its six-burner Aga range, a collection of Le Creuset Dutch ovens, and an assortment of Mauviel pots and pans hovering over the *île de cuisine*. The dining room table could accommodate twenty diners. All the rooms, including the bedrooms, had large stone fireplaces. Susan and I were delighted with our room. It featured a large, canopied bed, an elegance we had never experienced.

Risk-taking was part of Giles's DNA. Before he bought the house, it could have been called *Maison terrible*. It had been unoccupied and neglected for years, with a leaking roof, faulty plumbing, and wiring. Giles first negotiated a good purchase price, but he did not close the deal. Instead, he bought an option to buy from the owner, and then he set about recruiting investors for the project. He offered them timeshares. For a lump sum paid in advance, an investor could buy the right to use one of the apartments for one or more months of the year. When Giles believed he had enough investors to cover the cost of rehabbing, he completed the purchase with the help of a mortgage. He helped his bottom line by obtaining a mortgage from a bank in a country whose currency was weak and getting weaker, like the Japanese yen. This lowered the ultimate cost of the loan. He could pay off the mortgage with devalued yen.

What Giles saved on the mortgage, he spent even more on the rehab. He was a connoisseur of historical detail and gladly paid for things like vintage door handles, hinges, and *butées de porte*, doorstops. He rejected economy and chose elegance. He was not opposed to modern conveniences like step-in showers, but he had a fixation with baths. He considered bathing as important to proper British society as tea. Every en-suite bathroom included a claw-footed bathtub large enough to accommodate two people.

It was ironic that the flushing power of the château's modern toilets was put to shame by the whoosh of the *les toilettes sèches*, the outhouse, which was built in the 18th century and stood on one side of the courtyard. It was a three-seater affair and still had a working flushing system. The building sat above a small stream. When you entered the outhouse, you pulled a rope to lower a wooden barrier, which acted like a dam, stopping the flow of the stream and creating a small pond behind it. When your business was satisfactorily completed, you pulled another rope, removing the barricade. The onrush of the released water was truly impressive. Nancy was intrigued and insisted on repeating the process several times.

Lunch was a simple fare of bread, sausage, ten kinds of cheese, each one tasting better than the last, and wine. After lunch, Giles went to wheel and deal about another piece of Normandy real estate. I decided to explore the neighborhood. I walked along an unpaved road through the three-house village of Ravenoville. The land would have remained a marshland if the farmers had not cut numerous channels to drain it, creating islands of drier soil. I had no idea where I was heading. I assumed I could find my way back to the château since there was only one road. I walked up a slight rise and was overwhelmed by the vista—miles of open beach. It was not just any ocean beach; it was Utah Beach, the beach the U.S. 40th Infantry Division stormed on D-Day, June 6th, 1944. It was part of the largest amphibious invasion in history. I could picture thousands of GIs jumping out of Higgins boats,[1] struggling through the water, and charging up the dunes while dozens of MG-42 machine guns mowed them down. How could they do it? Why did they do it? Did they know it was for making such a soft life for us baby boomers? The debt I owed them brought tears to my eyes.

Nearby was a German concrete pillbox or blockhouse used to protect the machine gunners. I squeezed inside and looked out of the gun slits toward Utah Beach. New thoughts flooded my imagination. What did the German soldiers think when they saw thousands of enemy soldiers charging toward them? How could they do it? What were they fighting for? I concluded that the answers to those questions were probably very similar for the American GIs and the German soldiers. I walked back to the luxurious château I was living in with a different perspective. I was born into a lucky generation, and everything I had accomplished thus far was due in large part to the fact that I was standing on the shoulders of giants.

Giles was back when I returned and was eager to be our tour guide. We could not have had a better one. Giles spoke fluent French, had an encyclopedic knowledge of French history, and

---

1. A Higgins boat was a plywood landing craft used to carry a platoon of GIs ashore for amphibious landings in World War II.

knew the back roads and byways of Normandy like the back of his hand. Our first stop was Barfleur, where William the Conqueror had launched his invasion fleet in 1066, thereby seizing England from the Anglo-Saxon King Harold, the last successful invasion of England. Then it was on to La Hogue, where Giles told us that in 1692, the British had given a drubbing to the Dutch and French fleet, although many of the French ships had escaped into the harbor. Not satisfied with their partial victory, the Brits launched fireships into the harbor, and the remainder of the French fleet was destroyed. After Giles told us the British side of the story, he translated the bronze plaque erected by the French to commemo- rate the same event. The plaque proved there had been spin doctors back in the 17th century. It said the French had won the original battle, but perfidious Albion, avoiding a fair fleet against fleet battle, sneaked into the harbor like thieves in the night and burned the French ships.

I was not sure we were in La Hogue so much for the history lesson as for visiting one of Giles's favorite wine shops, where Giles could purchase some of France's finest wines at a tremen- dous discount. Why? They had flawed, half-missing labels or misshapen bottles. They were still not in my price range, but Giles bought six bottles.

Next on the Giles tour was the town of Sainte-Mère-du- Mont, an important crossroads town that had to be taken and held by the 101st and the 82nd Airborne Divisions on D-Day before the Army divisions came ashore on Utah Beach. One of the stories Giles told involved two soldiers in Sainte-Mère-du-Mont: one American paratrooper and one German. They were stunned when they met going around the corner of the same building. They fired simultaneously. The American died instantly, and the German was wounded. Another paratrooper took the wounded German to the American aid station, where a medic saved his life.

That story differed from Giles's description of an American sniper who hid himself behind a statue of the Virgin Mary in front of the village church. Whenever an unknowing German soldier left the building across the square, the paratrooper would shoot him. He killed or wounded twenty enemy soldiers.

Often, success or failure in a battle depends on pure luck, as seen in the anecdote about the French house painter who smuggled a German map showing their defense lines and strongpoints to the Americans. Two German officers had been examining the map in the belfry of the village church. A sudden gust of wind blew it away. The painter saw where the map flew, retrieved it, and delivered it to the first American paratroopers he saw.

As an American, one of the most moving sights we saw demonstrated that the people of Normandy still had a great affection for their American liberators. Normandy is the only place in France where the French and the American flags are flown on adjoining flagpoles, and the American flag was flown at the same height as the French flag.

Our final stop was a quick visit to the de Tocqueville estate to pay homage to Alexis de Tocqueville, who wrote "Democracy in America" in 1835, which is still required reading for history and political science majors. It seemed odd to me that the descendants of a person who so lauded the advantages of democracy had maintained their aristocratic status and still owned a large estate 150 years later.

Back at Maison Magnifique, dinner was what one might expect when surrounded by a group of gourmands. The first course was fish soup and dozens of prawns, which had been grilled in the largest skillet I had ever seen. Rather than allow the prawns to cool off, the skillet was placed in the middle of the table so we could pick them right from the pan. The second course was chicken cooked in goose fat and cauliflower smothered in a cheese sauce. In European fashion, salad came next. Complementing the meal were loaves of *pain brie*, a traditional Normandy bread, and an endless supply of wine. Dessert was a variety of cheeses and chunks of delicious, rich chocolate.

The next day, we had to catch the afternoon ferry back from Cherbourg to Portsmouth, which was ample time for Giles to do more exploring. He announced there would be no breakfast for me. I had mentioned my love for croissants, so Giles took me on a quest to find the best croissant in that part of Normandy. We sped along *routes étroites*[2] to five small villages: Saint-Floxel, Fontenay-sur-Mer, Saint-Marcout, Ozeville, and Saint-Aubin-sur-Algot. At each stop, I tasted a croissant at the local boulangerie. I did not understand how so many bakeries could survive economically when they were only separated by a few miles. Giles explained that it was the French demand for bread baked fresh every day. To serve day-old bread was uncivilized. Susan and I had learned that day-old baguettes could be dangerous weapons. If not eaten within a few hours, a baguette was hard enough to use as a club.

I did not expect I would be able to discern the difference among the croissants. They all tasted delicious, layered, puffy, with a crisp top producing a slight crunch when I bit into them. When I broke off a piece of the croissant, little flakes fell onto my plate, a good sign.

The most important ingredient was butter, some boasting as much as 50% of its weight. The croissants I ate would have appalled my cardiologist. To my surprise, I did have a favorite. It was the Boulangerie Les Co'Pains croissant, but I could not explain why.

We were not done. Giles insisted we share an omelet at the café next door. I knew better than to ask for ketchup. Then, after eating only half of my omelet, Giles told me no Normandy breakfast would be complete without a shot of Calvados, a kind of apple brandy we Americans call applejack. It could not be sipped. The proper etiquette was to touch glasses and toss it down our throats in one gulp. The liquid burned all the way and lit a small fire in my belly.

The final stop was the summit of one of the few real hills in an otherwise flat landscape. It was a crisp, cloudless day, so we could see from horizon to horizon, from Utah Beach to Cherbourg, all

---

2. Routes étroits are narrow winding roads.

the farms and villages laid out like a map. On the crest of the hill stood a petite, quaint chapel projecting an aura of serenity and normality, an aura distorted by a German pillbox close to the chapel's west wall. The pillbox had clearly been peppered with hundreds of bullets. What was it doing next to the church? Why was it not removed, leaving the chapel as the only structure on the hill? I assumed the juxtaposition of a symbol of peace with a symbol of war was meant to convey a message, a question, really. How can humankind reconcile such contradictions?

As for contradictions, Giles's attitude about the French was becoming clearer to me. Giles loved everything about France except the French. How could he be so enamored of the country and yet maintain a visceral animosity towards its people? Giles's opinion was mirrored by many Brits.

On our croissant excursion, I asked Giles what it was about the French he disliked so much. He said he objected to the French inquisitional legal system, which was the opposite of the British adversarial system. Giles's antipathy was understandable considering the French had little use for barrister-like lawyers. For example, Giles had been sued by a contractor who wanted to be paid for his work on Maison Magnifique. Giles refused to pay, claiming the contractor had done shoddy work. Giles disregarded the adage, "A lawyer who represents himself has a fool for a client." The French judge severely limited Giles's opportunity to question witnesses, especially the chance to subject adverse witnesses to his withering cross-examinations. Several times, the judge told Giles to sit down and stop making objections, lecturing Giles about the British Rules of Evidence not applying in French courts. To Giles, that was the equivalent of telling a priest that the Ten Commandments are irrelevant. Giles lost the case.

After Giles's rant about the French courts, his reasons for disliking the French resorted to the usual tropes, or actually one trope: how France had behaved in World War II. It begins with, "We (meaning the British) won the war," overlooking the contributions of Russia and America. This mantra was quickly followed by the gist of the complaint: "The French surrendered to the Nazis too soon and left Britain to fight on alone against the German juggernaut." Although the French would disagree with this assertion, there is a case to be made. In June 1941, the French still had an intact army, and it occupied over half of France. The fact that all the French leaders who had decided to surrender to the Germans were long dead did not alter Giles's visceral animosity towards the French. After the World War II surrender harangue was exhausted, Giles was hard-pressed to say what else it was about the French people he disliked.

It was time for a quick lunch back at Maison Magnifique, with the *pièce de résistance,* thinly sliced potatoes fried in the left-over goose fat from the Saturday night dinner. Of course, the potatoes were accompanied by fresh bread, cheese, sausages, and wine. Lunch was followed by a dash to catch the ferry, and Giles pulled up to the pedestrian entry gate with five minutes to spare. After a 6-hour trip across the English Channel, we were back in Portsmouth on Sunday evening.

NINE

Just Another Adoring Client

While a few of Giles's clients wanted to punch him, some of them wanted to hug him and kiss him on both cheeks, like Elizabeth Strong. Liz had been charged with embezzlement. She was the bookkeeper for the King Alfred Theatre and had stolen £27,000 from its bank account. Liz had a serious drinking problem. She pleaded guilty, and Giles's task was to try to mitigate her sentence. In England, mitigation with no prison time was rare in white-collar crime cases. Unlike in America, British judges regarded theft by persons in positions of trust as a more serious crime than the burglary of an unoccupied home. The British Sentencing Guidelines made sense to me. The prospect of serving time in prison is more of a deterrent to people who are likely to embezzle and commit other white-collar crimes than it is to thieves who break into homes. People who like good food, soft beds, and clean sheets will think twice before stealing from their employers or clients. They would know they could be serving time in a 10x12 cell with a cellmate who doesn't use deodorant, eating mass-produced food on a tin tray, sleeping on a steel cot, and having roaches crawling over them at night.

Giles told Liz that her chances of serving no time in prison and getting probation were practically nil. He advised her to pack her clothes and her toothbrush before coming to court. If Liz were given prison time, she would be led directly from the courtroom to her prison cell. Liz came to court prepared. She had her electricity shut off and put her cat in a cattery. My cynical side thought Giles may have downplayed Liz's chance of getting probation and wanted to stifle any glimmer of false hope, which would traumatize Liz even more if she were marched off to prison. Giles would vigorously deny it, but he may have also been lowering expectations about what he could accomplish through mitigation. If his performance kept Liz out of prison, his star would burn ever more brightly. I wondered if Giles was aware of the rumor I had heard a few days before Liz's sentencing. A probation officer told me his boss joked that probation officers should be more generous in recommending probation because the prisons were overcrowded.

Whatever Giles's motivation, his plea in mitigation was brilliant. First, he packed the courtroom with Liz's family and friends. He also managed to persuade Charles Taylor, Liz's former boss and the owner of the King Alfred Theatre, to submit a sworn statement on Liz's behalf. He told the court that Liz had been an excellent employee until her drinking led her astray, and that she had paid back the entire amount she had stolen. Most importantly, Charles said he forgave Liz.

Giles was at his rhetorical best, describing how Liz had turned her life around and how she tried to undo the harm she had caused. Liz reimbursed the King Alfred Theatre for every penny she had stolen by selling her home and borrowing from her parents. Giles stressed that Liz was enrolled in Alcoholics Anonymous and had been sober for four months. A major mitigating factor was that Liz herself had reported the theft to her employer and the police *before* it was discovered. Finally, Giles described in graphic detail how imprisoning this young woman would not foster her rehabilitation. Subjecting Liz to harsh prison conditions and surrounding her with hardened criminals would undermine the progress she had already made. Giles's speech overflowed with so much sympathy for Liz that I was prepared to hear Giles conclude that Liz should be rewarded for her actions, not punished. He did not do that. Giles knew when to stop gilding the lily. I am not sure if his eloquence discouraged the prosecuting barrister from arguing for imposing a prison sentence on Liz, but he told the judge, "I have nothing to add."

When Judge Warren recessed the hearing to consider the sentence he would impose on Liz, I had time to ponder Giles's performance, for it was a performance worthy of a skilled actor. Did Giles believe in what he was saying? Did he have to? Did he really feel sorry for Liz and would have been saddened by the sight of her being led off to prison? I do not think so. Paradoxically, my opinion of Giles was not diminished by thinking that once Liz left Giles's sight on her way to a small prison cell, he would think much more about her. I pondered whether such indifference may be a vital trait for any barrister. If a barrister representing a defendant felt sympathy for a convicted client, would he or she necessarily feel some self-reproach over the result? *What did I do wrong? Is Liz going to prison because of me?* That could be a slippery slope for Giles or any barrister. Barristers do reflect on how they could have improved their courtroom performance and incorporate those lessons for their next cases. Yet, too much self-reflection may also generate a sense of remorse, which, over time, could forge a heavy chain of guilt.

Judge Warren returned to the courtroom and pronounced his sentence—two years of probation and no prison time. The courtroom erupted in a cacophony of cheers and applause. Judge Warren gaveled for silence, but he did not seem to have his heart in it and could not suppress a smile. Liz hugged Giles, and she may have been aiming for two pecks on Giles's cheeks, but she missed and planted a large kiss on his lips, which Giles took in his stride.

A victory celebration was held at a nearby pub with a river of champagne. Our glasses—Giles's and mine—were constantly refilled, and lunch was free. I noticed Liz did not sip the champagne. Giles was in his glory, surrounded by people telling him how brilliant he was. When it was time for toasts to Giles and Liz, I was mortified when Giles toasted Liz and added a piece of advice: "Keep your hand out of the till." Curiously, I seemed to be the only one in the room who was troubled by the comment. Liz just responded with a hearty laugh. I was envious. Giles had the knack of getting by with comments that, if said by me, would provoke a chorus of criticism. This was my first experience with the phenomenon of people giving Giles a *pass*, letting *Giles be Giles*.

I did have a chance to chat with Liz. She had been convinced she would be sentenced to prison and was still finding it hard to accept Jude Warren's lenient sentence. Liz said she imagined a bailiff barging into the pub and saying there had been a mistake and hustling her off to prison. She was surprised and gratified by how her friends had rallied around her. Liz had thought they would shun her.

In contrast, Giles offered her no emotional support during her ordeal. Liz liked that. She said Giles took a hard and objective look at her case and told it like it was. Everyone else was so supportive that she needed someone to be candid with her about her situation. With Giles, Liz could be open and honest, expressing those negative feelings she had to suppress with her friends. She had not wanted to hurt their feelings. Giles was not being 'nice' with her, so she did not have to be 'nice' with Giles. Liz then hesitated a moment before adding with a winsome smile that it helped her to accept the hard truth Giles was delivering because he was "so good-looking."

TEN

The next day at Chambers, Giles shoved a large file box toward me, filled with all the materials connected with a case he had recently tried and lost. He told me he wanted me to draft a brief for an appeal. I asked Giles if the case was going to be appealed to the Court of Appeals, and he quipped, "You only get one appeal, David." He had filed in the Court of Appeal (singular) Criminal Division. I tried to disguise my panic. I assumed Giles was asking me to review all the materials in the box, including documents, statements, and the trial transcript, and to unearth all possible grounds for appealing the jury's guilty verdict, a monumental task. Adding to my dread was the distinct possibility that drafting a brief would display my ignorance. Up to this point, I had managed to avoid opportunities to appear stupid.

Fortunately, Giles was able to allay one cause of my dread. He had already applied to the Court of Appeal for permission to appeal. In England, there is no automatic right to appeal a criminal conviction. In fact, until 1908, there was no right of appeal. Convicted defendants could only submit applications to the Home Secretary, claiming a wrongful conviction and requesting a new trial—applications that were often never read and rarely granted. Today, under the rules for appeal, permission to appeal would be denied unless at least one judge on a three-judge appeal panel agreed that there is a substantial appealable issue. Giles had scaled that hurdle.

Giles, being the self-confident person he was, had decided to put all his eggs in one basket during the jury trial in the Crown Court. Those same eggs were the basis of his appeal to the Court of Appeal. One might say he put just one egg in the defense basket. It was the hearsay egg. I felt relieved. Tossing me this brief on the hearsay issue was like Brer Rabbit being thrown into the briar patch; the hearsay thicket was a cozy home for me. For law students, the *hearsay rule* is like the rope climb requirement in a high school gym class. To get a passing grade in gym, every student had to climb a twenty-foot-long, thick rope attached to a steel beam, touch the beam, and slide down. Similarly, law students must demonstrate a basic understanding of the rule against hearsay to pass *Evidence*, a required course. [1]

Giles's appeal in the attempted murder case of The Crown vs Sam Jordon and Margot Welch was based on an erroneous application of the hearsay rule by Judge Nelson.

Giles had only represented Welch and maintained that the entire case for the Crown against Welch was based on hearsay evidence. So, Giles took the risky route of not calling any witnesses for the defense, including Welch, and only put the one hearsay egg in his defense basket. Giles's strategy proved ineffec-

---

1. This brief footnote is intended for those readers who want to know more about the Hearsay Rule because they aspire to attend law school or hope to critique TV lawyers for their lack of understanding of the Hearsay Rule.

Hearsay occurs when person #1 tells person #2 something person #3 had said. Hearsay law considers #2's testimony about what #3 had said as inherently unreliable, unless #3's statement was made under oath and subject to cross-examination, which enables the judge and the jury to assess #3's statement for its trustworthiness. For example, Robert says, "Mary told me that John shot Alice." The Hearsay Rule prevents Mary's assertion that "John shot Alice" from being used in court to prove John shot Alice. Why? Because without being able to question Mary, we have no idea if Mary actually saw the shooting, or saw the shooting and was confused about how it happened, or Mary was lying outright about the shooting and it was Mary who pulled the trigger.

tive at trial. The jury found Welch and Jordon guilty of attempted murder. It was my job to draft a brief that would convince the Court of Appeal that Judge Nelson had erred in the case against Welch when he allowed the jury to consider improper hearsay evidence in reaching its verdict, and that Giles's hearsay egg was sufficient to reverse the guilty verdict.

The gist of the Crown's case was simple. Margot Welch had hired Sam Jordon to kill her husband. Both were charged with attempted murder. As I began to read the testimony from the trial, however, the plotline may have been more accurately described as *Laurel and Hardy attempt murder*. The entire scenario was so bizarre it would have been beyond Agatha Christie's imaginative powers, starting with the fact that the would-be victim, Mathew Welch, kept a troop of tarantulas as pets.

The Crown's case was based almost entirely on the testimony of three witnesses: Detective Chief Inspector Boney, victim Mathew Welch, and Blake Watson. Watson had also been originally charged with attempted murder, but he pleaded guilty and agreed to cooperate with the prosecution. Neither Margot Welch nor Sam Jordon testified on their own behalf, a wise decision.

Blake Watson was the first witness called by the Crown. He testified that he had been approached by his friend Sam Jordon to assist him in a little caper Jordon was planning. Jordon had told him that he had been offered a lucrative deal by his next-door neighbor, Margot Welch. She said she would pay Jordon 2000 quid[2] if he would kill her husband, Mathew. Jordon was intrigued by the offer because he detested Mathew Welch and his hobby of raising tarantulas, which often found their way into his garden. Jordon demanded that he be paid 3500 quid. Margot Welch agreed. Jordon told Watson that he could earn 1000 quid if he helped Jordon free Margot Welch from an unhappy marriage.

---

2. A quid is slang for one British Pound (£). One £ equals approximately $1.50.

Jordon described to Watson how he and Watson would take Mathew Welch out drinking and get him drunk.

With the alcohol smoothing the way, Jordon would invite Mathew to join them in a little enterprise that night, which could earn Mathew 500 pounds. Jordon would tell Mathew he would only need to help unload a cargo of marijuana from a small fishing boat that would come ashore at a nearby beach at 1:00 AM. In Dorset, of course, the beach was at the base of a 150-foot limestone cliff. Jordon said the three of them would leave the pub and go to the footpath along the nearby cliffs to watch for the imaginary boat. Jordon would encourage Mathew to keep an eye out for the boat, which was to flash three times with a torch.[3] Then Watson would excitedly ask Mathew if he could see what looked like a boat on the beach. When Mathew looked over the cliff, straining to see a boat, Jordon would push him off, and the 150-foot fall would do the rest. When, and if, Mathew's body was found, the autopsy would reveal a large amount of alcohol in his blood. Based on that fact, along with Mathew's reputation for often being drunk, the police would conclude he had accidentally fallen off the cliff. Watson thought it sounded like a surefire plan and agreed to participate.

Watson further testified that the next night, he and Jordon put the plan into action, and all seemed to go just as planned. Mathew looked over the cliff, Jordon shoved him, and they heard Mathew scream while falling. Jordon and Watson did not check on the results of their handiwork and quickly ran away from the cliff.

Jordon told Watson the following day that he had immediately returned home, knocked on Margot Welch's door, told Margot the deed was done, and that he would be back in the morning to collect his money. However, the best laid plans sometimes do go awry. Jordon told Watson that an hour or so later, there was pounding on his door. Jordon peeked out and saw what

3. Flashlight

he thought was a ghost. It was Mathew Welch wielding a cricket bat. Jordon wisely chose not to answer the door. Before dawn, he sneaked out of his house and went to a nearby town, where he rented a hotel room.

Jordon was not a quitter, though. He had a Plan B. Jordon again sought the help of Watson. Watson needed some persuading, so Jordon pointed out to Watson that their incentive to kill Mathew had doubled. In addition to the money, they had to keep Mathew from going to the police. Jordon then proposed another foolproof plan. Mathew Welch worked at a local pub, the Ugly Swan, and when the pub closed at 11:00 PM, as required by law, Mathew would leave the pub and walk home. To walk directly home, Mathew would have to cross the road in front of the pub. So, Jordon proposed to Watson that they steal a van from the Dorset Truck Rentals' lot and wait at the top of the hill in the van until Mathew left the pub. Then, when Mathew began to cross the road, they would zoom down the hill, hit Mathew, drive away, return the van to the rental lot, and the police would be none the wiser. Watson testified that he was not sure about the plan being foolproof, but he agreed to help for an additional £500.

Watson's story continued. As planned, the next night, Jordon and Watson were perched at the top of the hill in the stolen van overlooking the Ugly Swan. When Mathew left the pub shortly after 11:00 PM and was in the killing zone, Jordon revved the engine and tore down the hill. Except that when the van was fifteen meters from Mathew, they realized the man in their headlights was not Mathew. Jordon stood on the brakes and swerved into a hedgerow, narrowly missing the unknown pedestrian. The would-be victim was so grateful to have escaped certain death that he helped Jordon and Watson push the van out of the bushes. The bumbling would-be murderers returned the slightly scratched van to the Dorset Truck Rental lot.

Abiding by his mother's advice that "If first you don't succeed, try, try again," Jordon concocted yet another way to end Mathew's charmed life, and he once again proposed it to Watson.

Watson listened, but the two failed attempted murders had increased his skepticism about Jordon's crime-planning ability and reminded him of his own mother's advice, something about not being fooled twice. So, Watson listened very nicely and then went out and did precisely what he wanted to do. He contacted the police.

At first, Detective Sargent Hardy, who took Watson's garbled statement, did not believe him. Watson's tale that mixed tarantulas, a man surviving a fall from the Dorset cliffs, and being hit by a van was clearly a figment of Watson's overactive imagination. Hardy filed the report in the 'No Further Action Required' drawer.

After Watson's testimony, Giles only asked one question. "Mister Watson, did you at any time talk with, or even meet with Mrs. Margot Welch?"

Watson said, "No."

The next witness for the Crown was Detective Chief Inspector Boney. Inspector Boney explained how the case was resurrected from the 'No Further Action Required' drawer. She said, the next day after Watson visited the station, Detective Sargent Hardy was telling the other officers in the West Bay Station about a crazy guy named Harper coming into the station to confess to trying to kill a man who raised tarantulas and who was pushed off a cliff and survived. Constable Casey interrupted the story and recalled that several days earlier, an inebriated man by the name of Mathew Welch had come into the station complaining about being pushed off Chesil Cliff and surviving. When Officer Casey asked Welch what he was doing on Chesil Cliff at midnight, Welch said, "Forget it," and walked out of the station. Detective Boney told the jury that she connected the dots and believed the two tales of Welch and Watson had to be more than a coincidence. She ordered her team to make further inquiries, which led to the complete unraveling of Jordon's "foolproof" plan. Detective Boney concluded her testimony by describing how she interviewed Mathew Welch and Blake Watson with a station house solicitor present, and that at the end of their interviews, they provided written statements. In contrast, Detective Boney said that when she attempted to interview Margot Welch and Sam Jordon, they chose to exercise their right to remain silent and say nothing.

Again, Giles asked only one question of the witness. "Detective Boney, did Mrs. Welch say anything else to you except, 'no comment?'"

"No."

The final witness was Mathew Welch, who confirmed much of the preceding testimony. He described how he had gone out drinking with Jordon and Watson and consumed a few pints of the pub's Best Bitter. Mathew testified that Jordon told him how he could earn 500 quid in just a couple of hours by helping unload marijuana from a small fishing boat. The boat would arrive on the beach beneath Chesil Cliff shortly after midnight. He agreed to help. They walked to the top of the cliff along the footpath and waited for the boat's signal—three torch flashes. Mathew told the jury that Watson began acting all excited and said he thought he saw the boat on the beach, and asked Mathew if he could see the boat. When Mathew leaned forward to look, he was shoved from behind. Mathew staggered and fell off the cliff. About thirty feet down the side of the precipice was a large bush growing out of the cliff-face. Mathew said the bush stopped his fall, and he was able to hold on to keep from falling further. Mathew said he did not remember how, but he managed to scramble back up the cliff to the footpath. By then, Jordon and Watson were gone.

Mathew said his first instinct was to tell the police about Jordon and Watson trying to kill him, so he walked to the West Bay Station and began telling his story. He admitted he was still under the influence of alcohol and the trauma of being pushed off a cliff, so he may have sounded befuddled. When the constable asked him what he had been doing on the cliff at midnight, he realized he would be admitting to the crime of smuggling illegal drugs into the country, so Mathew walked out of the station and went home. After quietly letting himself in with the key, Mathew went up to the bedroom. He was trying to be quiet, but he stumbled over a chair. Margot Welch sat straight up in bed and shouted, "What are you doing here?" Mathew said he was puzzled by what Margot meant since he lived in the house and slept in that bedroom. Mathew testified that it was at that point that he went next door with a cricket bat and pounded on Sam Jordon's door. When Jordon did not open the door, Mathew returned to his house, crawled into bed with Margot, who seemed to have calmed down, and immediately fell asleep. The next day, Mathew said he tried to talk with Jordon, but Jordon was not home, or at least did not answer the door. Mathew admitted to the jury that he did not tell the police about what happened until Detective Hardy contacted him.

Finally, Mathew acknowledged he had sometimes slapped Margot in the face when he was drunk. He said he also liked to put one of his pet tarantulas on Margot's pillow before she went to bed to remind her who was boss. Mathew added that the tarantula trick made Margot very angry and said she felt like killing him in his sleep some night.

Once again, Giles posed just one question to Mathew. It appeared to be a risky one, and probably objectionable, but, as I was learning, Giles got an intoxicating rush from taking such risks. "Mr. Welch, did Margot Welch ever say anything to you about her alleged involvement in the plot to kill you?" Mathew's answer was, "Yes, she said she had nothing to do with it and that she loved me."

After the Crown rested its case, Giles did not call one witness. His closing speech was entirely focused on his assertion that the Crown had not introduced one iota of direct evidence linking Margot Welch to the attempt on her husband's life, and the entire case for the prosecution was based on hearsay testimony by Blake Watson. Everything Jordon had supposedly told Blake Watson about Margot Welch saying she wanted Jordon to kill her husband was hearsay. Giles argued that such hearsay evidence was unreliable, adding that Judge Barth would instruct them not to consider Margot's alleged statements to Jordon when determining the guilt or innocence of Margot Welsh.

In Judge Barth's summation of the case, he attempted the impossible. He instructed the jury that they could only consider Blake Watson's testimony regarding what Jordon told him about Margot Welch's involvement as evidence against Jordon. However, they were to ignore Jordon's hearsay statements about his conversations with Margot Welch when deciding if Margot Welch was part of the plot to kill Mathew Welch. How could the jury possibly determine what that instruction meant?

The gist of our appeal and my brief was that the jury obviously ignored or misunderstood Judge Barth's instructions and found Margo Welch guilty based on the inadmissible hearsay evidence. In fact, the judge was asking the jury to undertake an impossible analytical task. It was a reversible error to allow a jury to use what Jordon said to Watson to convict Jordon, but also instruct the jury **not** to use Jordon's hearsay statements to convict Margot Welch. The prosecution made a mistake by trying Jordon and Margot Welch together in one case. Now, I *just* had to draft the brief.

After reading the transcript from the trial, I had to ask Giles if, in his conversations with Margot Welch, she had admitted being involved in the attempted murder of her husband. Giles smiled and said, "David, attorney-client privilege, you know." I took that as a *yes*. That would explain, of course, Giles's decision not to let Margot testify. I also probed him about his cross-examination strategy, or lack thereof, especially with Blake Watson. Watson had a bullseye on his chest. He was not the brightest bulb in the pack and was easily befuddled. Giles could have made him look like—well, the Laurel half of the slapstick Laurel and Hardy comedy team. Giles correctly pointed out that beating up on Watson would not have enhanced the main defense based on the use of improper hearsay. Besides, one could not be sure that in the process of skewering Watson on the witness stand, Watson might have blurted out something that could hurt our defense.

I then began to speculate whether Margot Welch's admission of guilt to Giles, if it happened, influenced Giles's risky decision to roll the dice and rely entirely on his hearsay defense strategy. It was like shooting craps with someone else's money, money they may have stolen. Giles could play fast and loose because if he lost his gamble, Margot Welch would only be getting what she deserved. If he were playing with his own money, would he hedge his bet? I know how I would answer that question—hedge. As I learned more about Giles, however, I am sure he would go all in. He was inherently a risk-taker. The barrister system encourages emotional distance from clients, so guilt over a client's conviction is minimized. With little empathy for the client, the barrister is psychologically liberated to approach the whole trial as a chess game filled with attacks, defenses, feints, and gambits. A chess player may be tempted to try the ultimate gambit, the Queen's Gambit, sacrificing one's queen—the most powerful piece on the board—in the hope of gaining a decisive strategic advantage. Giles was willing to make that gamble with Margot Welch.

So, all I needed to do was draft a brief for the Court of Appeal. In England, writing a brief for the appeals court is not as onerous as in the States. The Court of Appeal demands *Skelton Briefs*. It is an apt description. The judges want the bare bones of an appeal, and scorn the fleshy, fatty, rhetorical baggage we lawyers like to add to the skeleton. "Cite the relevant statutes and cases, and do not waste our time telling us what the cases mean. We can do that for ourselves." I finished the brief in two weeks, but could not resist adding a few rhetorical flourishes.

What would Giles think of it? Suddenly, I had sympathy for my students when I evaluated and critiqued their writing assignments. Fortunately, Giles declared my brief "Brilliant!" He did need to correct my spelling of a couple of words, so they complied with the King's English, like replacing 'labor' with 'labour.' A few days later, Giles confirmed that his enthusiasm for my brief was not meant to flatter me, something that would be totally out of character for Giles. Giles and I were in the courthouse chatting with another barrister, who mentioned having a thorny hearsay issue to deal with. He reached into his briefcase, pulled out a copy of my brief, and urged the other barrister to read it. After a quick perusal, the barrister asked, "This is very good. Who wrote it?" Giles pointed to me and said, "My pupil, but I suppose I should put pupil in quotation marks since I am learning more from him than he is from me." I tried to accept the compliment modestly, but I was bursting with pride. It was a watershed moment. Our relationship changed in an instant. From then on, it was clear that Giles would treat me as an equal, and more importantly, I would feel like an equal, knowing that my analysis and opinions would carry weight.

Although Giles probably did not consider this exchange to be a teaching moment, it was from my perspective. I realized that when students feel their views are respected and valued by the professor, their enthusiasm for learning increases. A more confident student is better prepared to learn and is eager to engage with and even challenge a professor, creating richer learning opportunities.

The final test of my brief did not occur until two months later, when oral arguments were scheduled in the Court of Appeal Criminal Division in London. The timing for me was not ideal. The weekend before, we were on a family trip to Penzance, Cornwall. We had booked a sleeper train back to London, which was due at Paddington Station not long before our appeal was scheduled to be heard. To save money, we only reserved a two-berth compartment, so Nancy had to curl up and sleep on the wood panel covering the sink. My dressing for the court was comedic, at least for my family. Trying to shave on a rocking train was treacherous, but I only cut myself once. Wriggling into my non-Savile Row suit while periodically falling backward onto the lower berth sparked pithy comments from Susan.

Fortunately, the train arrived on schedule, and I hailed a cab to avoid possible delays on the Tube. When the cab stopped to let me out, I thought the driver had misunderstood my directions and had driven me instead to a Gothic cathedral. The two main black oak doors were set back under five concentric arches, providing a covered entrance. The façade was a jumble of towers, spires, gargoyles, and statues, bedecked with stained glass windows, the largest of which mimicked the Rose Window in Paris' Notre-Dame Cathedral. Except for the absence of an altar and ranks of pews, the cathedral aura was not diminished inside the Great Hall. The ceiling replicated the nave of a European Gothic cathedral. The courtrooms radiated out to the left and right of the Great Hall. As I entered Courtroom C, I wondered what small forest had been used to supply all the wood that covered the walls in a room three stories high. Surrounding the third story was a passageway screened by dense wooden lattice-work. It was rumored that the hidden corridor enabled the Lord Chief Justice to snoop surreptitiously on Court of Appeal judges.

While sitting in this ornate edifice and courtroom, I mused on the irony of lavishing such extravagance on a Criminal Court of Appeal that did not even come into existence until 1908. Prior to that date, individuals found guilty in a Crown Court had no right to appeal the verdict or their sentence. The judge might have committed the most egregious error in conducting the trial. Yet the convicted defendant had little to no chance of having a higher authority review those errors. These errors may have helped convict and hang an innocent person. The only remedy available to a convicted felon was to petition the Home Secretary to review the case. Those requests gathered at the bottom of the Home Secretary's *to-do list*. It was only after a long and determined public campaign, led in part by Arthur Conan Doyle, the creator of Sherlock Holmes, that Parliament was forced to create a criminal appeal process.

My haste in getting to court turned out to be needless. Giles neglected to tell me how appeals were scheduled. The Appeal Court published the order in which the cases would be heard, but did not designate a specific time slot for each case. If a case is fourth on the list, like our case, a barrister must make an educated guess as to when the case will be called. The unknown factor was how long the judges would allow barristers to talk. There is no set time limit. No, "You have two minutes left, Counsel." A barrister can ramble on until exhausting the topic and everyone in the courtroom, or until the presiding judge says, "Thank you, counsel, that is sufficient." There were a few ramblers in the earlier cases, so Giles's oral argument was held over as the first case on the afternoon docket. I ate my takeaway sandwich sitting on a marble bench in the Great Hall. It felt both sacrilegious and satisfying at the same time, profane in that I was eating my lunch in the nave of a sacred judicial cathedral and pleasing that an Ohio rube could eat his vending machine ham and cheese in such a magnificent restaurant.

When *Crown v. Margot Welch* was announced, Giles took his place behind the council table, and I sat alone in the public gallery. Giles summarized the grounds for the appeal and cited the relevant case law. There was no emotional content in the words he chose, nor was there an appeal to rectify a travesty of justice. There were several desultory questions from the bench. Then, with a glance at his fellow Justices, the presiding judge said, "Thank you, Mr. Adams-Smyth," and Giles sat down. I was caught up in my own hubris, assuming the arguments I made in my brief would carry the day. I was convinced the court had no choice but to reverse Margot Welch's conviction.

Then it was the barrister for the Crown's turn. He began with perfect intonation. "My Lords..." followed by a stream of perfect prose which was devoid of sound and fury, and in my opinion, signified nothing. However, as he droned on, drip by verbal drip, I began to worry. Would his trickle of words erode the logic of my brief? After half an hour, my worry produced a hollow feeling in my stomach, and perspiration broke out on my forehead. The judges were silent, asking no questions, and Giles was lounging back with one arm flung over an adjoining chair.

I had attached my personal self-worth to that brief, and it was now in jeopardy. Finally, the droning of the Crown's barrister ceased, and the judges retired to a room behind their bench. Nobody moved. We sat there. In less than five minutes, the judges returned and announced that the panel had reached a decision. At least we did not have to wait months for the court's judgment, as so often happens in the States. I quickly realized that this well-crafted opinion had been drafted before the oral arguments. My pins and needles disappeared in an instant when the presiding judge announced that all three Justices agreed that Margot Welch's conviction was not "safe" and would be reversed. Margot was now a free woman. I felt a rush of pride when I realized the judges had made up their minds before the hearing and that the oral arguments were mostly window dressing, providing the barristers with an unlikely opportunity to change the panel's mind. The judges had decided the case solely on the persuasiveness of my brief.

I floated out of Courtroom C and congratulated Giles on his victory. I confessed to him I had been worried the Crown's barrister might eventually wear down the judges with his never-ending speech. Giles laughed. He said he knew we had won the case the moment the presiding judge told Giles he could sit down. It was not a dismissal of Giles's argument, but a signal that the Justices agreed with it. Giles further explained that the court allowed the Crown barrister to take as much time as he wanted to try to change the judges' minds. There could be no complaint that he was not given a full and fair opportunity to persuade the Appeal Court to accept his view of the case. I was not angry with Giles, but I did scold him for not telling me we had prevailed sooner. He shrugged. "It was a good opportunity to practice controlling your emotions, David, and realize that you should avoid measuring your self-worth by how a judge, or a jury, or even the Court of Appeal decides your case."

The final wacky twist in the Margot Welch case occurred within weeks of the Court of Appeal's decision. Margot and Mathew apparently reconciled. Mathew forgave Margot for hiring Jordon and Watson to push him off a cliff. Mathew was allowed back into the house and readmitted to the conjugal bed, sans tarantulas.

They sold their story to a tabloid newspaper for 20,000 quid.

ELEVEN

Once More Into The Affray

In a sense, Giles had to don a different kind of wig for Monday's case. He was prosecuting for the Crown two yobs[1] who were charged with 'Affray,' the American equivalent of 'Assault,' and sometimes labeled 'Assault and Battery.' A person is guilty of affray if he or she uses or threatens unlawful violence towards another person, and the conduct would cause a person of reasonable firmness to fear for his or her personal safety. The tricky part of prosecuting a person for affray is proving that the perpetrator intended to use violence or threaten violence and was aware that his or her conduct was violent or appeared to threaten violence. An added incentive for obtaining a conviction in this case was that a female constable, Martha Cross, was the person who was assaulted and injured.

As the prosecuting barrister for the Crown, Giles assumed his 'honest guide' persona. Oozing neutrality from every pore, he stripped his opening speech of any language that would appeal to the jury's emotions or suggest the need for good citizens to protect the community from bad actors like the defendants. Giles described to me his approach.

---

1. A yob is a loud, loutish, thug type.

98

"You must convey the impression that you do not deal in tricks, and do not hold with the trickery of others... that you, unique among barristers, will tell it to them straight, that you will grapple honestly with every problem and every difficulty they may at first blush have with your case, and without any clever stuff, or long lawyerly words thereby inveigle them into allowing you into the jury box as the dead straight 13th juror."

I was not sure our case was going to be much of a test for the efficacy of Giles's tactic. There was overwhelming evidence pointing to the guilt of the defendants, Yates and Harper, including the statements they made to the police. Consequently, Giles's direct examination of our witnesses bordered on boring. The fun part for me was listening to the cross-examinations by the defense counsels, Arthur Cooke and Bram McDonald. I wished their questioning had been video recorded so I could show my Trial Practice students how *not* to conduct cross-examinations.

An important consideration for planning any cross-examination is the decision whether to scuff-up a witness or obtain the testimony you want from the witness by playing firm but nice. If the witness is a person the jury is inclined to sympathize with, launching an all-out attack on their character is likely to backfire. Yates's counsel, Arthur Cooke, made the mistake of trying to transform the victim of the assault, Constable Martha Cross, into the villain of the affray. Cooke not only failed to scuff up the officer, but it was unnecessary to try. Officer Cross could only identify the defendant, Guy Harper, in the affray and did not see Yates join in the melee. Cooke should have asked one question. "Officer Cross, isn't it true that you cannot say today that Yates was a participant in the affray?" To which, she would have had to answer, "Yes."

During the lunch break, Giles and I went to the scene of the crime and ate our brown-bag lunches outside the restaurant where the affray occurred. Giles was appalled that I ate a peanut-butter sandwich. I told him to think of it as *pâté*.

Yates's defense counsel, Cooke, and Harper's counsel,

McDonald, continued to demonstrate how *not* to conduct a cross-examination. At first, I thought McDonald was making progress on a possible misidentification by referring to Constable Cross's prior statement that a "colored man" was involved in the fight. Harper was olive-skinned and had emigrated from Pakistan. Cooke asked the officer if what she meant by 'colored' was 'black,' to which she replied, "Yes." I was on the prosecution team, but my professorial instincts were urging me to shout, "Sit down. Do not ask another question." Cooke had made a good point that he could use in his final speech. "My client, Guy Harper, was not involved in the affray because he is obviously not black."

Did McDonald sit down? No, he felt compelled to drive the point home, but only succeeded in burying the point in his own chest. He asked Officer Cross to look at Mr. Harper and say whether she considered him a "Black man." Without missing a beat, she said, "Yes, I do. That is the man I have been talking about." If an American, like me, knew that Brits often referred to olive-skinned people from Pakistan and India as 'Blacks,' surely a London barrister should know that.

Giles was completely relaxed in trying this case. Cooke and McDonald were doing all the heavy lifting for the prosecution. The more they cross-examined the prosecution witnesses, the bigger hole they dug for their clients.

For example, McDonald sought to minimize the injury suffered by Officer Cross. She had testified that she was bruised in the chest when one of the defendants kicked her. The treating physician, Dr. Osborne, said nothing in his report about Officer Cross having bruises. When Giles reread the report, though, something did not seem right to him. He asked me to talk to the Crown Prosecuting Solicitor, Orla, and have her contact Dr. Osborne to find out if he had sent the complete report. Dr. Osborne hadn't. One of the pages had not been faxed. When we saw the missing page, we knew we had struck gold, but Giles bided his time. He did not object while McDonald labored to make the case that the constable had not been hurt because Dr. Osborne did not find any bruising. At that point, Giles stood up and made an application to Judge Read. The jury was excused while the application was discussed. Giles showed the missing page to Judge Read and asked for permission to call Dr. Osborne to authenticate it and have it included with the previously admitted report. Judge Read agreed.

In the afternoon, Dr. Osborne took the stand and explained to the jury that the initial version of his report, which he faxed to the Crown Prosecution Service, did not include the missing page and had been inadvertently left out. Then Giles delivered the *coup de grâce*. He asked Judge Read's permission to read the missing page to the jury, which Judge Read granted.

Giles paused for dramatic effect, building jury anticipation, before theatrically flourishing the missing page from Dr. Osborne's report. He first played the gracious adversary and absolved McDonald of not discovering the missing page from the original report. Giles followed up that introduction by hinting that Judge Read considered the missing page important evidence since he had allowed Giles to read the missing page to the jury. Finally, with the jury now eager to hear the report, Giles read, "In addition to other injuries incurred by policewoman Martha Cross, there was a bruise on her chest in the shape of a boot." He could not resist flashing a smug grin at the jury before he sat down.

I thought surely McDonald would not cross-examine the doctor, but he seemed determined to dig a deeper hole for himself and forfeit the benefit of his one successful skirmish. Officer Cross had answered "Yes" when Giles asked her if she had suffered a concussion. Although Officer Cross said she had a blackout for a few seconds, there was no medical evidence in Dr. Osborne's report that she had incurred a concussion. Neither Cooke nor McDonald objected to Officer Cross's testimony. In America, their failure to object immediately would be treated as a waiver of any objection.[2]

Giles did not contest the defense counsel's delayed objection. When the jury returned the next day, Giles apologized to the jury for offering Officer Cross's unsupported opinion that she had suffered a concussion. Judge Read instructed the jury to disregard any suggestion that Officer Cross suffered a concussion.

Was Cooke content with prevailing in this tussle with Giles? No. With Dr. Osborne on the stand, Cooke could not resist the temptation to transform the molehill he had constructed into a mountain. He asked Dr. Osborne: "Isn't it true that there is no mention of a concussion in your report?" To which the doctor responded, "Yes."

Cooke: "Isn't it true that the symptoms Police Constable Cross was exhibiting were inconsistent with a diagnosis of a concussion?"

Dr. Osborne: "No, Constable Cross's symptoms were common and consistent with a person having received a concussion."

Giles could not suppress a self-satisfied smile.

Cooke and McDonald then compounded their litany of errors by calling Yates and Harper as witnesses. They were not ready for prime time. The challenge for Giles was that he had so many ways Yates and Harper could be roasted and barbequed during his cross-examination, but he had to limit himself to just a few. It was like having a stack of Christmas presents and insufficient time to open them all.

The defendant, Yates, like a petulant teenager, could not keep

---

2. The U.S. Waiver Rule prevents lawyers from not objecting to a witness' inadmissible testimony on the off chance the testimony might turn out to be favorable. Without the Waiver Rule, lawyers could "Have their cake and eat it too." If the testimony was helpful the lawyer would not object to the jury hearing it. If the testimony was hurtful, a lawyer could object later and ask the judge to strike the testimony from the record and to instruct the jury to pretend the testimony never occurred. The British Rule of Evidence allows barristers to wait until the end of the day and the jury sent home before lodging their objections.

the smirk off his face as he gave his testimony. Surprisingly, he readily admitted to saying nasty, insulting things to the victim, like calling her a bloody bitch in blue, but blamed his rude language on the alcohol he had consumed. These admissions were a treasure trove that Giles tucked away to use when cross-examining a later defense witness Cook had included on his witness list. He was Alan Prichard, a friend of Yates and Harper, who had witnessed the affray but stood by and let Yates and Harper do the fighting.

Yates ended his testimony by boldly asserting, "I just want the jury to get the true story, and I am being 100% truthful." Before Giles began his cross-examination, I whispered to him, "This is too easy." Giles wasted no time in demonstrating to the jury that while Yates was well-versed in lying, he just was not particularly good at it. Giles forced Yates to admit the dozen lies he had told the police. Yates was toast.

As a last resort, Defense counsel Cooke called Alan Prichard, who testified in support of the defendants' versions of the fight. His testimony was a clear demonstration of the effect of the British rule, which forbade barristers from speaking with witnesses prior to their giving testimony. [3]In the British courtroom, a barrister is often unpleasantly surprised when the unprepared witness utters unanticipated responses. The essence of Prichard's direct testimony was that Yates had not verbally abused the victim and said nothing that could be considered insulting.

Ordinarily, a lawyer cross-examining a witness avoids giving the witness the opportunity to repeat and embellish their direct testimony. Giles, as I was learning, was not an ordinary barrister. He not only allowed Prichard to repeat his story, but Giles also

---

3. In America, reviewing a witness's testimony before they take the stand is often called horse-shedding. The purpose of horse-shedding is to review what witnesses will say during direct examination and test how they will respond to predicable cross-examination questions. Horse-shedding gives lawyers the opportunity to gently suggest how their witnesses' answers can be improved - without actually lying.

encouraged Prichard to embellish how considerate Yates's language had been toward Officer Cross. Prichard completely swallowed the bait. Giles, adopting his most polite and obliging tone, let him run the line out until Giles thought it was time to set the hook and reel Prichard in. He encouraged Prichard to wax enthusiastically about what a complete gentleman Yates was, a paragon of virtue who should be congratulated on his restraint.

Giles then smoothly transitioned from benign questioner to intimidating interrogator, taking Prichard by surprise. He played Prichard like a violin. First, he informed Prichard about one of the nasty things Yates had admitted under oath, like saying to Officer Cross, "You're a bloody bitch." Giles quickly followed by asking, "Was Yates lying when Yates testified under oath that he called Officer Cross a bloody bitch, or are you lying now?"

Giles hammered Prichard repeatedly with the contradictions between what Yates had admitted saying and what Prichard had just testified he did not say, always ending with a question about whether Yates had lied or Prichard was lying. I told Giles later that I could visualize Prichard's nose growing longer with each question. Roadkill.

Once again, this pupil was unable to follow his mentor's advice. I was getting personally involved in the case. What was it to me whether the defendants were convicted or not? Without making a conscious decision, I had invested my emotional capital in the prosecution winning the case. Anything done by the defense to weaken the Crown's case, I took as a personal affront. I silently fumed when McDonald was being sarcastic with a prosecution witness. I tried to suppress my increasing agitation by writing notes to myself. "Cool it, David! There is no reason you should be emotionally caught up in this case." Why was I so nervous about a case that had a 99% likelihood of ending in a guilty verdict?

Then, the 1% chance happened. I was shocked and furious. The jury did not return a not-guilty verdict, a result that would have upset me less than what actually happened. Instead, Judge

Read declared a "mistrial." The jury was dismissed, and the case of the *Crown v. Yates and Harper* would be retried from the beginning. What inflamed my ire even more was that Judge Read declared a mistrial for a completely bogus reason, in my opinion. At the end of the fourth day of trial, Defense counsel Cooke had requested a conference with Judge Read. With all the barristers and me present, Cooke informed Judge Read that Yates had told a different story to the jury under oath than Yates had told him. Consequently, he was unable to continue as Yates's counsel. If what Yates said on the stand was not true, Cooke would not be able to cross-examine witnesses or give a final speech that supported Yates's lie.

On the other hand, if Yates's testimony was true, then Yates had previously lied to Cooke. There was a complete breakdown of trust between the barrister and the client, and this motivated Yates to discharge Cooke. Therefore, Cooke contended that the trial could not proceed, and a declaration of mistrial would be required.

I wanted to shout, "So what?" Cooke could adjust his trial strategy, not ask cross-examination questions that lent support to the lie, and then give a generic, boilerplate final argument that did not promote Yates's lie but emphasized the prosecution's burden of proof. Or, Yates could fire Cooke, hire a new barrister to continue the defense, or represent himself. Either way, the case could proceed, and the four days spent in trial would not be wasted. That was exactly what an American judge would do. How could the court and the criminal justice system reward Yates by declaring a mistrial for his lying under oath and firing his counsel? And since he and Harper were tried jointly, Judge Read also declared a mistrial for Harper. I was livid. Giles did not utter a word in protest.

Everyone lost except the defendants, who swaggered out of the courtroom with smug faces. The public lost the cost of holding a public trial, including the barrister and solicitor fees. The victims lost because they would have to endure the trauma of testifying again against thugs they feared might retaliate against them for their testimony. The jury lost four days sitting in the jury box. And Yates, Harper, and Prichard would have the opportunity to get their stories in sync for the next go-around.

The thought crossed my mind that Cooke acquired his concern about a possible conflict of interest only when he knew his defense was going down in flames. I did not blame Cooke so much as I blamed the British criminal justice system. I especially blamed the *Good Ole Boys* barrister culture of mutual back-scratching, the need to nurture barrister congeniality by avoiding public squabbles about the propriety of the unwritten barrister code. Giles did not object to Judge Read declaring a mistrial because next week, next month, or next year, Giles might be requesting a mistrial himself and would expect his honorable opponent to acquiesce to his request.

The next day, when I arrived at Chambers, I was still angry about the mistrial. Without saying, he was trying to distract me, Giles announced we were going to spend the day "skiving." The affray case had ended a day early, and the Clerk had not added anything to Giles's calendar to fill in the gap, so we had a day off. Skiving is jargon for avoiding work. Giles did not bother asking me about how I might be interested in spending my day off. He also did not tell me what he was planning.

Spontaneity was Giles's stock-in-trade. He had heard me mention how excited I was to have discovered Jane Austen's grave in Winchester Cathedral and how I had indulged in a moment of silent reflection standing over the grave of my favorite English author. So, our skiving was devoted to touring Jane Austin's home turf. We visited her home in Chawton, where I reverently stood next to her writing desk. While sitting in Jane's Garden, I fantasized that the cat that nestled at my feet might be the spirit of Jane, approving of my pilgrimage.

The highlight of the day was roaming the countryside on lanes strewn with potholes and ending up at a country manor house, the Grange. It could easily have been the stately home Jane had in mind when writing *Pride and Prejudice*. It was built in 1628, but in Jane's day, it had been rebuilt in a neoclassical style with Doric Greek columns. The building could not be seen from the road, and the lane leading to the great house had water-filled potholes laced together with deep ruts, just the kind of challenge Giles loved: "Damn the shock absorbers, full crawl ahead." The winding lane was lined with bushes and trees, partially obscuring the house until we edged our way around the last turn.

The great house had been abandoned after World War II. It was a wreck until it was acquired by the National Trust. The Trust had done little more than reinforce the walls and roof to keep them from falling down and replace the broken glass in the Orangery. It was the mansion's unaltered elegance that intrigued me.

There was only one National Trust person. Peter, that we could find. We must have missed the 'No Visitors Allowed' sign. Giles charmed Peter into letting us walk through the house and around all the grounds. Giles only slightly embellished the truth by explaining to Peter that I was a visiting professor from the United States, who had come to Hampshire with an interest in its manor houses, and that the Grange was one of the few that was still in its raw state.

The unspoiled condition of the house gave my imagination free rein to picture what life might have been like back in Jane's day. Instead of relying on some designer's vision of how the rooms would have looked, I could envision Jane's characters and recreate scenes from her novels. It was easy to picture footmen setting a meticulous table: forks on the left, knives and spoons on the right, glassware above the knives, knife blades turned toward the plate. They would even use a line gauge to ensure all the silverware was evenly spaced and aligned at the bottom. When the hot dishes were rushed up from the cellar kitchen, the footmen would smoothly lift the silver from the platters and serve the guests—silent, invisible, yet hearing everything.

I was fascinated by the Orangery. It is a structure whose name perfectly describes its purpose—growing oranges. It demonstrated to me the vast difference in wealth between those who occupied the Grange and most of the rest of British society. The aristocrats had the luxury of eating fresh oranges every day in a climate totally unsuited to their cultivation. Peter told us that now, instead of raising oranges in the Orangery, they sometimes staged operas.

Our long drive gave me the chance to raise a sensitive topic with Giles, which had been on my mind since the third day of the affray trial. During witness questioning, Giles was confused by the names of the defendants. He called Yates 'Harper' and referred to Harper as Yates. More troubling still was that Giles was not realizing he was doing it. I tried to raise the issue with Giles by describing Yates and Harper as two peas in a pod and how all thugs look alike, so it was easy to get them confused. Giles did not take the hint, so I had to take a more direct approach. I reminded him that he had mixed up Yates and Harper, referring to them by the wrong names. Giles looked puzzled. "Did I?" I assured him he had mixed up the names. I also reminded him about the third day of the trial, when he had difficulty asking a question and asked for a brief recess in the middle of his direct examination of Constable Cross. Finally, I mentioned that he got temporarily lost while driving to the scene of the crime. Giles did not deny or try to explain what had occurred; he said, "I was worried that might start happening."

"Okay, Giles, what's going on?"

Giles made me promise to keep everything he told me confidential before he told me about his medical condition. He said he had been diagnosed with an advanced case of cirrhosis and hepatitis, and his life expectancy was six to nine months. One of the symptoms of the disease was bouts of disorientation and mental lapses. They did not last long, but they could occur at any time. Giles had not told anyone about his condition, including Dana Cooper, his most significant other. I was the first person he had told. I asked if there was anything that could be done about it. He laughed. "I could add a few more months, perhaps, if I gave up wine and went on a strict diet. I think I would rather die." He added that there was a relatively new operation of a liver transplant that might add a couple of years, but he would not be put on a waiting list for transplants unless he promised to give up wine and eat like a Trappist monk. Giles said such a regimen could hardly be called living.

Neither was Giles planning to curtail his work as a barrister.

While abstaining from wine and good food would rob Giles's life of joy, abandoning the courtroom would deprive his life of meaning. Giles admitted he was worried about more incidents of his lapses in the courtroom. I told Giles that I sympathized with his dilemma, but I could not think of any advice to offer, and I could not help worrying selfishly about how his medical condition would affect my pupillage. Our drive back to Winchester was uncharacteristically subdued, with both of us lost in our own thoughts.

TWELVE

A Clash Of Egos

I had a sleepless night trying to decide if I should end my pupillage with Giles and return to Dayton or continue with the prospect of staying aboard a sinking ship. Would Ishmael have joined the crew of the *Pequod* if he had known Captain Ahab was determined to pursue the white whale, Moby Dick, even at the cost of his life and the lives of his crew? Although Giles could be shortening his life by continuing to try cases, my life would not be any more at risk if I continued the pupillage. Nevertheless, I felt my reputation and ego could be damaged by being associated with a barrister who accumulated a string of losses due to his increasing incompetence.

Then, just when I thought I had decided to end the pupillage and return to the States, I added my personal relationship with Giles to my analytical scale. Was our pupillage agreement a contract that could be terminated by either party at any time, or was it a binding agreement until death do us part? Only six months of the one-year pupillage had passed. Did the implied obligations of friendship also need to be weighed? Giles and I were certainly not best friends. In fact, if we were in the U.S., Giles would be no more than an eccentric acquaintance, an entertaining dinner guest, or someone to meet occasionally at a café for coffee. In Winchester, though, I was in unfamiliar foreign territory. Giles tried his best to ease my entry into the enigmatic world of the British criminal justice system, and he also facilitated my access to the broader British society by introducing me to people beyond the law courts. Wasn't that a token of friendship? Besides, I genuinely liked Giles. On the other hand, I dreaded the thought of sitting by Giles's hospital bed watching him die.

When morning finally arrived, my mind was still in a muddle and no closer to a decision. I ignored Giles's desire to keep his medical condition secret since I needed the benefit of Susan's wisdom to resolve my dilemma. Her one question to me was all the guidance I needed.

"Would you be able to help Giles if you stayed?"

Susan wisely did not suggest I should remain in my pupillage, but I could read between the lines.

"If you can help Giles through this difficult time, you should do it."

So, the muddled mess in my mind could be purged by answering Susan's question. Giles's condition would have the greatest impact on his courtroom performance, but as a pupil, how could I prevent a possible in-court train wreck? I did some research on the role of a barrister's pupil, and I found a possible answer, assuming Giles would agree with my solution.

I was already a well-qualified American trial attorney, and I had completed six months of my pupillage. Giles could certify to Grey's Inn that I had successfully completed the *non-practicing* time of my pupillage and that I was ready to begin my *practicing time*. As a Practicing Pupil, I would have appearance rights in the court and be able to litigate my own cases, under Giles's supervision, of course. In essence, I would be Giles's co-counsel. As a senior barrister of Northgate Chambers, he would have little problem persuading his fellow barristers that I was ready to begin trial runs.

My plan had the additional attraction that it dovetailed nicely with my personal desire to be more than an errand boy, an occasional consultant, and a brief writer. Although it was a worrisome prospect, I believed my experience as a pupil would be incomplete without an opportunity to perform in a British courtroom. I pictured myself taking over from Giles during a trial once his illness began affecting his performance. I only needed to convince Giles.

By the following day, when I met with Giles in Chambers to discuss a pending case, I had settled on my strategy. After a brief discussion of possible defenses in the next case, I opened the topic of my beginning my practice time as a pupil. Giles was surprised I knew about pupils being able to transition into a more active role, including in-court appearance rights. I avoided mentioning anything about Giles's slip-ups in the courtroom and focused on my belief that I was ready for prime time, under his supervision and guidance, of course. Giles demurred and said he had not thought about my transitioning into a practice time pupillage. It had seemed an unnecessary complication since I would be returning to America in a few months. Besides, he said we were working well together, and he saw no need to change, but he added that he would think about it.

This was not enough for me, and it did not address the underlying problem of Giles's deteriorating health. I needed to turn up the pressure, so I told him I was growing bored with being a law clerk and an occasional consultant and that if I were going to get full value from my pupillage, I would have to experience a more active role inside a British courtroom.

Giles laughed and jokingly asked if I really thought I was ready to go head-to-head with skilled British barristers and to cope with overbearing British judges? My overreaction to Giles's gybe may have shown I was not prepared to deal with a barrister's tart wit. Instead of trying to match wits, I let my ego dictate the dialogue. I reminded Giles that I was a fully qualified trial attorney, and I had, by Giles's own words, been an excellent pupil for six months. Furthermore, on numerous occasions, I contributed critical, case-winning advice on everything from opening and closing speeches to direct and cross-examinations of witnesses. I had written a brief for the Court of Criminal Appeal, which he had brandished to numerous fellow barristers as an example of exemplary writing and legal analysis. In short, I told Giles that he had often relied on my judgment and that I was a valuable, if not vital, element for our success in the courtroom. I said that my organized and disciplined way of reviewing a case file complemented his tendency to leave things to the last minute.

If I had been wise, I would have stopped my professorial lecture at that point. Giles may have tried to defuse the tension by politely praising my fine speech while flashing a wry smile and saying he would seriously consider my request. I did not stop. I raised the stakes and my voice by talking about his debilitating illness, which, over time, would manifest itself during future trials, and that his mental lapses would only get worse. I concluded by telling Giles he would need me to take over for him during a trial when he was incapacitated, and the only way I could do that would be if I had appearance rights in a British courtroom.

I now realize I had crossed a red line for Giles. In his mind, I was not only showing unwanted pity for him, but I was also questioning his ability to continue as an effective barrister. In an instant, Giles's ego became a powerful dynamic force in a discussion that was rapidly deteriorating into an emotional argument. Giles loudly proclaimed that he neither needed nor wanted my pity. He said, "You are patronizing me, and you do not believe I have the moral strength to cope with my medical condition." Giles brushed aside my attempt to explain the semantic difference between pity and empathy. Giles continued, "You have worked closely with me for six months and yet you doubt my ability to professionally conduct a case. That is insulting."

I had watched Giles feign anger in the courtroom and client conferences, but this was the first time I had seen him lose his temper. It made me think: *the barrister doth protest too much*, and Giles was far more troubled than he let on.

Giles's face turned crimson. He nearly shouted, "I do not need you, David, to try a case. You have been helpful from time to time, but I am sure the verdicts would have been the same regardless of your input."

Giles's poignards uncaged my own overwrought ego, and what began as a prickly debate deteriorated into a war of attrition, with no restraint on our arsenals of weaponized words. I told Giles I had no intention of sitting in the courtroom and being associated with a barrister who was determined to make a fool of himself and demonstrate such incompetence that he could be referred to the Bar Standards Board for possible disbarment.

I said, "If you are primed to navigate the courtroom minefield with one blind eye, I am one pupil who is not going to tarnish my reputation by following you across that no-man's land. I am ending my pupillage and will be returning to Dayton as soon as I can make the necessary travel arrangements." It would be a cliché to say I stormed out of the conference room, but I did close the four-inch-thick oak door forcefully.

Two days later, a worried Dana Cooper knocked on our townhouse door. She wanted to talk to us about Giles. Dana, the actress, knew how to make a stage entrance. There were no preliminary inquiries about our mutual health and no prologue. Dana simply said, "David, Giles needs your help." She told us she had seldom seen Giles more distraught than he was after I told him I was returning to America. "His monumental ego will not allow him to admit, even to himself, that if he is going to continue practicing as a barrister, he will need David Walker in his corner."

Dana's comment was a substantial boost to my ego, and it put me in a hubristic state of mind. I responded, "I would be happy to take up my pupillage again if Giles would ask me to do so, and if

Giles would agree to certify that I was ready to begin my practice time as a pupil." Then I paused. There was a loophole in my conditions, assuming Giles would agree to them. There was no assurance that, although I was qualified to appear before the Crown Court, Giles would actually ask me to take over any part of a case. So, I added, "Giles would need to promise I would be an active participant in trials."

Dana said Giles would not be capable of making the first move by asking me to come back as his pupil. That would be the equivalent of an apology, and Giles's ego would not allow him to admit he may have made a mistake. I shrugged my shoulders and said, "Then there is no solution."

Dana was unfazed by my reaction, and she had carefully prepared her part of the performance with the hope that I would follow her cue and not go off-script. "David, you need to talk with Giles and tell him you are willing to continue as his pupil and would be willing to defer to his judgment as to when you can begin your practice time pupillage." I did not like Dana's plan and retorted, "Dana, that is tantamount to my apologizing to Giles for our dust-up." To which Dana smoothly replied, "Now that you mention it, David, it would be helpful to rebuild a cordial relationship with Giles for you to first offer an apology." My reaction to this piece of advice was, "I suppose the next thing you will propose is that I kiss Giles's ring and wash his feet." Dana laughed and bestowed on me her best indulgent smile. "David, I do not think you would need to go that far, but knowing Giles, he probably would not object to a bit of ring kissing."

At this point, Susan interjected, "Okay, now that we have completed the preliminary skirmishing, let's consider the fundamental issues dividing Giles and David. First, there is the clash of two inflated egos, which essentially cancel each other out and need not be considered."

Dana could not resist quoting Shakespeare: "And where two raging fires meet together, they do consume the thing that fuels their fury."

Susan continued, "You, David, want to maximize your learning experience from the pupillage, and right now you are only halfway there. Giles, on the other hand, needs a legally astute person, and someone he can trust, to help him continue to practice as a barrister." Dana added, "Giles would insist on trying cases even when it became apparent to everyone he should not be appearing in a courtroom."

I interrupted and asked, "Did the two of you devise your tag-team tactic before Dana knocked on our door, or are you both improvising?"

Susan ignored me and concluded with, "Besides, Nancy and I like being here in Winchester and want to stay another six months." Suddenly, it dawned on me that the steamroller was on the move, and I had the choice of getting flattened or climbing aboard. "Okay, what do you and Dana want me to do?"

Dana summed up the plan. "Nothing will happen until you and Giles have an honest conversation, and that will not occur unless you first apologize to Giles for your outburst."

I sighed, "Eat crow in other words," to which Susan said, "Maybe only a Starling."

Dana continued, "Agree to continue as Giles's pupil but strongly suggest that the value of the pupillage to you will be spoiled if you do not get an opportunity to litigate at least part of a case in the Crown Court. He will feel obliged to propose some kind of compromise. Then it will be up to the two of you to negotiate specific terms. You are lawyers—isn't that what you are good at?"

I heard the trap Dana and Susan set for me snap shut. At least it was a humane one, and my neck was not broken.

I arranged to meet Giles at the Green Man pub two days later. I was early, and Giles was late, of course. I ordered two pints of Bowman Ale and waited for Giles in the booth furthest from the smokers. There was time for me to think about my strategy for our meeting. Giles did not know that I was planning to apologize with the hope of resurrecting my pupillage. He likely thought I was on my way back to America and that I would orchestrate a more cordial goodbye than when I had stormed out of the conference room.

I decided to take a page out of the script Dana used when she and Susan induced me to meet with Giles and quickly apologize. So, when Giles arrived at the table, I stood up, shook his hand, and before the exchange of any predictable pleasantries, I said, "First, Giles, I want to apologize for my boorish behavior the last time we met, and secondly, I was hoping you would still be willing for me to continue as your pupil."

Lacking Dana's acting ability, I was unable to convey any heartfelt contrition that I did not feel. Giles knew my apology was a mere formality. Still, it offered him sufficient protection for his ego to say, "No apology is necessary, David. It is all water under the bridge."

As Dana had predicted, Giles would not admit that he needed my help, but he readily agreed to resume our pupillage arrangement. Giles then unknowingly stayed on Dana's script and said he had been considering my request to step up to being a pupil with court appearance rights. He said I was already a well-qualified American trial attorney. So, he would certify that I had successfully completed my non-practicing time of my pupillage, and I was ready to begin my practicing time.

Giles assured me that Chambers would agree I was ready to make the transition. As a Practicing Pupil, I would have appearance rights in the court and be able to litigate my own cases under Giles's supervision. In essence, I would be Giles's co-counsel. Giles did not admit there could be a time when his illness would require me to stand in for him, but he did say I would be doing some direct examinations and cross-examinations of witnesses.

Giles had granted my wish, and my trepidation began immediately. The odds of my making a fool of myself had increased exponentially. The Giles tide was in full flow, however, and I let myself be swept along. It did mean that my mentor believed I was ready for prime time.

THIRTEEN

Masquerading As A Barrister

Status does not come without a price. Now that I had acquired appearance rights with supervision in the Crown Court, I had to purchase the required regalia barristers need so they can "strut and fret their hour upon the stage." Would wearing a wig provide me with a dose of pomposity along with an itchy scalp? I was about to find out.

The day after my conversation with Giles at the Green Man, I took the train to London, the Tube to Chancery Lane, and entered the shop of Stanley-Ley. I told the clerk about my new status, and he graciously offered to provide me with everything I needed. The size of a barrister's gown only varies by length, so selecting one took only a couple of minutes. The wig was a bit more complicated. I had to try on several wigs to find one that closely matched my head size. Too large, and the wig would slip off; too small, and it would have a similar problem. Next was a tunic shirt. I chose two—one pale blue and the other gray with thin Bengal stripes. A tunic does not have a collar, so next on the list were two stiff collars with rigid butterfly wings sticking out in front. The collar was attached to the tunic with studs, an additional purchase. Finally, there were the barrister bands, two heavily starched bib-like flanges that looped over the collar. Other than being black, there are no official barrister socks. Still, I could not resist adding to my wardrobe two pairs of black socks inscribed with "Trust me, I am a lawyer."

I thought, and hoped, I was done, having spent nearly £1000, but the salesclerk was on a roll. "Surely you will need cases to protect your wardrobe."

I added a wig case, a case for bands, and a collar-stud box made of thuya wood. Finally, he advised, "Surely, sir, with your new status as a barrister, you will want to have a bespoke suit. There are a couple of Savile Row tailors I could recommend." Had Giles gotten to the salesclerk and urged him to push me into an upgrade of suits? I had to draw a line somewhere in my expenditures. I declined his offer.

I returned to Winchester in time for my afternoon echocardiogram test at the Royal Hampshire County Hospital. An echocardiogram shows how much blood pumps out of a filled heart chamber with each heartbeat. It also displays cardiac output, which is the amount of blood the heart pumps in one minute. If the heart does not pump enough blood for the body's needs, heart failure can occur. Although I was mesmerized by watching my heart beating on the monitor, the test results were disturbing.

The test showed that in addition to partially blocked arteries, I had a leaky aortic valve, which was reducing my blood flow. A normal rate would be over 55%, and mine was a mere 40%. The only procedure that could improve my condition was open-heart surgery, cracking open my chest, and substituting a cow's heart valve for my faulty one. I was devastated and angry. I was fifty years old, and my life was transformed in an instant. I wallowed in self-pity as I contemplated the Sword of Damocles dangling over my head.

What was I going to do? Have an immediate operation in England? End my pupillage, return to the States, and have the operation? Postpone the operation until I have completed my pupillage? Complicating the issue were Giles's terminal liver condition and his need for my help in the courtroom. Another factor to consider was the joy and satisfaction I could have by playing that support role. Dr. Taylor hedged his prognosis. On the one hand, he said it was possible I could have a heart attack the next day.

On the other hand, since I had been living with my defective valve and partially blocked arteries for years and had not had an attack, I could well go several more years and escape a serious heart issue. However, I would need to alter my lifestyle and avoid strenuous exercise. I did not tell Dr. Taylor I had been avoiding vigorous exercise all my life.

I had a lengthy conversation with Susan and Nancy about the diagnosis and the prognosis. They were as shocked as I was, but they were never ones to allow their decisions to be dictated by emotions. We constructed a list of the pros and cons of staying in England for the rest of my sabbatical. The 'con' side of the list was easy and consisted of only one consideration—my having a heart attack. We ended up assessing Dr. Taylor's prognosis by assuming there was a 10% chance that I would have a heart attack in the next six months. The 'pro' side of the list covered two pages of a legal pad. Many of the listed items stemmed from the fact that we all loved Winchester, had settled into the culture, and had made some good friends. Weighing heavily was the fact that I enjoyed working with Giles and litigating, with the prospect of becoming even more actively involved. Finally, there was the reality that an opportunity like this was unlikely to come our way again. The decision was to stay.

I intentionally did not consult Giles about our decision, knowing he would carry me along whatever way his tide was running. He might also resent my taking into consideration his medical problems, which he would regard as "pity." I did tell Giles about the doctor's diagnosis and my family's decision to stay in Winchester. His response was, "Good, let's talk about our next case."

The brief was tied with a pink ribbon, so I knew we would be defending. Briefs we received from the Crown Prosecution Service were tied with a white ribbon. Giles summarized the facts for me. Our client was Ava Daley, a 24-year-old woman living in Southampton. In December 1993, shortly before Christmas, she walked into the Southampton Police Department holding the hands of her two children, aged two and four, and asked to see a detective. She told Detective Morgan that seven years earlier, she had killed her infant baby. The autopsy report at the time listed the death of her child as crib death. There were none of the usual signs of forced suffocation. Ava was sixteen years old when she got pregnant with her Welsh boyfriend, Dylan Davies. Davies wanted Ava to have an abortion, but Ava, still clinging to vestiges of her Catholic upbringing, refused. At that point, Davies abandoned Ava. She continued to live in their shabby flat, where she gave birth to a baby boy with the help of a midwife. She named the baby Peter.

Ava told the police a startling story. When Peter was four months old, she came home after working the late shift at McDonald's. She was exhausted. Peter would not stop crying despite everything she tried to do. Just to have a few moments of silence, Ava put a pillow over Peter's face with one hand, and after about ten seconds, she said he stopped breathing. Ava told the police she knew the baby was dead. Ava went to her bed and fell asleep. The next morning, Ava called 999, and the emergency crew took Peter's body to the morgue, where an autopsy was performed.

Detective Morgan asked Ava why she had waited seven years before telling the police what really happened. She said it was because of her fear of her abusive Scottish boyfriend, Bruce Campbell, the father of her two other children. Ava had told Campbell about what she had done to Peter, and every time they had a row, Campbell would call her a murderer and threaten to tell the police what she had done. Ava thought it would be better for her to tell the police herself and face the consequences. After her confession, Ava's two children were taken into custody by the

Department of Social Services, and the case was referred to the Crown Prosecution Service (CPS). The CPS brought charges against Ava for murder and included a lesser charge of manslaughter.

I thought the CPS was stretching to include the murder charge, but based on Ava's confession, the CPS had a solid case for manslaughter. Giles and I assumed the Crown Prosecutor, Cade Palmer, would offer Ava a plea deal for pleading guilty to manslaughter, and the murder charge would be dropped. It was a deal Giles would not discourage Ava from taking. The guilty plea to manslaughter seemed like a no-brainer solution to me. How could we craft a plausible defense that would depend on Ava taking the stand and admitting to killing her baby? The best result we could hope for after a trial would be a jury verdict of manslaughter. A not-guilty verdict was a flight of fancy, and by going to trial, Ava took the risk of a murder verdict and spending most of the rest of her life in prison.

Giles was not so sure, but there was something about the facts of the case that did not seem right to him. This was Giles at his best, when his instinct trumped pure logic. He was not convinced that Ava had killed her baby. The pieces of the puzzle did not fit. He said we could not rely on our solicitor's interview of Ava and needed to talk with Ava, face-to-face.

We arranged to meet Ava at Southampton Jail. She had not been released pending her trial because she was charged with murder and was also considered a suicide risk. When Ava was escorted into the interview room, she didn't look like a person who could have committed the murder of a baby. She was small, dwarfed by her female guard. Her handcuffs did not look like they could be squeezed tight enough to fit her wrists. Ava's eyes were green, and her hair was white blond, tied back in a ponytail. Elfin would be the best description.

After Ava's handcuffs were removed, Giles did not spend any time exchanging pleasantries. He launched in with a line of questions designed to test her story.

"Tell us what happened on the night your baby died, beginning from the time you went to work that night."

Ava repeated a narrative that duplicated what she had told the police and her solicitor. Giles then summed up her story with the facial expressions and the skeptical tone of voice he often uses in the courtroom, suggesting he did not believe a word of what Ava was saying.

"So, you say you were working the late shift at McDonald's, a place which had not opened until a year after your baby died. When you returned to your flat, you were tired and exhausted. Your baby was crying, and you did all the usual things to quiet him: feeding him, changing his diaper, and rocking him to sleep. He would not stop crying and continued to cry when you laid him in his crib. You say you were frantic, angry, and at your wits' end. It was only then that you held a pillow over the baby's face for ten seconds. Let me count out ten seconds." Giles counted to ten. "Is that about right?"

Ava said, "Yes."

"You say the baby did not struggle."

"Yes."

"This is the same baby, you refused to abort even though your abusive boyfriend at the time insisted you get an abortion. In fact, because you refused his demands, your boyfriend walked out and abandoned you and the baby."

Ava nodded, yes.

"Although you were only sixteen years old, you chose to endure nine months of pregnancy and suffer the pain of childbirth to have this child. You would not give up this child for adoption and struggled as a single mother to provide and care for him. You loved your child."

Ava teared up but did not say anything. Of course, Giles did not really give her a chance to speak.

Giles continued.

"You removed the pillow after ten seconds and determined your baby was dead. You had just killed your only child. But you did not call 999. Instead, you calmly crawled into your bed next to the crib where your baby was lying dead and went to sleep. It was not until the next morning that you called 999. The police and the emergency crew arrived, and you told them you had gone to sleep about midnight, and when you woke up, the baby was dead. An autopsy was performed on your baby, and the coroner concluded that your baby had died of crib death."

Ava sobbed.

"Seven years later, you stroll into the Southampton police station with your two children, four and two, in tow and coolly describe to the officer how you had murdered your four-month-old baby seven years earlier. The police asked you why it took you seven years to report what you had done. The excuse you gave them was that your abusive Scottish boyfriend, the father of your other two children, was threatening to tell the police about what you had done. You thought it would be better if you told the police first."

The only response was Ava's tears.

Suddenly switching to a gentle, empathetic voice, Giles asked: "Ava, isn't it true that you did not kill your beloved baby and are only imagining you did?"

If Giles expected Ava to recant her version of events, he must have been disappointed. Ava replied, "I killed my baby."

When we walked out of the Southampton Jail, Giles said, "I know she is not telling the truth, but I know she is not lying either. She sincerely believes she killed her baby. How could we present a credible defense to the jury that rests on us proving Ava, our client, was lying?" I did not have a clue.

Adding to our dilemma was the fact that Ava was willing to plead guilty to the manslaughter charge if Prosecutor Palmer dropped the murder charge. I could not blame Ava for being eager to take the deal. If she were found guilty of murder, she would face a mandatory life sentence. In contrast, the maximum sentence for manslaughter was eight years. It would be unethical for Giles to ignore the wishes of his client to plead guilty and force a full-blown trial. Even assuming Giles could persuade Ava to risk the outcome of a trial, it was still probably unethical behavior, as Ava was the one who was risking her life on a roll of the dice. And yet, Giles sincerely believed Ava was innocent.

Giles needed much more information about the phenomenon of crib death, otherwise known as Sudden Infant Death Syndrome (SIDS). Technically, it is the unexplained death of an infant under one year while sleeping in a crib. To prove that the death of Ava's baby was due to SIDS meant proving what is unexplainable. We would have the impossible task of proving the absence of all other conceivable causes. Ava would be the only witness who could testify about other possible causes, and Ava would confess, under oath, that she was the sole cause of Peter's death.

Giles would not give up, however. He resorted to what I call "The Good Ole Boys Network," which exists among the graduates of the same public school. As I quickly learned, a public school in England is equivalent to an exclusive private school in the U.S. Attendance at a public school generates a loyalty among its graduates that lasts a lifetime. Even sporting a school's unique tie will often open doors that would ordinarily be slammed in your face.

Giles was a graduate of Wells Cathedral School, which claimed to be the oldest public school in England, founded in 909 AD. Its motto is *Esto Quod Es,* Be What You Are, an apt maxim for Giles. Giles decided to take advantage of the "Wells Network." He arranged to meet another Wells graduate, Professor Gerald Dowd, for lunch. Professor Dowd was an Oxford professor and was one of the first researchers to conduct an extensive survey of crib deaths. Professor Dowd's findings proved that the traditional way of putting babies on their stomachs to sleep was wrong and dangerous. He advised that the best way to reduce the number of babies dying of crib death was for babies to be placed on their backs to sleep. Professor Dowd followed up that work with an extensive study of mothers who had young babies who had died in their cribs. He found many mothers who believed they had smothered their own babies, even when all available evidence proved they could not have done so.

We traveled to Oxford to meet Professor Dowd. I thought it a bit juvenile of Giles to wear his Wells tie, but when Professor Dowd arrived with his Wells tie prominently displayed, I assumed the matching ties were like a Mason's secret handshake, confirming membership in the same fraternal order.

Giles explained the facts of the case, and Professor Dowd did not hesitate to say, "Ava does not fit the profile for a mother who smothered her own baby." He gave a list of differences between the mothers he interviewed and Ava. First, Ava could not have smothered her baby with a pillow within ten seconds. It would take more than a minute, perhaps two minutes, to kill the child. Second, it would require substantial force to hold the pillow down. Third, the baby would violently struggle to breathe, causing bruises and abrasions. Finally, all the mothers he interviewed were in a state of extreme agitation from doing the act and realizing they had killed their babies. Professor Dowd said, "It is inconceivable a mother could calmly go to sleep in the same room where she smothered her baby." We were especially grateful that Professor Dowd was willing to testify in Ava's trial for a modest fee. Fortunately, in England, defendants charged with serious crimes are allotted money to hire expert witnesses.

Professor Dowd's testimony would be one leg of our defense, but we still needed to supply the jury with a reason Ava would confess to a crime she did not commit. I was not surprised when Giles discovered another professor who was a Wells graduate and who just happened to be an expert in how people can generate *false memories*. Once again, matching Wells ties were on display when we met Professor Oliver Townsend for lunch. Professor Townsend described his research, explaining how people who experience a traumatic event can sometimes create a false memory of the event to satisfy a psychological need. Furthermore, he said that if that person also feels guilty about what happened, it makes the development of a false memory more likely. After hearing the facts of Ava's case, Professor Townsend said he could not conclude Ava was exhibiting a false memory, but he did say it was possible. That was all Giles needed. We did not need to prove Ava actually had a false memory. We only needed to raise a reasonable doubt about the validity of her confession to the police—and we could accomplish that without putting Ava on the stand. If Ava testified, we would have all the ingredients of a farce. Ava would admit under oath that she killed her baby, and we would be trying to prove that our client was—without relying on leading questions like these:

Question: "Ava, tell us what happened."

Answer: "I killed my baby."

Question: "Do you clearly remember what happened that night?"

Answer: "Yes."

Question: "Were you agitated?"

Answer: "Yes."

Question: "Did you know what you were doing?"

Answer: "Yes."

Question: "What happened after you killed your baby?"

Answer: "I went to sleep."

Question: "Did you lie to the police when you told them you had killed your baby?"

Answer: "No."

By the time Ava finishes testifying, all the elements of murder will have been proven out of her own mouth. *Murder is when a person of sound mind unlawfully kills another person, and they have the intention to kill or to cause grievous bodily harm.*

Another ethical issue for Giles was that he would be calling a witness whom he believed was lying. Under British law, he could not vouch for Ava's truthfulness.

To my mind, pleading guilty to the manslaughter charge was looking like the best solution. Also, it was what Ava wanted to do. I had never seen Giles so personally and emotionally involved in a case. Gone was the cool, objective barrister. Giles was determined to keep Ava out of prison. He knew what would happen to a pretty, tiny, naïve girl like Ava in prison. An 8-year sentence would be the equivalent of a death sentence. Even if Ava survived, she would be psychologically scarred for life.

Giles's proposed solution was so unique that he presented it to the Bar Council's Ethical Enquiries Service. He sought its advice on whether his plan was ethical and consistent with his professional obligations. The panel of barristers reviewing his proposal took three days to mull it over, ultimately concluding that what Giles was proposing did not violate the Bar Code of Ethics. The panel's favorable opinion provided Giles with some cover, but an opinion from the Ethical Enquiries Service is only advice. It would not keep Giles out of hot water if a complaint were lodged with the Bar Council.

Giles arranged a meeting with Prosecutor Palmer and the solicitor handling the case for the Crown Prosecution Service. He did not ask me to attend, which hurt my feelings. The agreement they reached may have been possible because of the *Good Ole Boy Network*. Or perhaps Palmer realized that, in the future, Giles might prosecute a case against his client, and Palmer might want a favor from Giles. Or, it might have been due to the prosecution team being sympathetic to Ava's situation. Nevertheless, the deal that was struck was one that no American prosecutor would ever agree to. American prosecutors are determined to put more pressure on a defendant to plead guilty, not less.

Prosecutor Palmer and the CPS solicitor agreed to give Ava the right to delay pleading guilty to the manslaughter charge until after the close of the prosecution's case-in-chief and before we opened our defense. If she did decide to plead guilty to manslaughter, the CPS would dismiss the murder charge. In America, if a defendant does not accept a plea deal before trial, the offer is withdrawn. Then the defendant must take the risk of being found guilty of the more grievous charge and be sentenced to a much longer prison term, or even the death penalty. Ava, with Giles's advice, could delay her decision, and we could assess the strength of the prosecution's evidence supporting the murder charge. If the evidence was strong, Ava could still plead guilty to manslaughter. If the evidence supporting the murder charge was weak, Ava could decide to take her chances with a full trial in the hope she would be found not guilty of either murder or manslaughter. Although Ava would still be rolling the dice, the odds would be in her favor.

Ava's odds improved after we heard Prosecutor Palmer's opening speech. Unlike many American prosecutors who take a vengeful tone or assume the mantle of protector of the community, he sounded sympathetic to Ava's plight while at the same time emphasizing how the evidence justified charging her with murder.

I occupied my usual position next to Giles, but for the first time, I was gowned and wearing a wig. I had not been too adept at donning my plumage in the barrister robing room, which provided a few barristers with an entertaining beginning to their day. Brits cannot resist the chance to showcase the foibles of their American cousins. After fumbling around trying to attach my winged collar to my tunic with studs and constantly dropping the studs on the floor, a fellow barrister offered to help. I paid the cost of enduring British wit while he inserted those annoying studs.

The first prosecution witness was Sergeant Detective Morgan, who introduced Ava's original statement that she had made to the police, in which she had confessed to killing her baby. The coroner's report was introduced to prove that baby Peter had died from unknown causes. Of course, after Ava's confession, the prosecutor would argue the cause of death was not unknown.

The coroner testified it was possible Peter could have died because he was smothered with a pillow held over his face. On cross-examination by Giles, however, the coroner had to concede there were no visible signs the baby struggled, and that to smother the baby, the person holding the pillow would need to apply significant force.

When Giles began our planned series of concluding questions, I noticed he was having difficulty getting his first words out. I quickly raised my pen about ten inches off the desk. This was our agreed-upon stop signal if I thought Giles should stop his questioning and consult with me. Giles stopped, leaned over to me as I whispered the word I knew he wanted to say. He repeated them to the witness, and then Giles was back on track.

Question: "So, Doctor, in your opinion, it would take more than a minute to suffocate a baby with a pillow."

Answer: "Yes."

Question: "Therefore, Doctor, if Ava was telling the truth when she told the police she had held the pillow over her baby's face for 10 seconds, her actions would not have killed the baby?"

Answer: "No."

Question: "On the other hand, Doctor, if Ava was lying to the police and did forcefully hold a pillow over Peter's face for longer than a minute..."

I did not raise my pen because I knew his hesitation and a slight misstep was Giles at his theatrical best, setting the stage.

Question: "Pardon me, Doctor, I am getting ahead of myself. Before I ask you the next question, would you indulge me and, using your watch, indicate for the jury how long a minute is?"

Answer: "Yes."

The doctor let a minute pass on his watch. In the silent courtroom, the minute seemed interminable, riveting the jurors' attention for the next and final question.

Question: "Now, Doctor, if Ava was lying to the police and had forcefully held a pillow over Peter's face for longer than a minute, there would probably be signs of bruising or abrasions on the baby's face? Correct?"

Answer: "I would say, likely."

Question: "Thank you, doctor."

The next witness for the Crown was Doctor Adams, a psychiatrist, who had examined Ava at the jail. Prosecutor Palmer had to prove that Ava intentionally killed Peter and was of sound mind at the time she did it. Doctor Adams testified that at the time she examined Ava, Ava was in complete control of her faculties, and Ava sincerely believed she had killed her baby. Furthermore, based on her interview, Doctor Adams was willing to say Ava had been of sound mind at the time she told the police she killed her baby.

Giles was able to poke numerous holes in Doctor Adams' testimony. He was helped by Doctor Adams, who appeared to be lukewarm about her own opinions, and the fact that her examination of Ava was conducted seven years after Peter's death. Doctor Adams also had to admit that Ava's behavior of supposedly smothering her baby and immediately going to sleep in a bed next to Peter's cot was inexplicable.

The prosecution rested, and it was decision time. To proceed or not to proceed? Prosecutor Palmer asked Giles during the lunch break if Ava was ready to plead guilty to manslaughter, reminding us that once we began presenting Ava's defense case, the offer was off the table. Ava was ever ready to plead guilty to manslaughter, but she was willing to defer to Giles's judgment. For my part, I was willing to offer my opinion on the strength of the Crown's case for murder, but I was not inclined to suggest any advice on Ava taking the plea deal. Thankfully, Giles did not ask for my opinion.

Giles and I agreed on the strength of the Crown's case for murder—weak. It was impossible to assign exact percentages to the likelihood of the jury returning a guilty verdict on the murder charge. Nevertheless, we concluded the Crown had a 10 to 20 percent chance of securing a guilty verdict for murder, roughly one chance in six. As a practical matter, it was solely Giles's decision to make about pleading to the manslaughter charge. This was completely contrary to the normal attorney-client relationship. Ava was more than willing to plead guilty to manslaughter. She genuinely believed she had killed her baby and deserved punishment. Ava did not want to serve a life term. So, without Giles's influence, she probably would not have been willing to risk the one in six chance of a life sentence. Instead, she would have pleaded guilty to manslaughter. The ethical and practical problem for Giles was whether he was willing to gamble with Ava's life. He had no skin in the game. In a craps game with just his money on the table, Giles would not have hesitated to gamble that he would get a number greater than one. After only a moment's hesitation, Giles told me he had decided to roll the die and put on our planned defense case, maintaining that Ava had not killed her baby and therefore was not guilty of manslaughter.

Giles's odds that Ava would be found not guilty of murder turned out to be better than 5-1. They changed to 6-0 when Judge Price told us he was dismissing the murder charge. He had concluded the evidence supported Ava's defense of diminished capacity at the time of her baby's death. Thus, the prosecution could not prove Ava had the requisite intent to kill.

The remainder of the case was an anti-climax. After the persuasive testimony by our two experts, the jury had to have a reasonable doubt about the prosecution's case. After three hours of deliberation, the jury returned a verdict of not guilty.

Even Giles could not disguise his emotions. He was ecstatic and greatly relieved; a huge burden was lifted from his shoulders. What pleased Ava the most was the realization that she would get her two children back. What did not change, however, was Ava's certainty that she had killed her baby. The jury verdict did not erase that belief. It would require months of therapy to accomplish that.

FOURTEEN

Sacked

In our next case, our client, Thomas Dixon, was charged with sexual abuse of a six-year-old girl, Molly. Molly claimed her mother's new husband, Thomas Dixon, had touched her with his "willy" and made her touch his "willy." Dixon had told his solicitor he may have "brushed up" against Molly while sleeping. Molly often slept in the same bed as Dixon and her mum, Freya. Dixon admitted that he and Freya did sleep in the nude. To a prudish Midwesterner like me, this was an unhealthy scenario. A conference was scheduled with the client in three days.

Based on the information contained in the brief, Giles believed the Crown had a compelling case, and he asked me to research what the defendant's likely sentence would be if the defendant pleaded guilty. I thought Giles was teasing me, like asking me to search in a dark room for a black cat that wasn't there.

In the U.S., the sentencing judge in a case like ours had wide, unpredictable discretion and could order a sentence from as little as one year to ten years. The length of the sentence could be influenced by which side of the bed the judge got out of that morning, or whether the judge had had a chance for a second cup of coffee.

If a plea deal had been struck with an American prosecuting attorney, one of the more serious charges, like rape, would likely have been dropped by the prosecutor. Also, as part of the plea deal, the prosecutor could promise to 'stand silent' and not argue for the maximum sentence at the defendant's sentencing hearing. Nevertheless, the defendant could still be looking at a 10-year sentence.

In England, estimating the likely sentence is a matter of addition and subtraction. That I could do. I learned that if our defendant pleaded guilty, he would be entitled to bonuses that could be accumulated over time. The total of those bonuses would be subtracted from the standard sentence. For example, if the normal sentence was five years, a defendant would be entitled to a six-month bonus for pleading guilty. There would be additional bonuses if it were the defendant's first offense, or if he had a spotless criminal record, or if he were gainfully employed, or if the probation department determined he was unlikely to commit such an offense again, or if the defendant were genuinely contrite. Therefore, based on Dixon's biography, I was able to calculate a likely sentence of two years and six months, plus or minus three months. I thought the British approach to sentencing was brilliant. Dixon could be confident he would not serve more than two years and nine months if he pleaded guilty. Alternatively, he could take his chances and face the prospect of the jury finding him guilty, after which the judge would then sentence him to five years.

If we made an application to Judge Dawson, who was assigned to the case, we would be able to learn the exact sentence he would impose in return for a guilty plea. Judge Dawson would then be obliged to impose the promised sentence at the sentencing hearing. We lacked the time to file an application with him before our scheduled con with Dixon. Still, Giles trusted my estimated sentence enough to adopt it as his own.

Dixon came to the conference with his latest girlfriend, Poppy Dunn, not Molly's mom. The Crown Prosecution Service had previously sent us a copy of the videotaped interview that little Molly had with the social worker. Giles planned to view it with Dixon. Giles had not anticipated Dixon's refusal to watch the tape. There was a bit of confrontation. Giles was doing his patrician best to establish a modicum of rapport with Dixon, to no avail. Finally, Giles told Dixon that he did not have to watch the video, but explained that we, as his defense, were obliged to do so. Giles suggested Dixon and Poppy sit outside while we watched the video recording.

We could not view the videotape immediately. I was the only one in the room who could figure out how to run the videotape machine. Giles was clueless when it came to mechanical and electronic devices.

After viewing the tape, Giles and I looked at each other and did not say a word. Our expressions said it all: "Dixon is in trouble." Molly was totally convincing, using an anatomical doll to demonstrate what the Dixon had done. The social worker conducted a skilled and sensitive interview, using no leading questions or suggesting possible answers, which might make the tape inadmissible in the trial.

I invited Dixon back into the conference room and asked Dixon if Poppy could also sit in on the discussion. Giles hoped Poppy would provide a voice of reason. Giles's assumption was proven the moment the discussion began. Poppy had persuaded Dixon to watch the video.

Re-watching Molly tell her story did nothing to improve my estimate of Dixon's chances for a not guilty verdict. I was curious about how Dixon and Poppy would react to the video. They had both been sitting on the edge of their chairs and leaning forward with their eyes glued to the screen. Dixon did not move a muscle, but Poppy shifted around in her chair and continually glanced at Dixon. What was she thinking? I guessed she was rethinking her relationship to this alleged child molester and planned to walk away from him as soon as she could.

When the tape ended, Giles cleverly asked Poppy whether she thought a jury would believe Molly. She said, "Yes." Even Dixon had to agree. Then began the delicate dance of informing the client of the risks of going to trial and the possible sentence if he were found guilty. It is a tricky tightrope for a barrister to tread, especially when a client directly asks the barrister what he should do. Giles never offered his opinion about the guilt or innocence of Dixon. He couched his answers in terms of what he thought a jury might do, and he pushed Dixon and Poppy to make their own predictions about the likelihood of a guilty verdict. Giles suggested their assessment should then be balanced by the likely sentence if Dixon were found guilty versus the likely custodial sentence if Dixon were to plead guilty.

Dixon was clearly not ready to make a decision yet, so Giles advised the couple to think about it for several days and to tell his solicitor what they had decided. When they left the conference room, I asked Giles if he believed Dixon was telling the truth. He chuckled and said Dixon should get an award for telling one of the biggest "porkies" he had ever heard. I then asked Giles how he could ethically represent a client he knows is lying, and wouldn't he have to withdraw as counsel? Giles answered my question with a question. "What is the difference between knowing and believing? I strongly believe he is not telling the truth; I cannot know for certain he is lying."

"If he had told me he never touched Molly with his willie and then later said he may have touched Molly inadvertently, one of those statements must be a lie. I could not vouch for his credibility or represent him in court. However, if he stuck to his story that he may have touched her inadvertently, then there was at least a slim possibility that he might be telling the actual truth. He might believe it is the truth even if it wasn't. Since I did not *know* he was lying, I could continue as his barrister."

The irony was that my ethical question became moot. Dixon wanted a barrister who truly believed in his innocence, and Giles's skepticism of Dixon's story fell well short of that desire. He sacked Giles. Giles told me it was only the second time in his career that a client had sacked him. Dixon, however, did not have to travel far for a replacement; it was just a step across the hall from Giles's office. The Chambers Clerk assigned Nigel Pigot the case.

FIFTEEN

Panic In Penzance

We had a surprise phone call from our neighbor, Sally, except she was not calling from Dayton. She was calling from Canterbury, in Kent. Sally said she was on a Rick Steves Tour of Southern England, and one of the stops was in Portsmouth, just south of Winchester. We had told Sally about my sabbatical in England and may have made one of those not-expected-to-be-accepted invitations to visit us if she had happened to be in England. She proposed skipping the Portsmouth tour and coming to Winchester on the train for the day. We agreed, and four days later, we collected Sally from the Winchester train station.

To describe Sally as perky would be an understatement. She had the energy level of a 12-volt car battery crammed into an AAA battery package. Just over five feet tall, and at 40, she still had the body of a gymnast. She had been on the Ohio State University gymnastics team. Her curly black hair was cut short, and her eyes were smoldering green. Sally had recently been through a difficult divorce, and her England tour was meant to be psychologically therapeutic.

After a tour of the cathedral and the house where Jane Austin died, we went to the Wickham Arms for lunch, where we unexpectedly ran into Giles. We invited Giles to join us for lunch.

After he had a quick word with the hostess, we were ushered into a quiet booth in the back room. He was in rare form, oozing charm and making Sally the center of attention. He rarely talked about himself and focused his barrister-honed questioning skills on encouraging Sally to talk about herself and her life. Sally did not try to hide her attraction to Giles. Giles, for his part, quietly basked in the adulation. When lunch was over, he offered to drive Sally back to her hotel in Portsmouth.

Later that afternoon, Giles called and wanted to meet for a drink at the Green Man pub. I speculated that he wanted to chat about our upcoming cases. I could not have been more wrong. He wanted to talk about Sally. Apparently, a lot happened on their drive to Portsmouth. According to Giles, he was telling Sally how unfortunate it was that Sally's tour did not include Leeds and the Yorkshire Dales. He told her he knew so many beautiful and historically interesting places in Yorkshire that she would enjoy. Without missing a beat, Sally said, "How about me dropping out of the Rick Steves Tour for three days, and I spend three days in Yorkshire with you as my tour guide. I will cover the expenses as long as we can share a room."

Giles, who is well-skilled in maintaining his sangfroid in the courtroom, said he was hard-pressed not to look surprised. In fact, Giles confessed he was gobsmacked by Sally's proposal. He delayed making any decision with the excuse that he would have to consult his diary for possible conflicts. In truth, Giles wanted to consult with me about the wisdom of going along with Sally's plans. It was my turn to be gobsmacked. Why would Giles, whom I viewed as the ultimate Lothario, want the advice of a man whose romancing skills had not been particularly noteworthy?

I teased, "Surely you have had women throw themselves at you before."

"Not so," he said. Giles confessed he had never met a woman like Sally before. He compared her to champagne—bubbly, easily consumed, quick to produce euphoria, yet just as capable of leaving behind a hangover no remedy could cure. Even water, he said, only made a champagne hangover worse. Giles's surprising insecurity made him seem more human and gave a boost to my appreciation of him.

It was the sexual side of the three days in Leeds that worried Giles the most. Sally was not a neophyte when it came to sex. She did not seem to be the type of lover who acquiesced in her partner taking charge. Sally would be proactive. With her athleticism, she might insist on lovemaking resembling a gymnastic event, with Sally adapting a routine she may have practiced on the uneven parallel bars. Perhaps for the first time in Giles's life, his sexual partner might respond to his "How was it?" question with, "It was fine," a devastating blow to the male ego. Would Giles be able to keep up with Sally? I had not pictured Giles as a one-night stand kind of male who could pick up a woman in a pub and take her to bed the same night. Those kinds of liaisons are driven almost entirely by how good the sex turns out to be. If, for some reason, the male is unable to perform, the evening is considered a disaster, and his prospects for a second encounter are slim to none.

From what I knew of Giles, picking up an unknown woman in a pub was not Giles's style. He sought a deeper relationship, but not too deep. It might not be long-term, but he wants to connect with a woman on more than just a sexual level. He wants to be thought of as a handsome, charming, erudite raconteur. He is not interested in being someone who, in America, would be considered a *stud muffin*. He wanted companionship that fosters liking, or even better, admiration. Considering the women I have met who had relationships with Giles, he had mostly succeeded.

Many of his ex-girlfriends—and even his ex-wife—have remained good friends.

Now that Giles had provided me with a better insight into his persona, I was willing to take the risk of offering him my advice, which is a bit like asking a high school physics student to explain quantum theory to a physics grad student. I encouraged him to take Sally on a tour of Yorkshire. I believed her attraction to Giles was much more than sexual. I suggested that Sally had likely never met a man quite like Giles before—a gentleman who enjoyed her conversation and wit for their own sake. Giles's suavity made her feel he was interested in her both as a woman and in what she had to say. Before Sally met Giles, she may have had an image of the well-spoken British aristocrat in mind, inspired by authors like Jane Austen. Giles ticked all the boxes, and Sally was besotted. Therefore, I told Giles that sex would not have to be great for him and Sally to have a good time together in Yorkshire. Their exchange of wit, stimulating conversation, and having Giles as a knowledgeable tour guide, plus, of course, superb food and wine, would more than compensate for just OK sex.

Giles took my advice, and the next day he and Sally left for three days in Leeds. I did not ask either Giles or Sally how things went, and they did not volunteer any information. Evidently, what happens in Leeds stays in Leeds.

Despite the code of silence, I felt confident one of the stops on Giles's tour would be Ripley Castle, which had been in the Ingilby family for over seven hundred years, a rather good trick in itself. In the 16th century, one Lord Ingilby had been hard-pressed and nearly lost the estate to the King. Ingilby was under the illusion that his wife had been unfaithful to him and that all three of his children were not his. In a drunken rage, he killed his wife and two of his children. The third child was safe in another location at the time. In those days, prosecutors liked to obtain confessions, which made trials quicker and less complicated. They did not have to present much evidence at the trial. To extract a confession, the accused was subjected to a procedure known as *peine forte et dure*. Heavy stones were piled on the accused until he or she pleaded guilty or died under the weight. The dilemma for Lord Ingilby was that if he pleaded guilty, his considerable estate would be forfeited to the Crown. His one remaining heir would be a pauper. Lord Ingilby chose to die unconvicted rather than plead guilty, thereby keeping the estate in the family. That was an extreme form of tax rebellion. He would rather die and have a person he did not believe was his son inherit the estate rather than let the Crown have it.

With Giles gone, Susan, Nancy, and I decided to make a trip to Cornwall. We rented a car with a standard transmission that I had to shift with my left hand. I also had to learn to drive on the left side of the road. It would be the first time I had driven in England, and little did I know I would be driving on some of the most challenging roads in the country. I was not sure if I was more intimidated by the motorways or by navigating the backroads of Dorset and Cornwall. Both proved equally scary, with white knuckles on the steering wheel at all times.

I gave a sigh of relief after negotiating my way out of Winchester's medieval streets, only to face my first roundabout. Three roads merged into a roundabout, and I needed to take the one leading to the M-3 motorway. I edged into the circling traffic, and before I realized it, I was past the M-3 exit. No problem, you can circle a roundabout as often as you want, but I got it right after my first loop.

The M-3 is a limited-access highway, similar to an American expressway, except you drive on the opposite side of the road with the higher speed lanes on your right instead of your left. I had no intention of jockeying for position with 80-mph drivers, so I hugged the left lane and never went faster than 55mph. I exited the M-3, maneuvered through another roundabout, and merged with the M-27 toward Bournemouth. From there, we picked up the A35 to Exeter and then the A30 to Penzance—over a hundred miles in all. The A roads were largely two-lane roads, with occasional stretches widening to four lanes. Most of the time, I remembered to drive on the left, but when I pulled out of a side road and into the right—the wrong—lane, Susan's shouting quickly steered me back into the left lane.

Usually, when I am driving on a long trip, I am intent on reaching our destination and curmudgeonly refuse any frolics and detours along the way. Giles's skiving jaunt showed me that gambols and diversions were often the best part of an excursion. So, I only gave a pro forma objection when Nancy saw a sign for the Cerne Abbas Chalk Giant and asked for a slight detour. She had heard about chalk sculptures being unique to England in school and was eager to see one. Much to our surprise, the Giant turned out to be a naked figure sculpted into a chalk hillside. It was 180 feet long. Its white outline was fashioned by an ancient Celtic people, stripping away the sod and grass overlying the white chalk hillside, creating an image of a Hercules-like figure holding aloft a huge club. I wondered who or what he was going to bash with his cudgel since he was also sporting a huge, erect penis.

As we were driving back to the A-35, I posed a question: "What do you think the message is?"

Susan quipped, "Nothing seems to have changed in two thousand years. Prehistoric men were still struggling with 'penis size paranoia.'"

We had one more detour on the way to Cornwall—a drive through Dartmoor, the backdrop for many English novels, including Arthur Conan Doyle's, *The Hound of the Baskervilles*. Dartmoor is simultaneously desolate and beautiful, or at least that is how Susan and Nancy described it to me. Although I was driving, I did not actually see much of the landscape. I was much more concerned about rental car scrapes. The road through the park had been generously described as one lane wide. It did accommodate the width of our car with a few inches to spare. I had to navigate between sharp drop-offs into ditches and vine-covered stone walls brushing by my side-view mirrors. Fortunately, the park managers had designated the road as one-way, so I never had to squeeze by oncoming cars. I emerged on the other side of Dartmoor unscathed and uninformed.

The last leg of our journey was likely intended by Giles as a test of my navigational skills. He had made reservations for us at a country house bed-and-breakfast located north of Penzance, which could only be reached by negotiating miles of narrow, twisting farm lanes. Giles, however, neglected to consider that we had Nancy to navigate. Road maps to her were not a confusing maze of lines and squiggles, but arrows and signposts guiding her to wherever she wanted to go. "Go right, Dad, at the next intersection and then an immediate left until you get to a fork in the road, and then you go right again." Meandering through Dartmoor had been a good warm-up for the backroads of Cornwall. The lanes were similar in width to the Dartmoor byways, a couple of feet wider than our car, but rather than being hemmed in by ivy-covered stone walls and deep ditches, we were wedged between long rows of seven-foot-high hedgerows. The hedges were a mix of shrubs and trees like hawthorn, blackthorn, hazel, and yew, which were woven together to form a solid wall. They are effective fences, keeping livestock in and people out. Although brushing against them will not damage a car like a stone wall, it would play havoc with the paint job.

Unlike the road through Dartmoor, which required cars to drive in only one direction, the Cornwall lanes were two-way roads. So, what happens when you slowly go around a bend and meet another vehicle heading your way? Well, every few hundred yards, the road widened just enough to allow two cars to pass. The polite British expectation was that one of the drivers would pull over to the side of the road so the other driver could squeeze by. I was not polite. There was no way I could back up my rental car for a hundred yards without running into a hedgerow, so I just sat there and looked helpless. It never failed. The more polite Brit would do the backing, and I would edge past with a grateful wave.

Nancy's directions were perfect, with never a wrong turn. The bed-and-breakfast was a large manor house owned by a young couple, Judy and Don Ford. They had purchased it five years prior and were trying to make a go of it as a bed-and-breakfast. The house was remodeled in 1640 and had been owned by the same family until 1920. Judy showed us a 1645 inventory, which listed the movable property in all the rooms. The total value was £548, which was a chunk of change then. We did not have time to chat, though, as we had reserved seats at the Minack Theatre in Land's End.

The Minack is probably one of the most uncomfortable venues in the world to watch a play. Yet patrons must reserve seats months in advance of a performance, and West End theatre troupes compete for the opportunity to stage a play there.

Start with the fact that Land's End is literally the last piece of England you will see as you head west to the USA, three thousand miles away. The Minack Theatre was carved into a granite cliff in Cornwall, perched a hundred feet above the English Channel, with its seats cast in concrete. Most of the design and construction was done over six decades by Rowena Cade, who bought the land for £100 in 1920.

A sign could have been posted at the entrance: "All ye who enter here do so at your own risk."

What was posted was, "Beware, the theatre is a steep cliff and includes many uneven steps which may be slippery when wet. Wear sensible footwear. Seating is available on either turf or concrete; cushions and rugs are advisable. If attending a Matinee, wear a hat and bring sunscreen. For evening performances, wear warm clothing. Average wind speeds are ten to twenty knots. Performances are cancelled only in extreme conditions. Plays will be performed in the rain."

I was skeptical about the last caveat. Surely the audience and the cast would not be forced to watch a play in a thunderstorm. Dana Cooper, Giles's girlfriend, had assured me it was true. She told us she was playing Lady Macbeth at the Minack in the middle of a raging thunderstorm, and the only concession to the weather made by the director was allowing Dana to shed her metal crown.

The conditions for us were more benign. A star-filled sky provided an incredible backdrop. It was cool with a 15-knot wind blowing, and our four layers of clothes were a welcome addition. When we carefully edged to our seats, I was sure the actors' voices would be completely blown away by the wind. I was wrong. The acoustics at the Minack were superior to many London theatres. The actors did not wear stage microphones, and yet we could hear every word.

The setting was more interesting than the play, *The Further Adventures of Don Quixote*. It was a largely forgettable farce, except for the memory of how nervous I was for the safety of the actors. The scenes were frenetic, with actors jumping from rock to rock and then onto the stage. All I could think about was what if they slipped and plunged one hundred feet into the sea? The Minack is well known among actors for its precarious stage, which has caused numerous broken limbs. The high point of the play occurred when a pod of dolphins went cavorting by in the distance, and the audience lost interest in the play. The director, however, knew when his troop of actors was being upstaged by a troop of dolphins. He stopped the play mid-scene and informed the audience that the play would resume when the dolphins were out of sight.

After the final scene, more adventures were beckoning. I had to find my way back to the bed-and-breakfast at night, piloting my way in the dark through the same maze of backroads and lanes I struggled with earlier in the day. In one way, the drive was less risky. At night, I could see the glow of headlights from oncoming cars before rounding a bend in the road and meeting them head-on. My memory of the journey has been erased from my brain, but I remember being chuffed when Don and Judy Ford told me how surprised they were that I managed to find my way back at night. Had I passed another Giles test?

Giles regretted not being able to give us a personal tour of Cornwall, as he was otherwise occupied in Leeds, so he had arranged for a substitute, Harry Safari. We never learned Harry's real surname. Harry operated a one-person tour service, which he called "Harry's Safaris," which was emblazoned on the side of his van. Ordinarily, I would be hesitant to hire a person as a guide who gave his business such a kitschy name. Harry, however, proved to be a charming eccentric who took us to places that were off the usual tourist map. Our first stop in the morning was a return to the Minack Theatre, where Harry arranged with the owner for me to step onto the stage and give the only Shakespearean monologue I remembered to hundreds of empty seats.

"Tomorrow, and tomorrow, and tomorrow, creeps in this petty pace from day to day, to the last syllable of recorded time..."

Remarkably, Susan and Nancy had no difficulty hearing me while sitting in the last row of the theatre.

The next stop was Carn Euny, a preserved Iron Age village that had been occupied by a Celtic tribe over two thousand years ago. This was probably the safari part of Harry's tours. We had to scramble over two stiles and then hike through a muddy field, avoiding a herd of dairy cows while gingerly stepping around cow pies. It was worth the trek. We were the only ones at the site except for the Celtic ghosts inhabiting the stone huts. We crawled into one of the huts and huddled together to escape the raw, damp wind blowing across the hilltop. It was easy to imagine a family doing the same thing two thousand years ago and realizing they were not all that different from us, with similar needs, hopes, and fears.

The climax of Harry's tour was another hilltop, where there was a ring of large boulders called the Merry Maidens Stone Circle. Nineteen upright stones, set in a circle, were erected during the Neolithic era, between 2500 and 1500 BCE. Hundreds of such circles are spread across England, and archeologists are still arguing why they were originally assembled. The local myth about the Merry Maidens was that the young lasses were so caught up in their dancing that they frolicked past midnight and were still dancing when the Sabbath arrived. For that sacrilege, they were turned into stone. Myths have a way of surviving exposure to facts. The fact that there were no Sabbaths 4,000 years ago had not destroyed the myth, proving the adage that a story once told is as good as true.

Harry wove a different story about the origin of the Merry Maidens. He said he believed Neolithic peoples were much more in tune with nature and could sense natural phenomena that we moderns had lost our capacity for. Harry described Ley lines, a concept new to us. He said Ley lines were caused by the earth's magnetic field, and they were like invisible power lines criss-crossing the earth's surface, similar to a vast spider's web. In places where those Ley lines crossed, there was a surge of energy much like what happens when two electrical wires touch. According to Harry, the Neolithic people could sense those places where the Ley lines crossed. It was there that they chose to construct their rings of stone, such as the Merry Maidens, as sites for their religious and other ceremonies.

Harry was a master storyteller, but he could not sell that tale to us. We were three skeptics, and he knew it. Like the magician he was, he encouraged us to build our doubts like a house of cards, which he could then knock down with a single believable trick. He smiled when he handed each of us two L-shaped copper wires, about the thickness of a coat hanger. We were standing outside the circle, and he positioned us so we would enter the circle from different directions. We gripped one end of a wire loosely in each hand with our arms slightly extended. Harry said it was important to keep the two wires parallel and pointing forward as we slowly walked to the center of the circle. Then came the tricky part. We should not force the wires to move or touch, but at the same time, we should not prevent the wires from moving on their own and touching. For me, this was like carrying a full cup of tea across a room while concentrating on not spilling a single drop. As the three of us approached the center of the circle from different directions, our copper wires moved entirely on their own. The two parallel wires were suddenly crossed like an X, thus giving credence to Harry's theory that two Ley lines crossed each other near the center of the Merry Maidens. I was not entirely convinced of Harry's notion. I assumed there could be numerous other explanations for the phenomenon. Still, I left the circle with a more open mind about our Neolithic ancestors. They may have possessed knowledge and skills that we 20th-century folks had lost over the centuries.

SIXTEEN

Paying Clients

Giles returned from his weekend tour of Yorkshire with Sally in a happy mood. However, he gave no hint that his joy had anything to do with his exploration of the moors and manor houses of Yorkshire. It may have had more to do with the fact that the Chambers chief clerk told him he had acquired two paying clients. This meant that the clients had too much money to qualify for Legal Aid. The chief clerk could set the fee at whatever the chief clerk thought the client would be willing to pay. In the first case, the client, Sir Robert Nixon, was a multimillionaire who owned a chain of furniture stores. Legal Aid paid about £50 per hour, so the clerk was able to negotiate a fee of £250 per hour. In the second case, the client, Thomas Sunderland, had just earned £700,000 developing a program for the Royal Postal Service, which was designed to protect the Service's computer server from a particularly dangerous virus. The clerk settled for £200 per hour.

Sir Robert was charged with aggressive driving and a lesser charge of driving negligently. Aggressive driving is using a motor vehicle in a deliberate and aggressive manner, which is likely to endanger life by increasing the risk of a collision with another vehicle, bicyclist, or pedestrian. If found guilty, a person could be fined an unlimited amount, face a driving ban, and be sentenced to up to 14 years in prison. Negligent driving occurs when a person is deemed to be driving without due care and attention. That occurs when a person's driving falls below what would be expected of a competent and careful driver. If found guilty of negligent driving, a person would not be incarcerated but would be fined and possibly have their license suspended for a limited time.

In materials sent to Giles from the solicitor, there was an eyewitness statement that supported the aggressive driving charge. The witness told the police that she had seen Nixon in his Mercedes about to pull into one of the few available spaces in the Garden Center Car Park when a man driving a Mini West, Sam Cohen, zipped in ahead of Nixon. According to the witness, Nixon accelerated his Mercedes, circled around the next row of cars, and came back to where Cohen had just gotten out of his car. Cohen had opened the Mini's rear hatch and was in the process of taking out a package when Nixon drove his Mercedes so close to Cohen that he had to jump out of the way. Cohen fell to the pavement, causing him to break his wrist.

Sir Robert told the police he was circling the parking lot to find an open slot when Cohen emerged from between two parked cars. According to our client, Cohen did not look before stepping out into the parking lane to open the Mini's rear hatch. Sir Robert insisted he did not strike Cohen, but that Cohen lost his balance and fell onto the pavement. Sir Robert did not deny that Cohen had broken his wrist in the fall.

After reading the file, we decided a trip to the Garden Center Car Park would be helpful. It was, but not necessarily helpful to our client's defense.

Giles and I staged a reenactment of the scene. The lanes were narrow, so it was easy to see that any car going down one of the lanes would pass close to a person standing at the rear of his car. The tricky problem was that there are many lanes for parking cars on the lot, and we could not come up with a good reason why Sir

Robert would choose to go straight back down the same lane. There had been no parking slots on that lane moments before. Why not try one of the other lanes first? We had thought the big challenge for the Crown Prosecutor would be to show that our client's driving was deliberately aggressive, which implied an element of intent. His choosing to return to the scene of the incident where Cohen had annoyed him was some circumstantial evidence of his intent to give Cohen a scare. Our first meeting with Sir Robert and his wife, Martha, was two days later. We arranged to meet them along with their solicitor in the conference room at Northgate Chambers. Introductions were barely over before Sir Robert launched into a diatribe about how the police had treated him. He ranted about how he had actually been arrested, taken to the station where he had been photographed, and subjected to the indignity of being fingerprinted. Sir Robert was charged with a serious crime, yet he fumed that the police had the temerity to treat him as a common criminal. My American egalitarian streak made it difficult for me to suppress a smile. Perhaps Sir Robert might now develop more empathy for the ordinary bloke who gets caught up in the criminal justice system, but I doubted it.

My being an American attorney also triggered another rant about how he disliked places in America, like Los Angeles and San Francisco, because they have been taken over by "What do you call them? Hispanics? Like London has been inundated with Jews." After that comment, Giles flashed a quick side-eye in my direction and explained to Sir Robert that he and I would need to leave the conference room for a few minutes to do a little legal research.

We went into Giles's office and closed the door. "David, what do you think?"

I said, "We have a problem. We cannot put Nixon on the stand."

Giles asked, "Why?" although I knew he knew the answer. The weak link in the Crown's case was proving that our client was intentionally driving aggressively. Motives were often used to supply an explanation of why a defendant's action was deliberate. If Nixon testified, he could easily supply the missing intent. First, the jury was not going to have much empathy for a privileged multimillionaire driving a Mercedes who acted privileged. A multimillionaire who raged about the impudence of the police arresting him and treating him like a common criminal; escorting him to the police station, taking his mug shot, and his finger-prints. Secondly, with his anger always boiling beneath the surface, any skilled cross-examiner could light Sir Robert's short fuse and show the jury how he likely reacted when Mr. Cohen had the temerity to occupy the parking spot he thought was his by right. Cohen's encroachment on Sir Robert's rightful territory supplied the motivation for him to circle back to scare the usurper and teach him a lesson. Finally, it would not help Sir Robert's defense if his antisemitism revealed itself during cross-examina-tion—especially since Sam Cohen was Jewish.

The dilemma was deciding what to do. Giles thought it would be best for Sir Robert to plead guilty to the lesser offense of negli-gent driving. He could not ethically urge that solution on a client, and the natural combativeness of Sir Robert did not make it likely he would see the wisdom of pleading guilty. Sir Robert did not become CEO of Nixon's by avoiding fights, especially when he had his enormous wealth to back him up. I thought it ironic that, from Giles's own economic perspective, it would be quite lucra-tive for him to enter the lists on Sir Robert's behalf and fight to the bitter end. Giles would have been offended if he suspected such a thought crossed my mind. He was a professional, bound to do what was best for the client, even if it diminished his own pocketbook.

Giles proposed a divide-and-conquer strategy. I would invite Mrs. Nixon to the break room for a cup of tea, and Giles would stay in the conference room with Sir Robert and his solicitor, where he would perform the delicate dance of describing his assessment of the case, including about a 30% chance of convic-tion for aggressive driving, and a likely sentence if convicted.

Balanced against that possibility was the likely sentence if he pleaded guilty to negligent driving. Though I am sure Giles laid out the options in an apparently neutral manner, I'm equally sure he managed to tilt the scales in favor of pleading guilty to the lesser charge. Giles said he would assure Sir Robert that he would fight the case to the end if that was what he preferred.

My task was to chat with Martha and make the case to her that it would be better for her husband to plead guilty to the lesser offense than to take the risk of going to trial and having a jury find him guilty of a much more serious crime. I was not constrained by the limitation on a barrister's ability to persuade a client to plead guilty. I was Giles's pupil, but I was only explaining to the client's wife the advantages of pleading to the lesser offense. Martha appeared to be a diffident, submissive spouse, but I suspected she wielded more influence over Sir Robert than he would ever admit —pillow-talk power.

It was clear that Martha did not relish conflict and confrontation, so I stressed how going to trial would be a battle in which she might personally have to participate as a witness. I told Martha we estimated there was a one out of three chance that a jury would convict her husband of aggressive driving, and if that happened, it was likely he would be in prison for some period. I asked her to imagine what spending any time in prison would do to the health of a 68-year-old man. I cushioned my next comment by first apologizing for having to raise a difficult and personal issue, but she needed to understand why there was a reasonable chance a jury would convict her husband.

"Martha, I think you realize that your husband is quick to anger and there is a good probability that during aggressive cross-examination by the Crown Prosecutor, he will display that anger, which would undermine his defense with the jury."

Martha did not disagree.

Finally, I emphasized how her husband might win the battle in the courtroom and still lose the public relations war in the media. Due to his status as CEO and owner of one of the largest chains of appliance stores in England, the print and broadcasting media would have a field day covering all the details of the trial. Inevitably, his reputation would be tainted regardless of the jury verdict.

When we returned to the conference room, it was clear Sir Robert had not yet been persuaded to plead guilty to the lesser offense. Rather than urge an immediate decision, which could be "No." Given Sir Robert's personality, his decision would be carved in stone. Giles suggested that Sir Robert and Martha take some time to think and discuss whether it would be better for him and Martha if he pleaded guilty to the lesser offense. I like to think that my chat with Martha tipped the scales because two days later, Sir Robert's solicitor informed Giles that he was prepared to plead guilty to negligent driving. Giles was pleased, even though at £250 an hour he could have earned something north of £25,000 if the case had gone to trial, and more if there had been an appeal.

Thomas Sunderland, our other paying client, was the polar opposite of Sir Robert. If central casting wanted someone to portray the quintessential computer nerd, Thomas was the one. He was tall, lanky, and awkward, with arms that extended several inches further than his coat sleeves. He may or may not have passed a comb through his unruly hair, and his shaving always managed to leave a few bristles sticking out somewhere. There was a wide-eyed innocence about him, naïve and trusting, as if he were lost in a world he did not quite understand. Tom was doubtless somewhere on the autism spectrum, as evidenced by his shyness and difficulty in relating to other people.

Normally, we would have been worried about Tom's ability to connect with a jury. Would his appearance and reticent demeanor lessen his credibility? We would certainly have advised him to dress for success and discard his charity shop wardrobe. This was not a normal case; however, our defense was premised on portraying Thomas as being a deer-in-the-headlights dupe, who was incapable of seeing that his so-called friends were entangling him in a web of criminal conspiracy. We did not want to sharpen Tom's answers or improve his disheveled appearance. Let the jury see Tom as he really was.

Tom's trial was set at the Bournemouth Crown Court. The Crown Prosecution Service had charged Tom with being part of a criminal conspiracy to grow and sell marijuana in large quantities. Tom admitted to having supplied £50,000 to his friend, Tony Barker, who used the money to construct a marijuana farm in an old warehouse. Tony had also enlisted several other friends to run the operation, including a local police constable. Our defense was simple. Tom loaned the money to Tony, his lifelong friend, to help him start a business, and Tom had no idea what Tony was up to. All the other defendants except Tony had pleaded guilty.

The first day of trial was consumed with a few preliminary motions, the finalizing of the guilty pleas, and the sentencing of the three co-defendants. To an American lawyer, it was a surreal scene—a flock of senior barristers, solicitors, junior barristers, and a pupil or two like me representing the Crown and the five defendants. What made the scene even more unreal was that the Crown Prosecutor, Brooks Gibson, and two of the barristers and their juniors, representing two defendants, were fellow members of Giles's Chambers, Northgate, with offices across the hall from Giles's. Other than me, no one in the courtroom, including Judge Hart, would consider such barrister incestuousness to be a conflict of interest. I wondered how the defendants must have felt watching the prosecuting barristers and their defense barristers joking, laughing, and teasing each other before Judge Hart entered the courtroom to decide their fates.

Liz Spenser was one of the junior barristers for the Northgate barrister representing Tony Barker, Cyrus O'Brian. She generously offered to drive me back and forth from Winchester in her

Volkswagen (VW) Beetle, saving me the cost of the train and taxi fares. Liz had one thing in common with the other barristers I had ridden with—she drove at 80 to 85 miles an hour, which was even more exciting in a VW Beetle than hurtling along in Giles's Citroën.

If I had ever entertained the notion of remaining in England and being a barrister, my conversation with Liz supplied a hefty dose of reality. Liz was a 30-year-old junior barrister who was just getting by. She had managed to buy a small, dilapidated two-bedroom townhouse in the Badger Farm neighborhood, which she was rehabbing. In addition to her legal acumen, Liz was a skilled carpenter. We shared stories about the pleasure of driving a nail into a 2X4 with only a couple of whacks.

Liz was seriously considering a major career change to become a landscape designer. In the U.S., a lawyer who was not making it as a trial lawyer always had the option of falling back on a general practice of writing wills, drafting contracts, and facilitating real estate transactions. Liz pointed out that in England, solicitors conduct that kind of legal practice. No solicitor firm would hire her because she was trained as a barrister and consequently not deeply knowledgeable about substantive civil law. To make the switch to being a solicitor, she would be required to complete a one-year Legal Practice Course and then undertake a two-year apprenticeship with a solicitor firm, assuming she could find a solicitor firm that would take her on.

If Liz continued as a barrister with Northgate Chambers, she anticipated that her financial situation might not improve much. She was at the mercy of the Head Clerk of Chambers, who had to market her skills to solicitors. Junior barristers were not in much demand unless they reduced their fees, which was the start of a slippery slope. With fewer fees being earned, Liz still had to contribute to the overhead costs of Chambers.

The irony is that barristers may be the cock-of-the-walk in the courthouse and look down on solicitors, but the solicitors actually rule the roost. Solicitors choose which barristers they want to litigate a civil case or to represent a defendant in a criminal case, and they hold the purse strings. Liz said that solicitors were known to delay paying barristers for months. This allowed them to invest the unpaid money and thus receive the interest as an unearned bonus. There is little a barrister can do about it. A barrister who had the temerity to sue a solicitor for a fee would soon have no fee-generating legal work. Solicitors do gossip about which barristers are good for the bottom line.

Liz added that recent legislation had squeezed barristers even more. She said that before she was admitted to the Bar, barristers were paid at a standard per diem rate for representing clients who qualified for Legal Aid. The money for the barrister, along with the solicitor's fees, was dispersed to the solicitor, who then paid the barrister—eventually. The solicitor, however, was obliged to pay the standard per diem fee set by Legal Aid.

Now, however, Liz said there was no set per diem rate for barristers. A lump sum was given to the solicitor for representing the defendant, which included fees for a barrister. The solicitor could negotiate the fee to be paid to the barrister. The solicitor was in the catbird seat, being able to say to the Clerk of Chambers, "If you want the case, you must accept our price. In fact, if you expect any of our future business sent your way, you have little choice but to accept our offer." But it gets worse. Under the new regime, large solicitor firms have more bargaining power and can enter long-term arrangements with barrister chambers.

"We will send to your Chambers all our Crown Court criminal cases, but you will have to agree to our standard reimbursement rate. If you do not agree to our arrangement, your Chambers will receive no more referrals from our firm."

The icing on the cake for solicitor firms (designed to save the government money, of course) was legislation that allowed some crimes previously exclusively tried before juries in the Crown Court to be tried now in Magistrate Courts with no juries. While cases in the Crown Courts require barristers to represent the parties, there was no need for defendants to hire a barrister for the

Magistrate Courts. Solicitors could represent clients in the Magistrate Court and collect their own fees plus the fees that would have previously gone to a barrister. Liz thought this so-called reform would be the equivalent of turning over a West End play, like Hamlet, to a troupe of amateur actors.

Liz was under additional pressure from her boyfriend, Kyle. He was not happy with the time Liz had to spend during evenings and on weekends when cases heated up. Kyle also resented the time she spent rehabbing her townhouse. He was uninterested and would not help by hammering one nail or weeding one square foot of garden. I was dismayed that Liz sacrificed so much to accommodate Kyle's demands. Kyle did not seem to be contributing much to the relationship beyond complaints. I did not expect their relationship to go anywhere in the long or medium term and hoped it would not, for Liz's sake. She was too bright and talented to be dragged down by Kyle's deadweight. I did not tell her that.

The Crown's case against Tom and Tony for operating a marijuana factory was exceedingly boring, and I expected a couple of the older members of the jury to nod off. A good deal of prosecuting barrister Janet Brook's case relied on cell phone messages and sworn statements made by witnesses to the police during their investigation. In an American trial, the people who had given statements to the police would still have to testify at the trial. Those written statements would be considered inadmissible hearsay. Under British criminal procedure, however, statements made to the police can be read to the jury or recorded tapes can be played for the jury. That can happen when defense counsel does not say they intend to challenge the facts contained in those statements. Then, according to British criminal procedure, there is no need for the witnesses to give live testimony. Once, during our affray case, the judge sharply chastised a barrister for not abiding by the practice. A witness was subpoenaed to testify. The witness testified under oath, and then opposing counsel informed the judge he had no further questions for the witness. The judge was irritated that the counsel would make a witness travel to court and waste much of the day for no reason.

Giles had previously indicated he had no questions for many of the witnesses and that he had no evidentiary reason to object to the cell phone messages. Other than confirming that Tom had given money to Tony, which Tom admitted, the messages and the other sworn statements were ambiguous, at best, regarding whether Tom knew the money would be used to create a marijuana farm inside an old warehouse. The challenge for Prosecutor Brook was to prove Tom knew, or should have known, what the money was for. The challenge for us in defending Tom was to make the jury believe that Tom was the kind of naïve, lost soul who would give such a large sum of money to a person without ever checking to see how it was spent.

There was a welcome break in the non-action when the audio technician was struggling to play only a snippet of the audio version of a witness's statement. The statement had been recorded on a reel-to-reel tape, and the poor technician, listening to the tape through his earphones, had to keep fast-forwarding and reversing the tape to locate the morsel of testimony Brook wanted played to the jury. The technician broke out in a cold sweat. Every eye in the courtroom was focused on him for 10 minutes while he struggled to isolate the relevant segment of the recording.

I suppose I should have learned to trust Giles's instincts when it came to selecting the best line of defense for a defendant. Once again, Giles was determined to rest our case on the single assumption that the jury would accept our "dupe defense," that Tom was so childlike and gullible he could be seduced to give his friend £50,000 to invest in a completely illegal enterprise.

I was more worried about our line of defense after our interview with Tom. He looked like the type of guy who was comfortable with computer hardware and programming, but who was at a loss in the real world. I could easily picture Tom not coming in out of the rain. I whispered to Giles that Tom did look like a deer in the headlights, an appearance that fit the persona we hoped the jury would accept. Giles said he liked the deer business and would use it.

A critical question was how Tom would hold up under cross-examination. He was such a space cadet. It was almost impossible to get him to focus on the questions we asked. I suppose it is a sign of genius that a person can hear a question and then fashion six different possible answers, and then be willing to offer all of them, any one of which could be red meat for a cross-examiner. Giles may have crossed the line with prepping Tom for his testimony, but the fact that Tom was our client gave Giles a bit more leeway in helping him prepare for his testimony. For example, the police made a thorough search of Tom's house, looking for cell phones. They only found two. Tom volunteered, "There may have been a third one." Giles told him there was no need to offer such speculation when he was testifying. Fingers crossed.

The Crown's case against Tony seemed open and shut. Yet, Tony's barrister, Cyrus O'Brian, decided to maintain a defense that required Tony to testify. Tony was a smooth-talking character who had an exaggerated belief in his rhetorical skills, thinking he could snow a jury with his slick words. He was convinced he would be able to prevail in any verbal jousting match with a cross-examining barrister. Prisons were filled with inmates who were sure they could outwit a barrister. Tony would be joining them.

Brook used a cross-examination technique that often leads to disaster in American courtrooms when used against witnesses who had been super-prepped and vetted before taking the stand. He fired off a litany of "Why" questions, the kind of questions that make me cringe when my Trial Practice students pose them. During a good prep session with a witness, the answers to potential "Why" questions are rehearsed until they are as smooth as a Shakespearean monologue. Another lurking danger is that the "Why" question may open the door for the admission of evidence that would otherwise be excluded.

"Why do you say it was the defendant who robbed you?"

"Because my friend Mary told me that the defendant robbed

her last year." That same testimony, if offered during direct examination of the witness, would be excluded, but the "Why" question makes the same answer admissible.

Furthermore, cross-examining counsel who asks the "Why"
question cannot un-ring the bell and have the answer stricken
from the record. Once asked, counsel is stuck with whatever
comes back. A well-prepped defendant can deliver a five-minute
monologue explaining why they are completely innocent.

In England, it is less risky to ask the "Why" question with
unprepared witnesses. They are forced to concoct a credible
response on the fly while standing in the dock, an answer which
may provide the barrister with more grist for the cross-examining
mill. Tony's story had so many holes in it, with multiple loose
ends, that it only required a little tugging to unravel the whole
thing. Tony had no innocent explanation for what he did. He had
sold cannabis to an undercover agent and was arrested while
watering his pot plants in the factory.

Although Brook's cross-examination of Tony did not help our
client, I enjoyed watching her dissect Tony's tale. Giles said
Brook's style was like "Jane Austin with an edge." I thought *a steel
hand in the velvet glove* was a more apt description because I was
mesmerized watching her long, delicate, and perfectly manicured
fingers while she eviscerated Tony's testimony. Like all barristers,
she stood behind a small movable podium while conducting her
examinations. Her right hand was resting on the back of her chair.
Brook was not gripping the chair as a way to reduce tension;
however, she caressed it in a slow, deliberate manner, a kind of
Tai Chi.

Tony's barrister, Cyrus O'Brian, must have been desperate
because the next witness he called was Tony's very pregnant wife,
Daisy. Her direct testimony was an attempt to corroborate Tony's
implausible story, which was made more improbable by Brook's
cross-examination of Daisy. Brook wrung out a litany of instances
in which Daisy's version of events contradicted Tony's. Perhaps
O'Brian's strategy was to provoke sympathy for Tony's family, and

especially his unborn child, who would be fatherless while Tony was serving several years in prison. Throughout Daisy's testimony, she would be gently stroking her belly like she had learned in her prenatal classes, attempting to remind the jury about her plight if they convicted Tony. The cynical side of me wondered if the whole scene was designed to be a melodramatic performance planned months before. Daisy did not get pregnant until after Tony had been indicted. It would not seem to be the best approach to family planning for a wife to get pregnant when her husband is facing the prospect of being incarcerated until the unborn child starts preschool.

After the lunch break, our client, Tom, was scheduled to stand in the witness box. Giles and I took a table in a far corner of the lunchroom, and I could tell he was not feeling well. He said he was feeling some dizziness, and he doubted whether he could conduct the direct exam of Tom. I held my breath and feared what he would say next. He said, "David, you will have to do the direct examination of Tom. We have thoroughly discussed Tom's testimony, and you can use my notes." The latter part of that statement provided little comfort to me, since his notes were not a roadmap but more a collection of snippets designed to remind him about the question he wanted to ask. Assuming I could even decipher his scratches and scribbles, and that they offered any hint about the questions to ask, I realized I would still need to craft most of my questions on the fly.

I decided to jettison Giles's notes entirely and resort to the advice I had given my mock trial teams for years. I urged them to abandon their detailed list of questions and focus instead on the picture they wanted to paint for the jury of what had happened. Then, to ask questions that assist the witness in filling in the blank canvas, brushstroke by brushstroke. I knew what scenes we wanted Tom to paint. I just had to ask questions from which Tom could figure out what parts of a scene I wanted him to fill in and in what order.

When Tom walked to the stand, he looked terrified and was

visibly shaking. I was not much better. I was thankful no one could see my shaking legs behind our counsel table and speaking podium. Oddly, the wig, gown, and other accoutrements gave me an aura of competence I did not feel. I remembered that I often felt the same way before walking into a classroom to teach my first class of the semester. I also recalled how the nervousness disappeared as soon as I uttered my opening lines. That magic reoccurred in the courtroom when I asked Tom my first question. "Would you say your name and spell it for the court reporter?" Answering that question also had a calming effect on Tom.

One of the benefits of the British not allowing prepping of witnesses is that judges give more leeway in asking quasi-leading questions. A barrister cannot literally put words in a witness's mouth, such as, "You had the walk signal when you stepped into the crosswalk, correct?" Instead, a barrister is like a theatre usher who may not place you in a particular seat, but who can guide you to the correct row. I had often observed Giles helping anxious, reticent witnesses testify, so it was easy for me to echo his usual preface to many of my own questions. Giles would begin his question with "Would you think about..." and then describe the topic in such detail that the witness had clear guideposts for responding coherently. For example, I asked Tom, "Would you think about the time Tony came into the *Queens' Arms* and you both ordered a brown ale, and Tony mentioned a business opportunity, do you recall what, if anything, he said?" In a U.S. courtroom, there would be no chance of asking such a leading question unless the opposing counsel was sound asleep.

Early in my questioning, I opened up the topic of Tom's wife, Heather, leaving him for another man in 1991. Brook objected on the grounds of relevancy. I welcomed the objection because Brook was playing on my home turf, the Rules of Evidence. Judge Hart did not excuse the jury and allowed me to respond in open court with a mini closing argument, heard by the jurors. I explained that Tom's wife leaving him was relevant because after she left, Tom was totally depressed, and it was Tony, his best friend, who provided Tom with the needed moral and psychological support to prevent a total breakdown. Therefore, when Tony asked Tom for money to start a business, Tom was happy to return the favor and give Tony the money with no questions asked. The objection was overruled.

I then asked Tom about his version of what I had just laid out in my argument to the court. Having been essentially "prepped" by hearing what I expected him to say in my comments to Judge Hart, he began his narration of Heather leaving and of Tony's support without much need for me to aid his testimony by prompting questions. When Tom paused and appeared choked up, I chose not to help with inserting a question unless it was clear he could not continue. His silence spoke volumes. When he finally broke down in tears, I decided to move on to another topic, even though there were other questions I could have asked.

Another challenge I faced with Tom was his tendency to try to read between the lines of my questions, looking for a hidden meaning that might trip him up, like looking for depth in a sidewalk puddle. Tom would shake his head and act like he did not understand what information my questions were intended to elicit. Tom was acting like I was the Crown Prosecutor, rather than being part of the team that he was paying £200 an hour to defend him. During lunch, I diagnosed the problem and devised a solution. Tom behaved very much like the computers he knew so well. The data one inputs, or the questions one asks, must be perfect, or the computer will respond with an "error" message. If one comma or dash is out of place, the machine will not compute. Tom was like that. He had trouble interpreting the meaning of a question if the language in the question wasn't exactly as Tom's mental program was designed to interpret. If Tom was programmed to only accept "black" for a description of a color, then when I used a word like "ebony" or "jet-black," Tom thought I meant some color other than black. My afternoon questions may have appeared like I was talking to a child, but in some ways, I was.

Giles was scrutinizing the jurors during my questioning of Tom to assess whether Tom was being believed. Giles thought Tom's apparent insecurity and awkwardness helped support our line of defense. Missing the gist of my questions from time to time demonstrated what an innocent he truly was. Giles's conclusion was reinforced during a break when a man who had been watching the trial approached me and said he thought Tony, the codefendant, was a complete liar and that Tom was telling the truth. I must admit that at first, I could not focus on what the man was saying because I was looking at his nose. It was completely black. I had never seen anything like it and could not fathom how his nose could get so black and still be attached to his face. I later learned that very heavy drinkers sometimes develop a black or dark purple alcoholic nose.

My black nosed observer friend also caused a bit of a kerfuffle, which delayed the trial. An usher saw him conversing in the hall with a juror during a recess. This could have caused a mistrial, and the two weeks we had spent on the trial would have been wasted if the man had mentioned anything to the juror about his views on the witnesses. Fortunately, when Judge Hart questioned the juror, the juror told Judge Hart that he and the man with the black nose had not discussed the trial.

Giles was feeling better, but he was happy with my performance thus far. He thought that somehow the jury might think I messed up if he took over the questioning, undermining the credibility of our defense. Giles did believe, however, that we needed to revisit the relationship between Tom and his wife in more detail, even though it was obvious how painful it would be for Tom to talk about it. Giles thought it important for our "dupe defense." Since the topic of the state of his marriage had been allowed by the court, any relevancy objection by Brook would likely be overruled.

It is usually not a wise defense strategy to make your client look foolish, or even worse, to portray your client as an absolute chump. Nevertheless, I needed to do just that when Tom took the stand again, and I could not warn him in advance that I was going to do it. First, it would have been unethical for me to prep him. Second, it would be counterproductive. If Tom were coached to act like a naïve fool, his aura of credibility that we hoped to establish with the jury would have been stripped away. It was far better for our tactics that Tom had no idea what was coming.

I did not give Tom time to settle in the box before I asked him, "While you were married to Heather, did she have an affair with one of your best buddies?" I was pleased that Tom immediately looked distressed. My questions did not get any easier as I took him year by year through Heather's five-year affair with Clint. Tom told the jury that Clint was often at their home, and Heather would dress provocatively and wear perfume. Tom testified that there were many hurriedly ended phone calls and the weekends she supposedly spent with girlfriends. Tom talked about his and Heather's occasional and perfunctory sex life. All of this went on for five years, which would have alerted any normal husband to his wife's infidelity. Not Tom. He was in no way suspicious. My final question was a rhetorical one. "Tom, how could you be so stupid?" Tom did not answer; he burst into tears.

The moment of truth had arrived. After I sat down, it was Brook's turn to cross-examine Tom. Could he stand up to the blows of the iron hand in the velvet glove? We need not have worried. Brook's style of asking unfocused "Why" questions and Tom's disarming demeanor meant Brook landed nary a blow. If ever there was a witness who had to be controlled by leading "yes" or "no" questions, it was Tom. Even with the questions Brook believed to be penetrating and incriminating, Tom would respond with a matter-of-fact "yes" or "no." He would often have a puzzled look on his face, like he was pondering, "What was that question all about?" Instead of the nervous look of someone forced to admit to a piece of damaging evidence, Tom produced a look of genuine, wide-eyed wonder, like he was thinking, "Why would a competent barrister ask such an irrelevant question?" Tom did it without being condescending. It was as if he assumed the question must be important, but he could not figure out why.

Brook proceeded to dig the hole deeper for herself by asking Tom the worst kind of "Why" questions. "Why do you think a particular fact is not relevant?" Or, "Why did you act the way you did?" For example, during her cross-examination, Tom had to admit that after Heather had filed for divorce, he had tried to hide some of the money he had earned from the Royal Postal Service. Brook could argue during her closing argument that Tom's previous acts of deception made him a less credible witness. Then Brook made a mistake that so many of my students had made. She asked one more question, which she believed was the ultimate gotcha question.

"Do you think jurors would believe a person who tried to hide money from his wife during a divorce when such a person had testified he had not funded a marijuana factory?" I was not sure of the relevance of the question, but I did not object. Tom's answer was far better than any objection I could have made.

"Then those jurors had never been in a divorce where your wife is trying to take your children away from you."

Tom continued to thwart Brook's questions with similar zingers throughout her cross-examination. Yet, he did it without being sarcastic or disrespectful, maintaining his doe-eyed aura of naivety.

Tom had a prodigious memory, and often he would quote what Brook had said earlier in the trial, which conflicted with the question she was asking at the time.

"I don't understand. You asked something different thirty minutes ago." Tom had also memorized his previous statements to the police. Brook would attempt to impeach Tom by ostensibly quoting from Tom's police statement, "Didn't you say to the police...?" Tom's response was often, "That is not what I said in the statement, I said... and you can find it on page 10, line 15."

Brook was like a bulldog trying to chew on a non-existent bone. Tom had a phone in his home. Brook had a list of people who had been called from that home phone line and laid a trap for Tom by asking him if he knew any of the names on the list. There were many names Tom said he did not know, and Brook believed she had caught him in a litany of lies. But it was she who was ensnared in her own trap: neither the police nor the CPS had ever contacted the people who had received the calls from Tom's phone to determine if they had actually talked to Tom. It was undisputed that Tony was living in Tom's house at the time of the calls and had access to Tom's home phone. The first three I called from the list said they had spoken with Tony and not Tom. The unchallenged sworn statements I obtained from them were enough to destroy any inference that Tom was lying when he claimed he did not know some of the people on the list.

Instead of folding her tent and stopping her cross-examination of Tom, Brook made one more futile attempt to get the best of him. She violated one of my cardinal rules.

When cross-examining an opponent's expert witness, do not play on the expert's turf and pretend you know more than the expert. You don't.

Computers and their operating systems were Tom's cozy, comfortable home turf. Perhaps Brook was misled by his apparent ditziness and tried to cross swords with him over a computer's Microsoft operating system. Rather than rattling Tom, the exchange made him more confident. He explained to Brook in great detail how a software program worked without a hint of condescension. A neat trick, though, with Tom, it wasn't intentional. There was one juror who must have had some background in computers because he kept nodding his head in agreement as Tom educated Brook about Microsoft operating systems.

I assumed Brook was more than happy to end her ragged cross-examination of Tom and take a seat. I felt sorry for her.

Giles was feeling better and was eager to give the defense's final speech. I was relieved because only Giles could pull off a convincing closing argument for Tom's defense in which he disparaged Tom, his own client, and described him as a fool while trying to evoke jury sympathy for him. Giles reeled off a chronology of the times Tom had been oblivious to being misled and cheated by family and friends. His wife, Heather, had carried on an affair with one of Tom's mates literally in the marital bed for five years, and Tom never had a clue until Alice finally left him for Clint. Tom's best mate, Tony, mooched off Tom's generosity for a year, living in Tom's house, and persuaded Tom to give him £50,000 to bankroll a fictitious business, which was a front for a marijuana factory. Tom was completely oblivious of what the money was used for until the police arrived at his home and led him off to jail in handcuffs.

Finally, Giles appealed to the jury's common sense. He described Tom's disposition as being painfully transparent, with a history of being scrupulously honest. Therefore, Tony knew that if he told Tom his £50,000 would be used to operate an illegal marijuana farm, Tom would have refused to provide the money. And, if Tony could manage to overcome Tom's reluctance to join the marijuana factory scheme, why would Tony risk joining forces with a co-conspirator as clueless as Tom, who could inadvertently leak information about the unlawful marijuana factory like water in a sieve?

The jury's verdict came as no surprise. Tony was found guilty on all counts, and Tom was acquitted on all counts. While I was inclined to bathe myself in the warm glow of victory, Giles was blasé and ready to move on. Time operated differently for Giles. His sense of time had no *past* component. He lived totally in the now, ignored the past, and was always planning for the future, including my future. Walking out of the courthouse, Giles informed me that he would like Susan and me to be his guests in Normandy at the end of the following week. He already knew we had booked cooking classes in Sorrento and Florence for the first five days of the week. He brushed aside my logistical concerns and said we could take the night train from Florence to Paris, arriving in Paris early on Saturday morning, catch a train to Valognes, Normandy, and be there in time for lunch. Does anybody say "No" to Giles? I couldn't.

SEVENTEEN

The Countess and a Castle

Only Susan and I took the Italian cooking classes. Nancy was wandering the canals of England in a longboat, which had been rented by the family of her best school friend. We enrolled in two cooking schools: *Fattoria Terranova* in Sorrento and the Apicius Culinary School in Florence. What they taught me about my cooking skills was invaluable. The most valuable lesson I learned was that I had no talent for gourmet cooking. The instructors did allow me to dice onions and to singe the hair on my arm while toasting bruschetta over a blistering charcoal grill with undersized tongs.

Aside from that charring experience, the Italian sojourn was delightful. On Friday evening, we were at the Florence train station, preparing to board the night train to Paris, but not before we fell victim to a scam that friends, including Giles, had warned me about many times. They said, "Do not under any circumstances allow anyone offering to help put your luggage on the train to pick up your bags." But I made the mistake of asking a man who was dressed in what looked like a Trenitalia uniform if he could direct us to our sleeping car. He graciously agreed and picked up our two small suitcases. When we reached our compartment, he plopped down the suitcases and held out his hand. A tip seemed in order, so I offered him 2000 lire, about two dollars. He refused. He wanted 10,000. He knew a gullible American like me was not going to make a scene. He was right—I gave him 10,000. When the genuine Trenitalia porter came by to take our tickets, he told us we had been scammed. The final insult: the fraud had left us in the wrong compartment, in the wrong railcar.

I do not remember much about the rest of the trip because the gentle rocking of the train quickly put us to sleep. We did not wake up until the porter knocked on our door and told us we would be at the Gare de Bercy in fifteen minutes.

I was not sure about the best way to make our train connection at Gare Saint-Lazare. Since we did not have much time to catch the train to Normandy and Volognes, I decided we would ignore the cost and take a taxi across Paris. Half of our fellow train passengers had made the same decision. There was already a long queue for taxis. We took our places at the end of the line, but the line was barely moving, and few taxis were arriving. We decided to try the nearby *Réseau Express Régional* (RER) subway station, along with the other half of our fellow passengers who were also deterred by the taxi queue. I could not believe how small the station was, considering it was adjacent to a major rail terminal. It was chaotic, with scores of people shouting and trying to purchase tickets from the only working ticket machine. There were no staffed ticket booths open, and the line for the one ticket dispensing machine was barely moving. There was a horde of non-Parisians struggling to grasp how to operate the machine.

One enterprising Frenchman saw an opportunity for making a profit; he stood by the machine, taking people's francs, inserting them, getting the tickets, and accepting a small gratuity in return. Our problem was that we were not sure of our destination and which RER train to take. The one map of the system I could see was only readable after we passed through the ticket turnstile. Panic was rising. I persuaded Kathy to push past the turnstile with me, sans tickets. We had not even started down the escalator before I began doubting the wisdom of our scofflaw adventure.

What would happen at the end of the line if an agent demanded our tickets and we ended up in a French police station? We turned around and left the station. Susan was now crying. I knew we were at a crisis stage. For Susan, shedding tears was as rare as rain in the Sahara.

I was feeling desperate when a possible solution popped into my mind. Why not forgo the taxi queue at the train station and go out on the street and hail a cab? I stood on the curb waving both arms for a taxi. Miraculously, a taxi stopped on the opposite side of the street. We only needed to dash across a four-lane street in the middle of the block and hope the drivers would avoid hitting us. This was another symptom of Susan's state of mind. Ordinarily, she could not be persuaded to cross in a crosswalk if the sign had just changed to "don't walk." Now she was running across the street, dodging Parisian drivers.

Taking that taxi was the best 150 francs I have ever spent. We explained in our halting French about the need to catch the train, and the driver eagerly accepted the challenge of negotiating the clogged Paris streets. He knew all the back routes, and whenever we ran into heavy traffic, he ducked down a narrow side street or an alley. We made it to the station with ten minutes to spare.

With our Eurail passes, we were entitled to ride in the first-class section. Being one of the last passengers to board, we took the first available compartment, which already had six Frenchmen inside. After the "Bonjours" were exchanged, we noticed that it was a smoking compartment. Fortunately, none of our fellow passengers smoked. They also did not speak English, and we only had rudimentary French, so there was no cross-cultural conversation all the way to Volognes. What struck us Americans as curious was that the six Frenchmen did not even chat with each other. Pushy American that I was, I would have gladly spent the two-hour train ride eliciting their life stories, if not for the language barrier.

The train arrived at Vologne precisely on time. Giles was waiting for us on the platform, eager to bustle us off on another

Giles adventure, about which we knew absolutely nothing. Our first stop was the Grand Hotel du Louvre restaurant. I was surprised to see a *fermé* sign on the door. It was past the time for dejeuner or lunch. Giles was not deterred, and without a moment's hesitation, he opened the door and walked in. The place was empty, but a distinguished-looking gentleman said, "Bonjour," and guided us to a white linen-covered table set for eight people. It was laden with more plates, silverware, and glasses at each chair than any one person could use, or so I thought. I was wrong.

At the center of each place setting sat a large gold-rimmed plate, shining like the sun and anchoring the dishes, cutlery, and crystal glasses that orbited around it. I later learned that particular plate was called a *charger*. It seemed a shame that such a beautiful piece of dinnerware was soon removed from the table and never seen again. Atop the charger was a gold-edged bowl. To the left of the charger lay a cloth napkin and two silver forks of different sizes, and to the right were a knife and a large spoon. There was a small dish on the upper left with a butter knife lying horizontally across the top of the plate. Separating the small dish and the three glasses of different sizes was a tiny spoon, like a hyphen linking them. At the top of each setting stood the tiniest crystal salt and pepper shakers I had ever seen. Everything was laid out with meticulous precision. When I sat down, I stealthily measured the distances between the pieces of silverware. They were exactly the same.

Shortly after Susan and I sat down, we were joined by two other couples, Nick and Sarah, Thomas and Rosemary, and a man who introduced himself as Matt.

Somehow, Giles had persuaded the owner of the restaurant to keep his entire staff around just to serve us. When we were all seated, a parade of servers marched out of the kitchen. Two were carrying soup tureens, and two were holding ladles, which they used to fill our bowls with onion soup. Two other servers were each cradling a bottle of Pinot Gris wine wrapped in a towel, and they filled what I assumed were our white wine glasses, while two more servers were filling our water glasses. They moved with such precision that it was like watching a ballet.

The rest of lunch went by in a blur of waiters distributing plates of boeuf bourguignon, filling bread plates, topping off wine glasses, exchanging used dishes for clean ones, producing a salad course like magic, only to make it disappear and be replaced with individual ramekins brimming with Crème Brulée. Of course, no meal in Normandy would be complete without a glass of Calvados, apple brandy.

Giles had made sure we would all be in a receptive mood for his sales pitch, which he began while we sipped our after-lunch coffee. He unveiled the biggest real estate scheme he had ever attempted. He described how he had the option to purchase one of the largest châteaux in Normandy, with over a hundred rooms. His plan was to convert the building, including the extensive horse stables, into more than sixty luxury apartments. He would sell two-week timeshares in the apartments for $25,000 to $35,000. I made a quick calculation in my head that the total he could raise from the project, assuming he could sell all the time-shares, was something north of $38,000,000. He could sink $20,000,000 into renovation costs and still make out like a bandit. I knew Giles was not averse to taking risks, but his venture boggled my mind. His trial skills were on display. He knows when a jury is buying his story, and he sensed this audience sitting around the table was in a purchasing mood. Without even seeing the château, Susan and I were whispering to each other that $25,000 was not too bad.

Giles had set the stage for a visit to the scene, a tour of the château. His tour guide and partner in the project was straight out of central casting, the Countess Elyna de la Roche, but she insisted we call her Elyna. She reminded me of Grace Kelly, the Hollywood actress and Princess of Monaco. Elyna had elegantly coiffed blond hair and pale blue eyes. She was wearing a camel-colored cardigan with light blue denim trousers and a navy-blue scarf knotted around her neck. She validated the oft-heard quip that French women have an innate knowledge of how to tie a scarf. Although dressed casually, Elyna had the poise of a lady on her way to a ball. When she held out her hand for me, not to shake, not to kiss, although I was tempted, but lightly touched, I noticed her fingernails were neatly manicured with a clear polish. Somehow, Elyna had the ability to be extraordinary while appearing indifferent to whether she made a favorable impression or not. She was clearly confident in her own skin.

Her aura of modest self-confidence was not diminished when Elyna spoke in her alto voice. Her English was perfect, but she spoke it with a French accent. What is it about accents and their impact on Americans in particular? When a British man speaks with an Oxbridge accent, we subconsciously add ten points to his IQ. When a French woman speaks English spiced with a French accent, we assume she is subtly exuding her sexuality. Elyna confirmed that assumption.

It would be wrong, however, to think Elyna was only eye candy for us, potential investors in Giles's project. She held a master's degree in international law and international relations from the University of Amsterdam, chaired the Normandy Institute, and served as president of the American Friends of Bierancourt. In short, she took charge.

Giles, who was usually loath to yield the limelight to anyone, disappeared into the background like the Greek chorus, occasionally offering a helpful comment or a humorous quip. Susan and I thought Giles seemed slightly smitten with Elyna. Although we did not think Giles was in an intimate relationship with Elyna at that time, some hints suggested he and Elyna had had more than a business partnership in the past. What was it about Giles that allowed him to keep ex-lovers not only as good friends but even business partners after their affair was over? With Elyna, the question was even more puzzling, since Susan and I presumed she had ended the relationship. Ultimately, our thoughts remained speculative. Neither Giles nor Elyna dropped any clues as to what had happened, if anything.

The entrance to the château was a gravel lane lined with oak trees and flanked by abandoned German blockhouses, remnants of the war. Except for its size, my first impression of Château Latour was not enthusiastic. The château was a hodgepodge of architectural styles, which were only tempered by the extensive gardens surrounding it. The building may have been neglected, but someone had spent countless hours trimming bushes and trees and planting flowers. The connected buildings were L-shaped, four stories high, each with a gabled roof broken up with a line of dormers. The walls were made of stone, punctuated by floor-to-ceiling casement windows containing twenty-four small panes of glass separated by grids of muntin bars. What a nightmare to wash.

Elyna introduced us to Andre, the current owner of the château, who gave us a short account of the château's long history. The first structure was a defensive tower built around 1400 CE. A small manor house was added in about 1500 CE, with multiple additions built by Count Guillaume Cardot and his descendants over the next couple of centuries. In case any of us had doubts about the property's chain of title, Andre showed us a document written on velum and signed by King Louis XIII, confirming Guillaume Cardot's title to Latour. In 1940, the Nazis occupied the buildings and placed an anti-aircraft gun on the tower. When the U.S. Fourth Army Division landed on nearby Utah Beach, the Germans abandoned the château. It remained unoccupied until 1981, when Andre purchased it. Evidence of the German occupation was everywhere: a rusting Panzer tank, blockhouses, and pockmarks in the stone from bullets. It was like being in a time machine when we entered the Great Hall, which had once served as the German army's headquarters. The room was a duplicate of the German army's Operations Rooms, which were often depicted in American war films. There were the large wooden tables with green-shaded lights suspended over them, and, of course, the immense stone fireplace where reams of records were hurriedly burned to keep them out of American hands. It was the chapel, however, that served as a vivid reminder of the sacrifice made by the paratroopers of the 101st Airborne. Three paratroopers who had been captured were lined up against a chapel wall and machine-gunned. Their blood still stained the stone.

It soon became clear we were not going to do a haphazard wandering around the château and grounds. Elyna had our tour perfectly choreographed. She started with a meandering stroll through the garden, during which she told us the backstory of how Andre had acquired the property and what he had intended to do with it. Andre had been riding his bike along the road and was intrigued when he passed the Latour entry lane, flanked by two German pillboxes. He could not see the château, so he rode in. Although the building had suffered forty years of neglect, it was love at first sight. He quickly arranged to buy the property. His plan was to move his antique furniture building business to the château. I could not help asking, "How can you build antique furniture when by definition, antique means something over a hundred years old?" Elyna explained that Andre could build a Louis XV chair that was indistinguishable from the original. So, a person who had a dining table with four original Louis XV chairs could add two more chairs without anyone realizing they were fake. Andre also repaired antique furniture to as-good-as-new condition—or more accurately, as-good-as-old.

Andre had had the unrealistic hope that he could use his skills to rehab the château little by little, room by room, and convert the entire property into a luxury resort. Unfortunately, Andre's rehab progress up to that point in time suggested it would take him over forty years to complete the project. In the meantime, he needed to make mortgage payments and pay taxes. Furthermore, Andre was clueless about hiring workers to make repairs that were beyond his furniture-restoring ability. He was also completely at sea when it came to marketing. In brief, Andre was in a pickle, and selling the property to Giles was a lifeline. Giles was shrewd, however. He only purchased a six-month option to buy Château Latour at a specific price. During that time, he and Elyna could test the waters to see if their time-sharing plan for such a large property was feasible. Elyna had links with the local contractors and tradesmen who would be hired to do the rehab work. Giles had connections with Brits who would be interested in purchasing a timeshare in advance of actual construction, thereby raising the funds to finance the rehabilitation. He also knew how to market the timeshares to a wider British audience—and at least one American couple.

Elyna showed us two model rooms that had already been remodeled, complete with exquisite furnishings. Then she proved herself a consummate salesperson by leading us into the rooms that were in shambles after fifty years of theft and neglect, where large vats had been placed to catch the water dripping from the leaking roof. She described in meticulous detail how the room would be restored to its 19th-century look—what walls would be removed, and what window coverings and furniture would be chosen. In the next room we visited, Elyna stressed that the restoration would not resort to cookie-cutter rooms with identical architectural features, beds, carpets, drapes, tables, dressers, and paint schemes. Each unit would be unique. As Elyna explained, timeshare owners could be blindfolded and led into any unit in the complex. The moment the blindfold was removed, they would know at once they were in the wrong room. Elyna had the planned interior design of the entire Latour complex etched in her mind.

If we nurtured any doubts about Elyna's genius as an interior designer and property entrepreneur, they were dispelled by a quick visit to her home on the Île de Marie. It had been a French noble's hunting lodge, but with its two large defensive towers dwarfing the main structure, it was a castle in my eyes. Seeing how Elyna had restored the building and furnished it with her exquisite taste convinced us to buy into Giles's project. Giles was pleased.

We had a quiet dinner with him in an apartment he owned nearby in "just another" French château. One of his neighbors was the former head of the Directorate-General for External Security, the French equivalent of the CIA. I am not sure I felt more or less secure staying across the hall from the man who was responsible for sinking the Greenpeace ship, which had been protesting the French nuclear bomb testing in the Pacific.

I had hoped to impress Giles with my choice of wine—the $50 bottle I had purchased at a winery outside Florence and had been carrying in my backpack ever since. The wine did make an impression, just not the one I was hoping for. Giles was tactful after tasting the wine by describing it as "interesting." I am no connoisseur of wine, but even I could tell this bottle of wine was undrinkable, tasting more like vinegar than wine. I suspected the salesman at the winery found a way to unload a bottle of unpalatable wine for a hefty sum. He knew we were taking it out of the country as a gift. So, there was no risk we would drink it in Florence, return to the winery, and make a scene in front of other visitors. Since a meal without wine was unthinkable to Giles, he uncorked a bottle from his ample stock.

The guest room for the château was located on the third floor. The view from our window was a vast expanse of meadows, with not a single structure in sight. That seemed odd to me until Giles explained the meadows were water meadows and, in the spring, they were covered with water when Île de Marie was literally an island.

The trade-off for the third-floor panorama was the absence of a bathroom. We had to use the bathroom in Giles's apartment three flights down, a bit of a trek in the middle of the night. Giles said that negotiating three flights of stairs was a small price to pay for being able to luxuriate in his enormous claw-footed bathtub. He was aghast when I told him I hadn't taken a bath since I was a young child. My mother used to wash my hair while I was sitting in the bathtub. Giles was inspired. He had a new case to argue, his theme being that I had led a deprived life if I had not experienced the bliss of lolling up to my neck in a tub full of hot water. Giles won his case, and I agreed to forgo a shower before going to bed and to take a bath instead. Although it seemed like a prodigious waste of water, he insisted that I fill up the tub completely with water as hot as I could tolerate. Damn, Giles was right again. It was a luxurious and indulgent experience to lie back and let the hot water loosen every muscle in my body while gazing at the crystal chandelier glittering overhead. By the time I climbed out of the bath, my legs were rubbery, and I could barely manage the three flights of stairs to the guest bedroom.

The next morning, Giles was occupied with consultations and meetings with Elyna, Andre, contractors, and various other players in his château restoration plans, so Susan and I decided to relax and read in Elyna's lovely garden.

Our whirlwind visit to Normandy was nearly over, but not without one last Giles escapade. Dana Cooper was due to arrive in Cherbourg on the 3:00 PM ferry, and since Giles was constitutionally incapable of arriving at any meeting early, he decided he could squeeze in a few errands before her boat docked. The first stop was an antique store that Elyna patronized. Giles did not buy anything but spent much of the time chatting with the owner about the future of Europe, in French, of course. We could not escape the shop because it was clear that the owner and Giles were enjoying themselves. I kept looking at my watch. When we finally got back in the car, Giles announced that we needed to go grocery shopping. We flew through the Intermarché Superstore. I steered the trolley, and Giles threw food and other items into it. Then, just when I thought we should get in a checkout line, Giles decided that since it was such a pleasant day, we should have dinner on the terrace. But we could not have a civilized dinner on the terrace unless we had an umbrella to cover the table. We circled back to the Garden Shop, where Giles agonized over the color of the umbrella, and I worried about the time.

We plunged the umbrella into the cart and cruised back toward the checkout lanes with the umbrella protruding five feet in front of the cart like a ship's bowsprit. Other shoppers cleared the aisles for us rather than risk being impaled on the tip of our umbrella. At the checkout line, Giles commandeered an extra bagger to speed things along. Finally, the car was loaded, and we were headed to the ferry terminal, or so I thought. Giles swerved into a petrol station because we were nearly out of gas. Why did I even worry? Giles led a charmed life. He did not bother to park the car in the ferry parking lot. He simply coasted to the main entrance of the terminal, arriving just as Dana emerged with her luggage in hand.

Sadly, Giles's charmed life was beginning to turn unlucky shortly after we arrived back in Winchester. His liver condition worsened and may have contributed to his inability to juggle half a dozen balls and retain details of testimony and transactions without notes. One lapse cost Giles £100,000 and Château Latour. Giles had a six-month option agreement with Andre to purchase Latour. During that time, Giles and Elyna invested large sums of money in restoring and furnishing several rooms to showcase to prospective purchasers of the timeshares. Giles had also launched an advertising campaign in Southern England. What he did not do was to renew the option agreement in writing. Andre's decision to not renew the option agreement did not improve Giles's opinion of the perfidious French. There may have been a nod, an affirmative shrug, and assumptions made, but Andre adamantly refused to renew the option to purchase. Andre assumed that with the repairs to the property and a promotion campaign that was drawing interest from potential buyers, he could finish the project himself and make a fortune. He was wrong. He lacked the business sense and vision of Elyna or the connections Giles had to the British timeshare market. Château Latour continued as a neglected, largely abandoned estate.

I am sure it was not Giles's intention to teach me a life lesson out of his failure, beyond the obvious one, "Get it in writing." Still, I gleaned a valuable insight about managing one's expectations. Uncharacteristically, Susan and I had been hooked with the prospect of owning a timeshare apartment, which would provide us with a bolt hole whenever we, or our children, visited Europe. We envisioned spending a delightful two weeks at Latour, followed by weeks of exploring all the European countries. In short, we had allowed the prospect of owning a particular piece of property to create an illusion that possession of a thing would, in itself, produce contentment and happiness. Consequently, when that "cup was dashed from our lips," our distress was sharper than it should have been. We had not actually lost anything but a speculative anticipation. So, the lesson for me was: "Do not overvalue ownership," or thinking possessions were essential for happiness. More of my mother's words of wisdom came to mind: *a thing is only dear the day you buy it*. I did not tell Giles about my epiphany; he would have found it amusing. The need to acquire beautiful things was in Giles' DNA.

EIGHTEEN
Stalking A Stalker

Giles's life was full of paradoxes, and it should have been no surprise to me that our first case after returning from Normandy had an ironic twist. He transitioned from stalking investors for his timeshare scheme in Normandy to prosecuting a person for stalking. When the Clerk of Chambers first told Giles he was assigned to prosecute a stalking case, he was irritated. Most stalking cases are dealt with in the Magistrates' Court. Giles considered having to appear in front of a panel of often inexperienced magistrates a waste of his talent. When Giles read the file, however, he saw the case was in the Winchester Crown Court. The defendant was charged with a type of stalking that threatened violence or serious harm to the victim, making it a felony. Giles was more intrigued when he saw that the alleged stalker was a woman, Carmen Marsh. He realized that prosecuting a woman would be a challenging case. It would test his advocacy skills. He also knew that while the mere sending of adoring love notes and emails might constitute harassment, they lacked the necessary element of instilling fear of violence in the victim.

After reading the Crown Prosecution Service's file, I told Giles I believed the case against Marsh was based entirely on circumstantial evidence. There were no witnesses who could testify they had seen Marsh anywhere near the victim, Dr. Jan Falk. Marsh, on the advice of her solicitor, refused to talk to the police, so there was no statement of hers for us to dissect. If Marsh had stalked the doctor, she was clever about not dropping any careless hints to her family or friends about what she was up to. It was the kind of case Giles loved to prosecute. At the same time, Giles was well aware that his health condition might impact his ability to conduct a vigorous prosecution, so he told me to be ready to step in if necessary. Giles especially wanted me to conduct the direct examination of the forensic expert who would testify about the results of DNA tests. He said he did not know anything about the methodology used to analyze DNA. When I pleaded my own ignorance of the process, Giles assured me it was time for me to learn.

The first question I had to resolve was how much I needed to know about DNA analysis. Was it necessary for me to know as much about DNA testing as an expert to conduct a good direct examination? A perusal of the academic literature quickly convinced me that I would not be able to understand the underlying science of DNA testing, or more precisely, that I was not willing to invest the time and effort to acquire an in-depth knowledge of the process. I was also doubtful that an extensive understanding of DNA testing would help my direct examination of Dr. Pope, the DNA forensic expert. My first conference with Dr. Pope confirmed my slothful inclination. If I could not follow Dr. Pope's detailed explanation of the DNA testing process, I was sure a jury would be totally lost in the weeds. A detailed explanation of how the DNA was analyzed would also provide a better opportunity for the defense to nitpick the testing that Dr. Pope did.

I decided and told Giles that I was going to adopt the K.I.S.S. approach to the direct examination of Dr. Pope—*Keep It Simple, Stupid*. The first hurdle to such a stripped-down examination was Dr. Pope. He was justifiably proud of his methodical and flawless analysis of the DNA evidence and was eager to demonstrate his expertise to an attentive audience. I had to convince him that less was better, and if defense counsel had the temerity to challenge his forensic skills on cross-examination, he would have a splendid opportunity to not only demonstrate his brilliance but to have the satisfaction of embarrassing a presumptuous barrister.

I am sure I was pushing the limits of the British restrictions on prepping a witness. Nevertheless, I wanted Dr. Pope to know in advance what questions I would be asking and the answers I hoped he would give. I explained that my open-ended questions might suggest I was asking for a mini-dissertation, but I told him I wanted him to limit his answers to one-paragraph narratives. I did not conduct an exhaustive rehearsal of his testimony as I would have done for an American jury trial. Instead, I told him the essential questions I would ask and urged him to think about how he could craft simple, easily understood responses.

Who are you?

What is your occupation?

What is the basic purpose of a DNA test?

Do you perform DNA analysis often?

Are there other scientists like yourself who regularly conduct DNA testing?

What was the result of the DNA testing you did in this case?

How certain are you of your findings?

If my learned opponent were to dispute your conclusions, can your results be checked for accuracy by other forensic experts?

I did not believe I was violating the no-prep rule. I did not ask Dr. Pope what his answers to my questions would be, and I certainly did not suggest or hint at how his answers could be made more persuasive.

The defending barrister, Bert Newman, did his best to package Marsh as an attractive woman more likely to be a "stal-kee" than a stalker. Carmen Marsh appeared in court wearing an expensive lavender pantsuit, which emphasized her voluptuous figure. It was also obvious Marsh had spent considerable time applying the right touches of make-up. She did not cross the line of looking like a streetwalker, but as a woman who would have no difficulty in finding men eager to buy her a drink in pubs. Throughout the trial, I noticed a couple of male jurors frequently stealing glances at Marsh. I was not sure if their libidinous interest in Marsh would hurt or help convict her of stalking.

The testimony of our first three witnesses—Dr. Jan Falk, Deborah Pemberton, and Detective Inspector Hawkins—provided a comprehensive narrative account of the case. Carmen Marsh was a forty-year-old cheese counter assistant at Sainsbury's in Winchester in 1990. In May 1990, Marsh had taken her flat-mate, Doris Fletcher, to see Dr. Falk. At that time, Dr. Falk was a highly respected psychiatrist, but he was best known to the general public as a successful yacht racer whose photos often appeared in local newspapers. Dr. Falke had been interviewed on the BBC Breakfast program for winning the J/70 class trophy in the *Round the Isle of Wight* regatta.

Dr. Falk said he might have met Marsh when she brought her friend Doris Fletcher to the clinic, but he did not remember such a meeting, adding that Marsh would not have been permitted to attend Dr. Falk's therapy sessions with Ms. Fletcher.

In July 1990, Dr. Falk told the jury he began receiving an avalanche of anonymous telephone and text messages. Initially, the text of the messages declared the sender's "undying love" for Dr. Falk and expressed a desire to sleep with him. Then the messages became more threatening. One text said, "Dig your own grave." Another one threatened, "Your life will end, gunman paid." A phone message left on an answering machine whispered, "Bang, Bang, Bang is all you deserve." The threats were also directed at Dr. Falk's fiancée, Deborah Pemberton. They said such things as, "A hit man had been hired to murder Deborah," or "She will be burned down in her wedding dress." The final straw for Deborah was the text message promising to poison her wedding guests at the reception. Dr. Falke said Deborah contemplated suicide. Deborah was so distraught that she decided to call off the wedding two weeks before the scheduled ceremony.

Detective Inspector (DI) Hawkins testified that the police were not able to trace the phone calls or text messages. He assumed the caller/texter used some kind of Voice Over Internet Protocol (VoIP) to make the calls and to send the texts. With VoIP, users sign up with a service or download an app, which assigns them a virtual phone number. The virtual phone number is not connected with the user's identity in any way; it is virtually untraceable. A text message can be sent using VoIP from a desktop computer, phone, or any other device that is connected to the internet. DI Hawkins explained that only the sender's virtual number would show up on Dr. Falk's phone, ensuring complete anonymity for the texter. When a voice message is sent, the sender's voice is converted into a digital signal before being transmitted, so the voice heard by the recipient is unrecognizable. The recipient cannot even determine if the actual caller is a man or a woman.

Before Dr. Falk and Ms. Pemberton notified the invited wedding guests that the wedding was canceled, DI Hawkins proposed a plan to trap the harasser into identifying himself or herself. He suggested that Dr. Falk and Ms. Pemberton pretend the wedding would go forward as planned at the New Forest Hotel and that the event would remain on the hotel schedule. Two days before the phony wedding was to take place, the New Forest Hotel received a phone call making a bomb threat. The police had hooked up a "Trap and Trace" device to the hotel phone and were able to trace the phone call to a phone booth in Winchester. When Constable Cole arrived at the scene, she found Marsh standing close to the phone booth, near a newsagent's kiosk. Constable Cole questioned Marsh, but she denied ever being in the phone booth. Constable Cole also questioned several other people who were in the area, including the newsagent. No one could say they had seen Marsh or anyone else in the phone booth. Detective Hawkins testified that, at the time, he did not think there was enough evidence to charge Marsh with harassment.

The calls and text messaging stopped after the wedding was officially canceled. Dr. Falk tried to move on with his life, continuing to practice as a psychiatrist. A few months later, he met Sarina Templeton, who had recently emigrated from South Africa. After seven months, they were engaged, and their engagement was announced in the Hampshire Chronicle.

Within a week of the announcement in the Chronicle, Marsh walked into the Winchester Police Central Station on Tower Street and alleged that nine months earlier, Dr. Falk had raped her in his office. She claimed she had been too traumatized to report the attack earlier. Marsh described in some detail Dr. Falk's office and how the doctor sexually assaulted her. To support her allegations, she gave the police a pair of knickers she said she had been wearing at the time of the rape and that they likely had Dr. Falk's semen on them.

Forensic examination determined that the DNA of semen found on the knickers matched Dr. Falk's DNA. When interviewed by the police, Dr. Falk denied raping Marsh, but he could not explain how his semen was on her knickers.

Based on this evidence, Dr. Falk was charged with rape. For the next eighteen months, while he was awaiting trial, Dr. Falk had to endure numerous stories in the media, which were encouraged by Marsh.

Dr. Falk's license to practice medicine was suspended pending the outcome of the trial. Ms. Templeton did not abandon him, however, and it was she who eventually provided the clue that led to the dismissal of the rape charges by the Crown Prosecution Service.

Ms. Templeton remembered a day when their rubbish bin had been tipped over and its contents spilled on the ground. She added that it was likely the bin that contained a used rubber from the previous night's lovemaking.

Dr. Pope, a forensic expert, was hired to reexamine the knickers. He found traces of Ms. Templeton's DNA on the knickers, but found no trace of Marsh's DNA. That finding alone should have led to the dismissal of the rape charges against Dr. Falk, but the fact that Ms. Templeton had not arrived in England until two months after Marsh claimed she had been raped by Dr. Falk proved the alleged rape could not have happened. Not only was the case against Dr. Falk dismissed, but the Crown Prosecution Service also charged Marsh with stalking that threatened violence, or serious harm to the victim.

Defense counsel Newman barely challenged the testimony given by Dr. Falk, former fiancée Deborah Pemberton, or DI Hawkins. He conceded that Dr. Falk had been harassed by someone. His defense was simply that the defendant, Carmen Marsh, was not the harasser. The cross-examination questions were limited to just a couple of inquiries preceded by a bit of compelling theatre. Newman first had Marsh stand up in the dock, and then he asked Dr. Falk to look at her. Newman then asked, "Isn't it true, Dr. Falk, that during the months you were being harassed by phone messages and texts, you never saw Carmen Marsh once?"

"No, I did not."

"You never saw her near your home, your business, or on the street?"

Dr. Falk had no choice but to agree.

The same questions were posed to Ms. Pemberton, and her answers were the same as Dr. Falk's. She had not seen Marsh until after Marsh had brought the rape charges against Dr. Falk.

DI Hawkins conceded during his cross-examination that he had not seen Marsh until she was interviewed at the police station. Furthermore, DI Hawkins agreed with Newman's assertion that it was not possible to trace the phone or the text messages to Marsh or to conclude that the voice on the phone was hers.

If this had been all the evidence we had to convict Marsh of stalking, Judge Carr would have quickly dismissed the case against her. Our entire case rose or fell with the testimony of Dr. Pope. First, the jury would have to be convinced that Ms. Templeton's DNA was found on the knickers and that Marsh's DNA was not found. If the jury was sure about those facts, that still might not be enough evidence to convict her of harassment. How would the false allegation of rape prove that it was Marsh who was making the harassing phone calls and sending the vicious text messages? Such a connection was far from self-evident, and therefore, much would depend on Giles's skill to persuade the jury that the false rape claim proved Marsh had made the earlier harassing phone calls and had sent the threatening text messages.

Before Giles could make that final summation, however, I had to elicit the testimony of our DNA expert, Dr. Pope, whom I hoped would educate the jury about whose DNA was, and was not, on the knickers Marsh had happened to save for nine months.

Although reciting all of Dr. Pope's qualifications would be dull listening for the jury, it was necessary to forestall any attacks by Newman, suggesting Dr. Pope did not have the skill and expertise to conduct DNA testing. It also discouraged any attempt by Newman to claim that a DNA expert who might testify for the defense was better qualified than Dr. Pope.

The remainder of Dr. Pope's testimony was smooth, succinct, and easily understood by the jury. His narration needed little assistance from my questions. My pretrial conversation with the doctor provided him with a summary of the points I wanted him to cover and guidance on keeping his testimony simple and short.

Dr. Pope described how he had conducted hundreds of such DNA tests and had testified in scores of cases, appearing for both the Crown and the defense. He modestly told the jury that he was one of hundreds of forensic scientists who regularly do DNA testing. He readily admitted that scientists like him were not a dime a dozen and that he was well compensated for his time at £200 per hour. I had not thought to mention his fee in our pretrial conversation, but it was an adroit addendum because it lessened the impact of the inevitable defense counsel's question, "Now, Doctor, how much are you being paid for your testimony today?" Counsel could imply the doctor was a "hired gun" and would say whatever his employer, the prosecution (us), wanted him to say.

Judges prefer witnesses not to testify with lengthy narratives, so I interposed a question or two to head off an objection from Newman, or worse, a chastising comment from the judge. I asked, "What is the purpose of DNA fingerprinting?"

Dr. Pope replied, "The purpose is to determine if a DNA sample from a crime scene matches the DNA of a particular person. In this case, we wanted to find out if the DNA sample from Carmen Marsh's knickers matched the DNA sample taken from Ms. Templeton."

"Did it?"

"Yes."

"What are the chances you could be wrong, and the DNA you found on the knickers was the DNA of another person? Or put another way, what are the odds that the DNA you analyzed was not Ms. Templeton's DNA?"

"One in a trillion." Dr. Pope added the embellishment I had hoped for. "About the same number of people if you had one million Wembley stadiums with sell-out crowds."

My next question was. "What if you made a mistake while conducting your testing?"

I liked how Dr. Pope sounded a bit annoyed with me when he answered, "I didn't, but I would be happy if any other forensic scientists checked my work and conducted their own testing."

Dr. Pope had baked a splendid DNA cake, and it was time to spread the icing. Asked whether he found other DNA samples on the knickers, he said he had conducted a thorough search for other traces of DNA and did not find any other DNA except Dr. Falk's.

My final question was, "Dr. Pope, if Carmen Marsh had been wearing those knickers at the time she said she was raped by Dr.

Falk, how likely is it that no trace of her DNA was found on the knickers?"

After Dr. Pope responded, "Impossible," I thought it was a good place to end my direct examination and rest our case.

Newman adopted the best defense strategy for Marsh. He did not attempt to refute the overwhelming evidence that she had instigated a false rape claim against Dr. Falk. Instead, Newman argued there was a total absence of evidence connecting her to all the harassing texts and phone messages. Newman stressed in his opening speech that even if one assumed Marsh did make a false rape claim, that allegation alone did not prove in any way that she was the person sending the texts and leaving phone messages. In addition to our arguably weak circumstantial evidence, Newman had the law on his side. To be convicted of stalking, we had to prove Marsh persistently followed Dr. Falk or forced contact with him using texts and phone messages. Most importantly, to support a case of stalking that also engendered fear of violence or caused serious alarm, we needed to prove Marsh had done the stalking on two or more occasions and that her stalking had had a substantial adverse effect on Dr. Falk's day-to-day activities.

Our challenge was to use the incontrovertible evidence of Marsh bringing a false claim of rape against Dr. Falk to show it was Marsh who harassed and threatened Dr. Falk nine months before she had taken her rape story and her knickers to the police station.

It was relatively easy to cast Marsh as a vindictive and malevolent character. Giles would be in his element, combining his disdainful frowns with cutting sarcasm, laced with innuendo, to paint a picture of the defendant as Lady Macbeth. Unfortunately, or maybe fortunately, the Rules of Evidence do not permit a prosecutor to use a defendant's bad character to prove the defendant committed a crime. Otherwise, defendants would be convicted, not because they committed crimes, but because they were vilified by the prosecution as despicable, wicked people. The prosecutor would leave no stone unturned in the hope of discovering all the sins the defendants may have committed over a lifetime. Stole a candy bar as a teenager from the neighborhood grocery store? Admissible? So, to prevent a trial based on one's general character, the Rules of Evidence stipulate that the character of the defendant is not an issue in the case.

Giles was disappointed that the Rules of Evidence prevented him from attacking Marsh's general character and giving a detailed description of her malicious and amoral nature. Giles asked me if I thought he could portray her as a natural-born harasser. The evidence supporting his assertion, he argued, was that she proved herself a harasser when she made the false rape charge against Dr. Falk.

It dawned on me that our roles had been reversed. I was now the mentor imparting lessons, and Giles was the pupil. I explained that if he resorted to that line of attack, he would still be introducing Marsh's character into evidence, and Judge Carr would likely preclude it.

Giles began his final speech recapping the evidence and trying to connect the dots that linked Marsh's false rape claim with the earlier harassing text messages and the phone calls. He argued she had the same motive to disparage and threaten Dr. Falk for all her actions. Therefore, she was responsible for all the harassment of Dr. Falk. Giles did not suggest Marsh was an innate harasser and therefore likely to be the same person who sent the vile text messages. I maintained a poker face during this part of Giles's speech, although I was convinced the jury was not buying it.

Then Giles switched gears. He said, "Just ten steps, ladies and gentlemen of the jury. Just ten steps." Neither the jury nor I knew what he was talking about, but he had piqued our curiosity. "Just ten steps from the dock where Carmen Marsh is sitting and the witness stand." The jury may still have been clueless at this point, but I was getting nervous. Was Giles going to comment on the fact that the defendant did not testify and infringe on one of the basic rights of an accused—the right to silence, and the prosecution's inability to force an accused to testify in his or her own defense? An American prosecutor was forbidden from commenting on the fact that the defendant did not testify, as it would punish defendants for exercising their right to remain silent. This was a fundamental right embedded in the Fifth Amendment of the U.S. Constitution, and I assumed it was also a basic principle of British criminal law. Was Giles wandering off the rails? I picked up my pen and waved it in a tight circle motion, our agreed-upon signal that Giles was supposed to stop his comments immediately and consult with me. My expectation was that a word from me would put Giles back on track.

Giles ignored me and went on. "Carmen Marsh would only need to take those ten short steps, and many of the issues and the questions in this case could be resolved." My pen waving became frantic, whirling around like a propeller. He looked at me and winked. Was he toying with me and getting some of his own back for having to endure my lecture on the admissibility of character evidence?

Giles continued, "If Carmen Marsh made that short journey, I am sure she would be able to answer some of the many questions I would have for her, and questions members of the jury would have liked to ask."

My stomach was flip-flopping while my face remained unmoved. In the best-case scenario, I was sure Newman would object and be sustained by Judge Carr. The worst-case scenario would be for Judge Carr not to wait for an objection and proclaim from his lofty perch that Giles was completely out of order, rebuking him in front of the jury, just before declaring a mistrial.

The judicial silence was deafening. Giles proceeded to tell the jury the list of questions he would ask Carmen Marsh if she would only walk those ten steps and take an oath to tell the truth.

"Why did you falsely accuse Dr. Falk of rape?"

Everyone in the courtroom knew that Carmen Marsh could not offer any plausible answer. If she admitted bringing a false claim of rape, what could she say that would justify her actions? If she insisted her rape claim was true, Giles would point out to the jurors that she would have to explain why the knickers she supposedly was wearing at the time of the rape had no traces of her DNA on them.

Giles's final words were an adroit juxtaposition of defending a defendant's right not to testify and speculating how much easier it would have been for the jury to decide the case if she had taken those ten steps.

"Ladies and Gentlemen, His Lordship will instruct you that Carmen Marsh has an absolute right not to testify in this case, and that is as it should be. However, one cannot help but think her testimony would have made your task simpler."

Judge Carr called a recess before Newman's final speech, which would be followed by the judge's final summing up of the facts and his instructions to the jury. I cornered Giles in the hallway to find out what had just happened. One of the most fundamental protections for a defendant—the right to remain silent and not be coerced into testifying—was in tatters. I was convinced Judge Carr would declare a mistrial, and I was at a loss as to why he did not do so immediately. Giles laughed and asked if I would like to make a small wager about that. I knew better than to bet against him, so I merely asked him to explain how he could be so sure. He told me that Britain had recently changed the law, reaffirming a defendant's right to remain silent and not testify, but at the same time allowing the prosecution the opportunity to comment on the fact that the defendant had not testified.

As an American attorney nourished on the sacredness of a defendant's constitutional rights, I was aghast. The new law rendered the constitutional right to remain silent meaningless. Defendants could be coerced into taking the stand. If defendants did not testify, prosecutors could imply that the defendants must be hiding something. If defendants did testify, their right to silence would be waived, and they would be required to answer all the insinuating cross-examination questions put to them.

Giles said, "David, you must remember Great Britain does

not have a written constitution etched in stone. There are traditions, judicial precedents, and laws enacted by Parliament which
confer specified rights and privileges on British citizens, but as the
Bible says, 'that which is given can be taken away.' Parliament can
giveth and Parliament can *taketh* away."

I said the Puritans in Massachusetts had a similar process. A
suspected witch could choose between being burned at the stake
or being bound with ropes and thrown into the river. If she sank,
it proved she was not a witch. If she floated, she was a witch and
would be pulled from the river and then burned. Marsh was in a
similar position. She could testify and incriminate herself by
attempting to respond to Giles's shrewd questions, or she could
refuse to enter the witness box and be skewered in Giles's closing
speech, which implied Carmen Marsh was not trustworthy and
was hiding facts the jury should know.

Giles thought my analogy amusing but argued that the prosecution's ability to comment on the defendant's refusal to testify
was merely giving voice to what the jury was already thinking.
Furthermore, Giles said the new rule put the issue out on the
table, and the judge could instruct the jury on how they could, or
could not, use the defendant's refusal to testify in their deliberations.

Our friendly debate ended when the public announcement
echoed down the courthouse halls, instructing all participants in
the case of the *Crown v. Marsh* to return to Courtroom 6.

Newman did his best to mitigate Giles's insinuation that
Marsh had something to hide. He emphasized her absolute right
not to talk to the police or testify during the trial, arguing that she
should not be disparaged or falsely judged because she had chosen
to follow the advice of her solicitor. He exhorted the jury not to
make a mockery of Marsh's right not to testify and "ignore the
innuendo-filled remarks of my learned opponent."

Having done as much as he could to blunt Giles's attack on
Marsh's credibility, Newman focused on what I considered the
Achilles' heel in our case, the shaky evidence connecting the

defendant to the harassing phone and text messages. The major link of Marsh to the earlier communications was the false claim of rape. Giles maintained that her allegation of rape demonstrated her absolute motivation to ruin Dr. Falk's and his fiancée's lives, and therefore, Marsh was the only person who could be responsible for the prior harassment. Newman rightly pointed out to the jury that there was no similarity between the types of harassment. The modus operandi was entirely different. One involved anonymous messages through electronic devices, and the other was a person making a false public allegation to the police. I thought it wise that Newman did not claim Marsh's charge of rape was true. The jury would reject such a distorted version of the evidence. Newman's credibility with the jury would be shattered, and jurors would also reject his contention that Marsh did not make the phone calls or send text messages.

Instead, he made a valiant effort to make lemonade out of lemons. He invited the jury to assume Marsh did bring a false claim of rape against Dr. Falk. He then asked the jurors, "Would a woman with that level of vindictiveness be content to send petty harassing text messages to Dr. Falk for months? Would a person who robbed a Marks and Spencer's cashier at gunpoint necessarily be the same person who months before had shoplifted from the same store?" It was a persuasive point.

Of course, it was Judge Carr who had the last word on the issue, and this was the instruction he gave the jury on Marsh's right to silence.

"Ladies and Gentlemen, Ms. Marsh has the right not to give evidence, but she had been warned by her solicitor that her failure to do so may result in jurors drawing negative inferences from her refusal to testify.

"Ms. Marsh's failure to give evidence cannot, on its own, prove her guilt, but her refusal to testify can assist you in deciding whether she is guilty.

"Ms. Marsh has put forward a reason for not testifying; you should consider it, and if accepted, do not draw any inferences.

However, if you reject her reason, you may draw inferences, but you are not obliged to do so.

"If you conclude that the only sensible explanation for Ms. Marsh's decision not to testify is that she has no answer, or no answer that would stand up to cross-examination, then it would be open to you to hold against Ms. Marsh her failure to give evidence. It is for you, however, the jury, to decide whether it is fair to do so or not."

After Judge Carr's final instructions, the jury retired to deliberate, and Giles and I retreated to a nearby conference room to await its verdict. Although the judge's instruction to the jury on how to evaluate the fact that Marsh did not testify fulfilled a prosecutor's dream, and we represented the prosecution, I believed from Marsh's perspective that it was an injustice.

I told Giles the judge had just invited the jury to convict Marsh on the basis that she did not testify. There was the judicial fig leaf of instructing the jury that it could not convict Marsh solely because she did not testify. But it did encourage the jury to find some shred of circumstantial evidence connecting her to the prior calls and messages—and then they could use her silence to find her guilty. To my mind, this kind of evidence was far worse than the introduction of evidence focused on determining the defendant's character; it allowed the jury to assume imaginary facts from the defendant's silence. The logic was that if Carmen Marsh remained silent, she must be hiding something, which led to a huge assumption that what she was hiding was that she had harassed Dr. Falk. As Einstein quipped, "Assumptions are made, and most assumptions are wrong." Questionable assumptions should not be grounds for conviction.

Judge Carr attempted to add another fig leaf by instructing the jurors that if they believed Marsh had a good reason for not taking the stand, then they should not draw any inference from her silence. What better reason could Marsh have than being advised by her counsel not to testify? I did not think the jury should have been encouraged to speculate on why she did not testify.

The third fig leaf in Judge Carr's instructions was as thin as a wet T-shirt. Judge Carr told the jurors they could hold Marsh's silence against her if they believed her imaginary answers to the imaginary cross-examination questions would not stand up. However, in weighing the negative impact of her silence, you jurors should act fairly. In short, Judge Carr is essentially saying, "I am giving you an instruction which is totally unfair on its face, but I am trusting you to apply it fairly." It is like giving a pistol to a teenage boy with the caveat that he should not shoot at anyone with it. It is the responsibility of the judge to ensure the fairness of the trial and only admit evidence if it comports with a fair trial process. In my opinion, jurors should not be given the burden of deciding when not to use questionable evidence because it would be "unfair."

I surprised Giles when I hypothesized that if I had tried the case, I might have avoided commenting in my final speech about Marsh choosing not to testify. I was troubled about using a strategy that was perfectly proper according to the Rules of Evidence, yet, in my opinion, violated one of Marsh's fundamental rights.

Giles pushed back with unusual intensity.

"It would be unethical for you to allow your views on what you think the law should be to trump what the law is. As a prosecuting barrister, you represent the Crown and the British people. The Crown Prosecution Service has determined there is sufficient evidence for a jury to conclude that Marsh was guilty of stalking. It is your duty to prove that case, not help disprove it."

Although I had my doubts about the legitimacy of my position, I vigorously challenged Giles's didactic assertions.

I asked, "But Giles, what if you firmly believed it was totally an unjust law?"

His answer, "Lobby and advocate to get it changed. It would undermine the rule of law if barristers worked to nullify laws they personally objected to, even when the law was helpful to their clients. It would only hurt their clients and not alter the law itself. In fact, no one would know the barrister abstained from using the unjust law as a protest against the law."

I was not ready to surrender to Giles's logic, so I asked him to assume he was prosecuting, but that he believed there was a reasonable chance the defendant was innocent. Would he still resort to an unjust rule like being able to comment on the defendant's silence, knowing that the power of using that argument would tip the scales of justice and that the jury would return a guilty verdict?

Without hesitating, he said, "Certainly. My responsibility was to persuade the jury to find the defendant guilty, even if, in my heart of hearts, I thought there was considerable doubt about the defendant's guilt. It is the jury's duty to determine guilt or innocence, not mine. If a jury makes a mistake and convicts an innocent person—well, as you Americans say, 'that is the way the cookie crumbles.'"

I took a broader view of the prosecutor's obligations. A prosecutor's duty was more than just producing guilty verdicts; it was about achieving justice in a broader sense. To my mind, justice was not achieved if there existed a distinct possibility that the defendant was innocent.

We were not able to continue our discussion because an announcement blared over the speaker system, informing us that we were expected to return to the courtroom.

The time was 4:00 PM, and the jury had not yet reached a verdict. I assumed Judge Carr would declare an adjournment and have the jury back the next day. The judge asked the foreperson if the jury had reached a unanimous verdict or was at an impasse. The foreperson responded that the jury was at an impasse.

Uh-oh, it looked like a hung jury, which would mean the case had to be tried again. In America, when that prospect arises, the judge often resorts to what is colloquially called the "dynamite charge," or more formally, the "Allen charge." It is intended to blow up a jury logjam by gently urging the holdout jurors to reconsider their positions, considering the fact that most of the other jurors did not agree with them. Much ink has been spilled debating the legitimacy of a judge essentially telling the jury how it should decide the case. "Go along with the majority if you can."

But often, the TNT in the dynamite charge isn't enough to break the logjam. If the jury remains hung after more deliberation, a mistrial is declared.

In England, however, judges are loath to order a jury to return to the jury room for hours into the evening in the hope of ending the deadlock. It would mean that the jurors and all court personnel would have to stay in the courthouse, possibly missing their trains and buses, and return the next day for more deliberations. The British judge has a better impasse-breaking power than the Allen charge. The judge can tell the jury to return to the jury room and ascertain if ten jurors out of the twelve can agree on a verdict of guilty or not guilty. If so, then ten out of twelve would be sufficient for them to render a verdict.

The jury went out and returned in 15 minutes with a 10-2 guilty verdict. I had mixed feelings about the result. It is always satisfying to win, but the 10-2 verdict was troubling. It meant that two people on the jury believed Marsh was innocent, despite Judge Carr's instruction allowing them to infer guilt because she did not testify. In my opinion, that meant Marsh was convicted because we used a flawed and unjust rhetorical device.

The jury was excused with the court's thanks, and Judge Carr asked the barristers if they had any motions to present. Defense counsel Newman made a perfunctory motion for a new trial, which the judge denied. Then, my troublesome conscience was relieved when Carmen Marsh exploded with a hysterical rant about how she had been raped by Dr. Falk, and now Judge Carr was complicit in that assault. Marsh's outburst clearly demonstrated her vindictiveness toward Dr. Falk and her delusional version of events. I was now totally convinced that Marsh had sent the harassing texts and voice messages, and that justice had been achieved.

When Giles and I returned to the robing room, we were surprisingly subdued. Giles was not gloating or rehashing the case. He was already planning the next thing, a weekend excursion into London that included Susan and me. It was all planned. We would stay at his flat near Saint Pancras and King's Cross train stations.

NINETEEN

Breaking And Entering

On the surface, Giles's agenda for our whirlwind London excursion was simple, but I had learned that nothing was simple with him. On Saturday, Giles instructed us to take the train to Waterloo Station and ride the Tube to King's Cross Station. From there, we would walk to his flat in Ice Wharf, where we could stay the night. It was the first time I heard about his flat. Giles had not scheduled anything for us on Saturday afternoon, so we had free time. In the evening, we were to meet him and Dana at the Royal Academy of Art. It featured a temporary exhibition called "The Glory of Rome," which brought together a diverse collection of Italian Baroque art inspired by Caravaggio. Then the plan was that the four of us would have a late dinner at the Ice Wharf flat.

Our excursion began badly as soon as we left our Winchester townhouse to walk to the train station. It was *bucketing*. To live in England, one must adapt to the ever-present threat of rain showers. I thought I had acclimated to the wet weather, but five days of constant rain were eroding my patience. It did not help my mood to see an article in The Times reporting it had been the wettest twelve months in Britain since records were first kept in 1766.

The rain had not let up by the time we left King's Cross

Station, and we needed to find our way to Ice Wharf. We had to duck under awnings periodically to consult our London A-Z pocket map and determine our location, as well as how to get to New Wharf Road. When we finally discovered the street, we were hesitant to walk down it. The street was more like a wide, neglected alley flanked by boarded-up warehouses and clusters of homeless people huddling inside their make-shift shelters. Susan suggested waiting until we met up with Giles and Dana later in the evening. I insisted we push on. I reminded Susan of our trip to Penzance and the test Giles had set for us. I said, "This is another Giles challenge, and we cannot fail, or we will forever be hearing about soft, anxious Americans."

Arising like a phoenix from the debris of New Wharf Road was a modern six-story apartment building, a developer's aspirational first step, hoping gentrification would soon be transforming New Wharf Road into a housing Mecca. Buying a flat in the building was typical of Giles's risk-taking persona—to buy in early and cheaply with the anticipation that he could double his investment in a few years.

Following Giles's instructions, we rang the buzzer of Samuel White, the porter for the building. We asked Sam for the key to the flat. Sam was flustered. Giles had not told him we would be staying at the flat, and Sam mumbled that the Canadians who had been staying in the flat the previous week had not vacated the premises. Their car was still in Giles's parking space. Sam called the phone in the flat, but there was no answer. Neither could he reach Giles. We decided that the best plan was to leave our backpacks with the porter while we went to the National Gallery. According to Susan, there was a special exhibit of African art that she wanted to see. So, there was more sloshing about in the rain and a Tube ride to Trafalgar Square.

In keeping with the adage "When it rains, it pours," there was no African art exhibition at the National Gallery. When I asked a docent about the alleged exhibit, she acted like I had asked her to point the way to the room for starving artists. Fortunately, there is a remedy for rain-soaked, frustrated, and disoriented tourists in London—a hot cup of tea. Somehow, tea makes life seem less dreary, and our mood improved. If tea is comfort food, then revisiting my favorite paintings in the National Gallery provided a banquet of solace, and we were almost happy when we stepped outside and saw the rain had finally stopped.

My optimism improved when we returned to Giles's flat and spoke to Sam. He said the housekeeper told him she had cleaned the flat, and the tenants had left. Sam gave us the key, and we gratefully walked into the flat. It was immediately obvious the tenants had not gone yet. Clothes were still hanging in the closet, socks were draped over the backs of kitchen chairs to dry, and two well-used toothbrushes were lying on the bathroom sink. Susan and I assumed the Canadians were trying to scrounge an extra day in the flat, believing any new tenancy would not begin before Monday. We were determined to thwart their sneaky scheme by commandeering the flat and awaiting the return of the trespassers.

At least it was a beautiful place to while away the time. The entire living space was surrounded by floor-to-ceiling windows, giving the impression of being encircled by water. The flat stuck out like the prow of a ship where two of London's great canals met. From the first floor, I could almost reach out of a window to touch the water flowing by. Susan vetoed that idea by reminding me of all the nasty E. coli bacteria luxuriating there.

The confrontation with the overstaying tenants we hoped for and dreaded did not occur. It was time to meet Giles and Dana at the Royal Academy. We parked our backpacks in the middle of the couch. Susan drafted a terse, testy note to the Canadians. "Renters clear out. Owners returning momentarily," and taped it on the door.

Once more into the King's Cross Tube Station. This time, our destination was Piccadilly Circus. The exhibition at the Royal Academy was marvelous. The art was organized strikingly and logically, which made it easier for us to grasp how Italian Realism had developed from Mantegna, through Caravaggio, and ended with Raphael and Titian. As the mysteries of the Italian Renaissance were being resolved, the mystery of what happened to Giles and Dana went unanswered. They were nowhere to be found. I circled through all the rooms several times, looking for a man with blond flowing hair to no avail. It was almost 10:00 PM. What should we do? We opted to return to Giles's flat and await developments. Surely the Canadians would be gone, and at least we would have a place to sleep. It was not to be. Instead of handing us the key to the flat, Sam gave us a slip of paper with a phone number to call. Using his phone, I dialed the number.

I was expecting Giles's voice, so I was startled when a woman answered the phone. It was Dana, and she had unwelcome news. She said the housekeeper had finally been able to reach Giles, and she told him about the snafu. Giles had managed to track down the rental agent at her boyfriend's house in Kent. The boyfriend answered the phone and told Giles his girlfriend was taking a bath. Giles told him, "No problem, take the phone into the bathroom." While sitting in the bathtub, the rental agent explained to him that she had agreed the Canadians could spend another night and had forgotten to tell Giles about it. Dana did not say what Giles's response was, but I imagine that any expletives were composed in perfect prose.

I told Dana we would catch the late train back to Winchester and arrange to rendezvous in London another time. Dana insisted we take a cab and spend the night at her house in Hampstead. She said Giles was on his way, she had an extra bed, and was preparing dinner for us. I had learned by this time that if I were to follow in Giles's wake, I had to be prepared to trim my sails to navigate his sudden shifts in course. Sam ordered a cab for us. When the car arrived, it seemed suspicious to me. It was an unmarked cab, and I had heard how rogue cab drivers would take their passengers on a circuitous trip around London streets to run up the meter. It was comforting when the driver called his dispatcher to ask for directions to Dana's address on Parliament Hill Road.

Our taxi driver took the direct route to Hampstead, and we arrived at Dana's four-story townhouse in fifteen minutes. The dark red brick stood out even at night. There was a half flight of stairs leading up to a wood-paneled door on the first floor. Dana must have been watching for us because she opened the door and greeted us with a big smile before we could ring the bell. We hung our coats in the tiled entryway before being ushered into the drawing room, where Dana had laid out an immense selection of noshes to sustain us until dinner. The nibbles were welcome, as we had not eaten since lunch. While waiting for Giles, Dana told us about the history of the house. It was a Victorian design and built in 1870. There were only two rooms on the first floor, the parlor and the formal dining room, which Dana had converted into a sitting room. Both rooms had tiled, enclosed fireplaces with carved wooden mantels. The sitting room looked out onto a terrace and an extensive but overgrown garden. I was intrigued by the dumbwaiter, which had once transferred food from the kitchen below to the dining room.

As any reader could deduce from my bland description of Dana's home, I am no Charles Dickens. I would be a prosecutor's nightmare as an eyewitness to a crime. I have no eye for detail, and the best description of a robber I would conjure up would be, "the perp was male and wearing a blue coat—maybe." I also suffer from ADD, *Adjective Deficiency Disorder*. What stuck in my mind about our visit with Dana was the stories she told about living in the house. She began by telling us about her neighbor.

Dana only owned the first two floors. The third and fourth floors were owned by a woman, Corrine, who was the mistress of the head of the British Communist Party, Jordon McDougal. Corrine lived on the third-floor flat, while Jordon, in keeping with the communal aspect of Communist doctrine, lived on the fourth-floor flat with his wife, Sarah. Jordon was not exceptionally successful in the political arena; the British Communist Party was never more than an intriguing fringe organization, but he must have had a gift for attracting women. Maybe it was the kilt he occasionally wore. Dana said Corrine was so besotted with Jordon that when Jordon died and Sarah moved house, Corrine purchased the fourth-floor flat. She did not want the memories she had of Jordon tarnished by strangers living in the same rooms. She was distraught at the prospect of hearing their footsteps through the ceiling and knowing they were not made by Jordon. The fourth floor remained empty. Dana wanted to buy both the third and fourth-floor flats, but Corrine, who rarely left her flat, refused to sell.

Hampstead is a combination of Beverly Hills and Greenwich Village, a mix of rich and famous artists, writers, and actors, as well as those who aspire to become rich and famous. Keats, Shelly, Donne, and George Orwell had lived in Hampstead. Around the corner from Dana's house were the mansions of Boy George, Benedict Cumberbatch's parents, and Jeremy Irons.

Living close to the rich and famous, however, had not deterred the nasty and nefarious. Dana's flat had been burglarized twice, once while she was sleeping. Another time, a gang brought what looked like a moving van and proceeded to empty her flat. Her ten-year-old son Conor came home from school while the burglars were clearing out the house. Fortunately, they did not hurt him.

A fellow actor who needed a place in London stayed with Dana during her two-month stint as an actor at the Old Vic Theatre. She was so nervous about burglaries that she chose to carry her $50,000 worth of jewels with her rather than leave them in the flat. It did not help. One afternoon, after she had opened the door, a man pushed her inside and tried to take her purse. With exceptionally long nails, she put up a fight. Conor, now eighteen, was in the flat. He heard the struggle and tried to intervene. The robber knocked him down, but Conor was able to hit the panic button by the door, and the blaring alarm scared off the robber.

Dana had had two cars stolen, so she drove a battered Volkswagen, which she hoped no one would want. Despite those experiences, she still took walks on Hampstead Heath at night. She said she would not sacrifice her freedom to criminals.

Giles finally arrived, and dinner was served: grilled salmon, mushroom soup, mixed vegetables, fresh-baked garlic bread, and wine, of course. Much of the after-dinner conversation was about Dana's career as an actor. She had performed with many of the greats of British theatre, including Ian McKellen, Patrick Stewart, and Judy Dench. Dana still carried a modest resentment for not getting the lead role in the Poldark TV series.

Giles did not want to talk about his health, but Dana and I insisted on a discussion about his drinking after he drank his third glass of wine. The severe symptoms of cirrhosis were too hard to ignore. He had arrived at Dana's looking exhausted. His skin and eyes were yellowish, and he had abdominal swelling. He exhibited bouts of confusion, misremembering events, and stumbling over his words. We all looked at each other when Giles appeared to doze off in the middle of a conversation.

The three of us put Giles in a full-court press, urging him to stop drinking and to cut back on his cases. He laughed at us and said, "At the end of one's life, one should not stop doing the things one loves. Adding a few months to my life is hardly fair compensation for eliminating the very things that make my life worth living." Dana thought she had the perfect rebuttal to Giles's cavalier attitude. She looked Giles in the eye and, adopting her best Lady Macbeth tone, said, "If you think I am going to play nursemaid to you while you are dying, think again."

Giles, believing a good offense always trumps a good defense, chose that moment to announce he was planning a big party at his château in Normandy in three weeks. He was going to invite a group of friends, which, of course, included the three of us. The main event would be a banquet worthy of French royalty. He added that it would indeed be a tragedy if the weekend did not include uncorking the cases of the vintage wines he had been storing in his wine cellar.

Giles won again. We were trapped. We could hardly refuse to attend what could be his "Last Supper."

I could not help but appreciate the irony. Giles was an unlikely candidate for being Christ-like. He possessed many good qualities, but they did not include humility, patience, temperance, thankfulness, and self-control. The lack of these virtues was not a recipe for friendship, yet I considered Giles a good, but unlikely, friend. I usually cannot abide people with huge, selfish egos. Yet, here I was playing his sidekick, a Sancho Panza to a staunch narcissist. Why? Many times I had asked myself that question. The best answer I could fashion was that Giles made my life more exciting, like Sancho. He gave me entrée to worlds that I could barely imagine, let alone gain access to.

Most importantly, Giles educated me about law, advocacy, and how to live life—and how not to. I was sure it was not Giles's intention, but I also gained insights about myself that would have eluded me without the Giles effect. Cervantes said it best. When Sancho is asked why he follows Don Quixote despite the travails and irritations that come with being his squire, he answers, "I like him."

Maybe it is more accurate to describe Giles as a generous narcissist, odd as that may sound. That night at Dana's apartment captured that contradiction. Our evening of frustration and annoyance due to Giles botching the arrangements for his flat and not showing up at the Academy as promised was offset by his willingness to spend the night on a mattress on the floor of the parlor with Dana, while we slept in the only bed. When Dana had told us on the phone that she had a spare bed, she failed to mention that it was a pallet in front of the fireplace on an oak floor.

Giles's largesse continued the next morning when he cooked up a complete English breakfast: eggs, hash brown potatoes, bacon, sausage, baked beans, grilled tomatoes and mushrooms, toast, and pots of freshly brewed tea. He brushed aside our gratitude for preparing such a morning feast. "This is what I have every morning," which provided another reason for his health issues.

Unlike many narcissists, Giles's generous acts were not designed to elicit praise, adding additional fodder to his ego. All too often, narcissists display bouts of generosity, like working at a food bank. However, when telling friends and family about their charitable work, they expect lavish praise in return. Their ostensible bigheartedness keeps the narcissists at the center of the narrative. When Giles slept on the floor so we could have a comfortable bed, he did not expect us to sing "Hosannas" to him in the morning. He would have been silently irritated if we had. I had never met anyone more comfortable in his own skin than Giles. He did not appear to have any deep-set insecurities. His ego and his comfort level with his persona were already at maximum capacity and required no additional feeding.

Reverting to his more self-centered character, Giles left the breakfast debris for Dana to clear up. He bustled off to run errands. Dana refused our offer of help, insisting we sit on her terrace and enjoy another cup of tea.

With the dishes done, Dana was eager to take us on a walk around Hampstead Heath with her two Yorkshire terriers. The Heath, a 790-acre park, is permanently protected from development under the Hampstead Heath Act. The only structure permitted on the Heath is Kenwood House, which was donated by Edward Guinness, 1st Earl of Iveagh, the original owner and president of Arthur Guinness Son and Co. Brewery, and the richest man in Ireland. The view of London was impressive. Although it was cloudy, we could pick out St. Paul's Cathedral and the Houses of Parliament. We stood near a grove of trees, which, according to legend, was supposed to be the burial site of Boudicca. She was a Celtic queen who led a revolt against the occupying Roman army in 50 AD that almost severed Britain from the Roman Empire.

The park has three swimming ponds that retain vestiges of their Victorian heritage: one pond was reserved for men, one for women, and one for mixed couples. As a concession to modernity, the single-sex ponds allowed nude bathing. Dana said she often enjoyed sunbathing in the buff but had not done so lately because the "lesbians had become more aggressive." It was obvious there were no minimum temperature restrictions on swimming in the ponds. The temperature hovered around 60 degrees, and there were dozens of people demonstrating a variety of swimming strokes and showing off a similar assortment of bodies. The Brits appeared to be immune to hypothermia.

Giles had returned from his errands before we finished our walk, and it was time for us to catch the 1:00 PM train back to Winchester. We left in plenty of time, or so I thought, but Giles got a thrill from catching trains just before they left the station, preferably after the guard had signaled the engineer to start the train. I do not. I have nightmares about missing planes and trains.

British trains do add excitement for late arrivals. The doors are not locked as the train starts moving, and each compartment has its own door, so it is possible and dangerous to open the door to a compartment and literally hop in. Such antics must be common-place since other passengers in the compartment never look up from their books and newspapers and graciously slide over to make room for the late arriver. I had seen so many movies where the leading character chases the slow-starting train, flings open the door, and leaps in at the last second. I had a secret desire to attempt the feat myself, but Susan would be in no mood for such larks. If I had boarded the train at the last second and held out my hand to help her up, she would have glared at me and remained rooted to the platform.

I was not driving the car, however, and Giles took a detour through a London neighborhood of tired-looking Edwardian townhouses. It was the kind of shabby neighborhood Giles liked to invest in, one on the cusp of being gentrified. He would buy a house or two on the cheap, rehab them while sparing no expense, and resell them at a handsome profit. Giles showed us two adjacent townhouses he was thinking of buying, rehabbing, and reselling. This was vintage Giles. He did not only "Live for today," he actually "Lived for tomorrow," even when he did not have many tomorrows left.

Susan and I had to rush through the station to catch the train, but no leaping aboard was necessary. We were back in Winchester twenty-four hours after we had left. Another typical day with Giles.

TWENTY

Robbery Most Foul

If the stalking case delivered a thrill a minute, our next case promised nothing but tedium. At first glance, one might have expected it to keep the jurors on the edge of their seats. The two defendants, Jack Catesby and Trevor Ratcliff, were charged with twelve counts of aggravated robbery. A third member of the gang, Ronnie Bloodsworth, had pleaded guilty. A conviction on any one of the charges could lead to a lifetime custodial sentence, the same as for premeditated murder. The British considered the threat to society from aggravated robberies to be equal to or greater than the danger of being murdered. One reason for treating the two crimes similarly is that murders are exceedingly rare in England thanks to strict gun regulations. The second reason is the deterrence effect. The British understand, whereas Americans don't, that draconian penalties, including the death penalty, do little to deter murder. Most homicides are not committed by a person who first sits down over a pint of ale and ponders the pros and cons of killing another human being. The would-be murderer certainly is not contemplating what the punishment might be if caught. If the barroom shooter had taken a moment to consider the consequences of his actions, counting to ten, for example, he would not likely have shot. In contrast, a perp considering a burglary or an armed robbery of someone's home might be deterred by the prospect of an exceptionally long prison sentence and may opt for breaking into the corner tea shop, facing only a one-year custodial sentence. Thoughtful thieves would also know they would be less likely to be caught for breaking into a tea shop since the British police have a lower priority for investigating crimes against property than they do for assaults against people.

The case had also generated an avalanche of media attention. The Isle of Wight is normally as tranquil and quiet as the fog that regularly shrouds the island. For the anxious islanders, the rash of nighttime burglaries was a reign of terror. Not only were their homes broken into, but the residents were often bound to chairs, gagged, and threatened with knives pressed against their throats, forcing them to reveal where their jewelry was hidden. Even then, the horror did not end; they had to watch while the burglars raided the fridge, ate sandwiches, and drank wine.

So, how could the trial of such a case be dull? First, there was the Sisyphean task of proving a case when there were scores of exhibits to be introduced and eighty witnesses to be called. Adding to the recipe for tediousness was the British court's practice of reducing the number of live witnesses testifying in court. Instead, the sworn statements the witnesses had given to the police are read to the jury. There was a certain logic to this approach. If defense counsel had reviewed the statements of the witnesses and did not intend to cross-examine some of those witnesses, then there was no need to subpoena the witnesses and require them to waste hours of their time providing testimony that no one contested. The downside from an advocate's perspective is that live theatre is replaced by droning monologues, and jurors nod off despite their best efforts to stay awake. The reading of statements also drags out the trial. With a live witness, the examining barrister can cut to the chase and only bring out the essential points of a witness's testimony. When the statements are read, the entire statement must be read, including the plethora of trivial and irrelevant facts.

Catesby's and Ratcliff's barristers, Richard Park and Sir Roger Barrymore, did not challenge the witnesses' statements because they did not dispute what the victims described on the nights of the robberies. Their defense was simple: "It wasn't us behind the stocking masks."

Giles told me I would be reading the uncontested witness statements into evidence. I was not thrilled by the prospect, but Giles said he wanted to husband his strength for the two-week-long trial. He did seem weaker. He also booked a bed-and-breakfast in Portsmouth for that duration. At first, I assumed he did so to help conserve his dwindling energy. However, I was still annoyed that I would be required to take the train every day to Portsmouth and hike a half mile to the courthouse carrying a stuffed briefcase. It was only twenty-eight miles from Winchester to Portsmouth, and Giles at his normal rate of speed could make the trip in half an hour. The train, however, was a milk run with numerous stops, and it took an hour to reach Portsmouth.

The robbery gang seemed to have followed a checklist designed to guarantee the maximum possible sentence if caught, and they ticked all the boxes. As the prosecution, we had to prove:

1. The robbers targeted vulnerable victims.
2. The robberies were carefully planned.
3. Violence had been inflicted on the victims, or they had been threatened with serious violence.
4. The victims suffered substantial physical or psychological injury.
5. Victims were in their homes.
6. The robbers stole or damaged property, causing a substantial loss to the victims.

The Isle of Wight robbers did other things to make them a

dangerous, vicious bunch of villains worthy of exceptionally long custodial sentences.

1. They carried weapons.
2. They used face coverings.
3. The robberies were committed at a dwelling.
4. In some of the robberies, a child was in the home.
5. All the robberies occurred at night.
6. They tied up their victims.
7. Many of their victims were old and vulnerable.

On the first day of the trial, there were twenty observers. I assumed many of them were reporters. The law in England, which regulates how the fourth estate covers ongoing trials, presents a challenge for reporters. Reporters can only describe what occurred in the courtroom when the jury was present. They are forbidden from reporting or commenting on all the motions, applications, and arguments contesting what evidence may or may not be admissible. If the judge excludes an important piece of evidence, the reporter cannot mention it in the morning edition of the Portsmouth News or on the local BBC newscast. If they do mention the unmentionable, the paper or the TV station could be fined by the court. The rationale for suppressing the press is a good one. It creates an information bubble around the jury. In theory, the only evidence the jury hears about the case is the evidence presented in the courtroom. Jurors should see nothing on the television or read anything in the newspaper that would be different from what they saw or heard in the courtroom. Unlike in the U.S., there is no constitutional right in Britain guaranteeing freedom of the press. So, the American media is free to publish everything about the case that reporters can uncover. American commentators and pundits can float outrageous theories and engage in breathless, wide-eyed speculation. Lawyers can also try their cases in public if they think the publicity would help their clients. They trot out arguments and make questionable statements in front of the cameras. If they had engaged in similar antics in the courtroom, they could have ended up being led from the courtroom in handcuffs, charged with contempt of court. In the U.S., judges attempt to shield jurors from the hype, false statements, and speculation by instructing them not to read or listen to anything in the media about the case and not to discuss the trial with anyone—not even family or fellow jurors. In reality, American jurors are exposed to all kinds of outside information and opinions, and judges still naively hope it won't influence them.

I was surprised to see Francine sitting in the spectators' section of the courtroom. I remembered her from our trip to Normandy, when she shared our cabin on the ferry to Cherbourg. Before I could ask her why she was there, Francine volunteered that she had never seen Giles try a case and was eager to see him in action. The penny dropped. I realized why Giles had booked a bed-and-breakfast for the duration of the trial instead of driving the twenty-eight miles from Winchester. He never missed a chance to mix business with pleasure.

Giles delivered his opening statement in his usual prosecutorial style, acting as the honest guide whose sole duty was to present the evidence so the jury could make a fair and just decision. Unlike many American prosecutors, he did not take on the role of society's avenging angel on a moral crusade to rid the world of all criminals. It was unnecessary in this case to adopt such a posture. The crimes committed by the defendants were so horrible that they were enough to put jurors in an avenging mood.

Giles described how a gang of three men—Bloodworth, Catesby, and Ratcliff—conspired to commit dozens of robberies. Their planning was meticulous. First, they would explore one of the Isle of Wight's smaller villages, looking for homes that were off the High Street and more isolated. Once they had selected those homes, they would observe them to determine who lived there. They were looking for older people. Since the Isle of Wight attracts thousands of retirees who either reside there permanently or own a summer cottage, it was not difficult to find them. The homes of those select few were monitored by one of the gang members to find out the routines of the inhabitants, such as when they went to bed, whether they left lights on, or if there was a security system in place. Sometimes, the homeowners were followed while they shopped to learn if they paid by check, credit card, or cash. The gang paid particular attention to the watches and jewelry they wore.

Once the victims were selected, the robbers would pull stockings over their heads, break into the home after midnight, and rouse the sleepy residents, who would wake up to discover three men in their bedroom holding knives. The gang would then tie the couple to chairs. The gang knew what they wanted. They did not bother to ransack the home for valuables. Instead, they asked the frightened, tightly bound couple where the cash, jewelry, and silver were kept. Televisions or computers were never taken. Any reluctance by the owners would provoke one gang member to thrust his knife into the face of the hesitant victim, threatening to cut off an earlobe. Compliance always followed. The valuables were collected into black leather bags, and the victims were gagged and left bound in their chairs.

Only Catesby and Radcliff were on trial. Bloodworth had pled guilty and received a lighter sentence. According to the sentencing guidelines, Bloodworth's sentence was reduced for several reasons: he pled guilty soon after being indicted; he was 25 years old at the time of the robberies; he had no prior convictions; he had a learning disability; and he demonstrated remorse.

What struck me as unusual about the plea deal was that Bloodworth was not obligated to cooperate in the trial of Catesby and Radcliff. In fact, from the moment he was arrested, Bloodworth followed the advice of his solicitor and refused to talk to the police. His solicitor had also informed the court that if Bloodworth were subpoenaed to testify at the trial, he would assert his right to remain silent. As Crown Prosecutor, Giles was prohibited from telling the jury that a codefendant of Catesby and Radcliff had pled guilty.

Such a lack of cooperation by a codefendant would never happen in the U.S., where plea bargaining between prosecutors and defense counsel is the norm. An American prosecutor has the power to drop charges and ensure that if the defendant pleads guilty, he will obtain a significantly reduced sentence. But there is a proviso. If there are co-defendants in the case, the defendant who took the plea deal, like Bloodworth, must testify against his fellow robbers in their trials. To guarantee the cooperating codefendant does not change his mind and experiences a sudden loss of memory, his reduced sentence is not confirmed until he has testified and put his buddies in the frame.

The long slog of introducing exhibits and entering uncontested statements into the record began. Giles graciously gave me the chore of boring the jury by reading the statements. The cynical side of me thought he was trying to enhance the impact of his own witness examinations by showcasing my dullness. Reading testimony is inherently tedious, but under the court rules, it can be mind-numbing. I was not permitted to enliven my rendition with storytelling techniques, like a parent at bedtime, adding breathless tension, bursts of excitement, and animated gestures. Instead, imagine the big bad wolf responding to Little Red Riding Hood's question, "Why, Grandma, what big teeth you have," in a flat, droning monotone. "The better to eat you with, my dear." I was prohibited from using hand motions to emphasize certain parts of the witness statements. This was especially onerous to a person who has a habit of "talking with his hands." The result was that the jury and the judge were bored, and I was bored. Every person in the courtroom was bored. One elderly gentleman on the jury appeared to nod off. I even caught Giles "resting his eyes."

The victims of the robberies all told the same story about what the robbers did and how they acted. I had to break the soporific spell even if I risked incurring the censure of Judge Mills by calling a witness to testify whose sworn statement had not been challenged by either defense counsel. Perhaps Judge Mills welcomed a break from my droning voice. I elicited from Mr. Baker exactly what he had stated in his written statement to the police, except for one thing. He had told the police the robbers had Irish accents, and he said in the witness box that the robbers spoke with an Irish or Celtic accent. That variation meant nothing to me, but during the midafternoon recess, Giles told me that a Celtic accent could be different from an Irish accent because, although Scottish is a Celtic language, it is quite different from an Irish accent. It looked like a significant variation in Baker's testimony because the defendant, Ratcliff, was Scottish. Giles urged me to ask the witness to explain why he said, "Irish or Celtic." He thought the inconsistency and the witness's confusion could undermine the credibility of one of our most persuasive witnesses. Giles said it would be like the witness saying the robber had a French or a Romanian accent. I believed, though, that opening such a line of inquiry was too risky. Since we were not allowed to prep our witnesses, I said, "We have no idea what his answer might be, and it might be opening a Pandora's Box." I doubted that a Portsmouth jury would recognize any difference between a Celtic and an Irish accent and would assume both terms meant an Irish accent. Baker was my witness, so Giles acquiesced in my decision.

The discrepancy in the testimony, however, did not escape Radcliff's barrister, Sir Roger Barrymore. He believed he had good ammunition to undermine Mr. Baker's credibility and introduce evidence that would suggest one of the robbers was not Radcliff.

I was not looking forward to passively listening to Sir Roger's annoying cross-examination, consisting of a sneer and feigned outrage. To an American, he was the archetype of a superior, snobbish Brit with an affected accent. I described him to Giles as someone who acted like he had a poker up his ass. He drove me crazy. I wanted to jump up and slap him. Instead, as far as the jury was concerned, I just looked bored. Sir Roger was dull except for his condescending pretentiousness. He was like a baseball player who had struck out, but strutted back to the dugout like he had just hit a home run. With one witness, Sir Roger spent ten minutes working to get the witness to agree that he lived at 2012 Collingwood Lane. Then he turned to the jury as if he were expecting a round of applause.

Sir Roger's decision to delve into the accent discrepancy was not unreasonable. Still, he was violating one of the guiding principles of cross-examination: *Do not ask a question you do not know the answer to*, and *never ask the 'why' question*. First, Sir Roger wanted to show the jury that Mr. Baker was an unreliable narrator who could not tell the difference between a Scottish and an Irish accent. Second, he hoped to pin Mr. Baker down to the answer he had given in his statement that the accents were Irish. He could then argue Radcliff was not part of the gang because he was Scottish and had a Scottish accent.

"Please explain to the jury, Mr. Baker, why you characterized the accents as Irish **or** Celtic?"

Mr. Baker turned out to be like Henry Higgins in "My Fair Lady," an accomplished linguist living on the Isle of Wight, and not a professor lounging around Covent Garden, flirting with flower girls. He explained the varied accents one could hear in Ireland. He noted that the robber he identified had a lilt in his voice that was similar to the accents of the Irish residing in the northern three counties of Ireland. Their lilt was higher in tone than that of the southern Irish and remarkably similar to the Scottish accent. Without pausing for another question, Mr. Baker concluded that the robber could have been Northern Irish or Scottish.

I almost felt sorry for Sir Roger, and yet I could not resist leaning over and whispering to Giles, "The poker just went in deeper, and it was hot."

Things did not improve for Sir Roger during his cross-examination of the next witness, Sarah Bates. Sarah was a teller at the

Barclays Bank in Newport on the Isle of Wight. Sarah had testified during Giles's direct examination that Radcliff had exchanged one hundred £1 coins for five £20 banknotes within a week of the last home invasion on the island. In that robbery, a large cache of £1 coins had been taken. She did not know the customer was Radcliff at the time, but later her fellow teller told her it was Radcliff. During cross-examination, Sir Roger, rightly in my view, pointed out that Sarah's identification of Radcliff was dependent on the hearsay statement of her colleague. I was surprised when an obviously miffed judge intervened and asked Sir Roger if he was contending that the person exchanging the coins was not his client. Sir Roger's response did not improve the judge's mood.

"Your Lordship, I am not obliged to say if I contest the identification because the prosecution bears the burden of proving all issues in the case."

Apparently, Giles suspected what was coming next and remained silent. Under British law, defense counsel must inform the court as to which relevant facts offered by the prosecution they are contesting as not true. Sir Roger would not, and could not, tell Judge Mills he did not believe it was his client, Radcliff, who cashed in the coins, and that it was another person. Obviously, Radcliff had previously told Sir Roger that he had exchanged the coins for banknotes, and Sir Roger would be lying to the court to say otherwise.

Then came the chastisement from Judge Mills on high. He peered over the top of his reading glasses and said, "Sir Roger, you have wasted the court's time challenging a fact you do not contest. Please move on."

When it was time for defendant Catesby's counsel, Richard Park, to question Ms. Bates, he was not as constrained as Sir Roger. We did not claim Catesby had anything to do with the exchange of the coins for banknotes. It would have been reasonable for Park to forgo asking any questions. Maybe he believed that if he could weaken the case against Radcliff, it would also weaken the case against Catesby. Once again, it led to unintended consequences. Park reviewed with Sarah her direct testimony, a questionable cross-examination tactic in my opinion, because the witness can repeat the damning statements she had previously made. Park was attempting to establish inconsistencies between Sarah's direct testimony and what she had said to the police. The problem was that he was misquoting what Sarah had said during her direct examination. I whispered to Giles about the discrepancies, but he did not object. I wondered if his reluctance to object was again driven by the unwritten barrister code of conduct, not to embarrass a fellow barrister unnecessarily, especially when the barrister is a member of the same chambers. Since Sarah was Giles's witness, I could not and would not object myself, so I leaned over and whispered to Park's attending solicitor that Park was misquoting the testimony. My comment to the solicitor set in motion a chain of events that would be rare, if not unheard of, in an American courtroom.

Nothing immediately happened except that Park doggedly pursued Ms. Bates, trying to make her appear inconsistent. During the lunch break, I explained my concerns to Park. He and the solicitor reviewed the audiotape of Ms. Bates's testimony to determine if my memory of what the witness said during her direct testimony was more accurate than the notes they took. My memory was correct.

When the trial resumed, Park graciously, and with evident remorse, apologized to the judge and the jury for his mistake. He read to the jury the correct lines from the previous testimony and asked them to disregard his unwarranted attempt to show that Ms. Bates's in-court testimony was inconsistent with her statement to the police.

Thanks to the ineffective cross-examinations of Sir Roger and Park, Giles said Sarah was "copper-bottomed,"[1] a witness whom the jury could trust completely.

---

1. Wooden ships that are covered in copper sheets are immune to attacks by barnacles and teredo worms which can turn a ships planking into Swiss cheese.

Another day, another witness. We called Edmund Hardcastle to the stand, who should have been an easy witness to question. Hence, Giles gave me the opportunity to sound like a proper barrister, with negligible risk to our case. We assumed Edmund would testify consistently with his statement to the police. Edmund told the police that three days before the invasion of the Pearson home in Cowes, he had seen the defendant Radcliff lingering outside the Pearson home in the early evening, smoking a cigarette.

After the usual preliminary questions, I began laying the groundwork to put Edmund in a position where he could observe Radcliff on the night in question.

During the preliminary foundational questions, Edmund began to deviate from what he had stated in his statement.

"What time of night was it?'

"The Devil's *dancen* hours, about midnight."

"What was the weather like?"

"It was rimy, slightly foggy."

"Did you notice a person in the area?"

"Yes."

"Where was the person standing?"

"On the pavement."

The problem these answers posed for me was that they differed from what Edmund had said in his police statement. He had told the police it was "murky," at twilight, said nothing about fog, and had the person standing out of sight in a "lewth"—a sheltered spot.

I was rattled and stopped my questioning. I had a flashback to my very first trial when my client's testimony deviated from what he told me had happened. It was a civil case of assault and battery in which my client alleged that a burly, former football player pushed his way into his leased apartment and intimidated him in front of his family. The defendant was a realtor who had represented the owner and claimed he had a right to enter the apartment. My client was a small, frail 60-year-old man who suffered from black lung disease after decades spent in coal mines. My client had told me he had been terribly frightened.

After taking my client through a chronology of the confrontation, I asked him if he had been scared. Much to my surprise, he answered, "No." It was like whatever was left of his testosterone rushed through his veins, and he had to defend his manhood. I was at a complete loss of what to do, and meekly ended my questioning. Not surprisingly, the jury agreed the defendant had committed an assault on my client but only awarded $125 in damages.

I was now faced with the same dilemma on the Isle of Wight. Giles sensed my panic and passed me a note. "Ask to make an application to the court." I did, and Judge Mills said it was about time for a recess and adjourned the court for 15 minutes.

We found an empty conference room, and I explained to Giles my concern about Hardcastle's answers varying from what he told the police. I anticipated Hardcastle's responses were precursors to his changing his story and either denying he saw Radcliff or that he was not sure it was Radcliff. That damn British vouching rule prevented me from confronting Hardcastle when he returned to the stand with his prior sworn statements to the police. If it looked like I was challenging my own witness's veracity, Judge Mills would intervene and ask me if I was no longer vouching for Hardcastle's truthfulness, basically calling Hardcastle a liar. I would be in the "Catch 22" trap. If I responded "No," Judge Mills would preclude me from challenging Hardcastle with his prior inconsistent statements. The jury would never hear about what he had told the police. If I said, "Yes," Judge Mills would tell the jury I was not vouching for the truthfulness of my witness. Therefore, any fact Hardcastle might offer that was favorable to our prosecution case would likely be rejected by the jury since I could not ask the jury to accept it as true.

In the U.S., I avoided impeaching my own witnesses because I hoped the jury would accept most of what the witnesses said as true. It is permissible in the U.S., however, for me to point out inconsistencies between what witnesses said in court and what they may have said in prior statements, without having the judge instruct the jury that I was no longer vouching for the truthfulness of my witnesses.

I was at a complete loss of what to do. Giles came to my rescue with a superb strategy. He would make an application to the court that Mr. Hardcastle be considered as a "hostile witness." If the court agreed, I would be permitted to ask him leading questions and to confront him when his answers were inconsistent with his statements to the police. "But," I said, "How would that help? Judge Mills would instruct the jury that it could not consider those prior statements as relevant evidence in the case."

"David, without saying what is in the prior statements, we have to encourage Hardcastle to incorporate what he told the police into his in-court testimony."

I just shook my head. "How am I going to accomplish that?"

I was irritated; Giles was enjoying his "tutor the professor" moment far too much. Yet, damn, he was right again. He proposed that before I asked Hardcastle a question, I should have him read the pertinent part of his prior police statement to "refresh his recollection." After being refreshed, Hardcastle would not likely say anything different to the jury than what he had said in his police statement. He would be worried about being accused of lying under oath by Judge Mills if his sworn testimony to the jury differed from the sworn statement he had given to the police. Hardcastle would not know that under British law, he could not be charged with lying under oath for merely giving inconsistent statements.

Giles made the application to the court, and Judge Mills agreed to allow me to impeach Hardcastle by showing that his prior police statements were inconsistent with his in-court testimony. Judge Mills emphasized, however, that he would tell the jury they could not consider any prior statements by Hardcastle for their truth and could only be used by the jury to assess Hardcastle's credibility.

Giles's questionable, unorthodox strategy worked flawlessly. I handed Hardcastle a copy of his police statement with the passages marked that I wanted him to review. I then took back his statement and asked:

"Mr. Hardcastle, having refreshed your recollection, can you tell the jury if you saw the Defendant in Cowes on July 17th, three days before the robbery of the Pearson home?"

"Yes, I did."

"Where was he?"

"On the pavement outside the Pearson home."

"Did you know it was Mr. Radcliff at the time?"

"No."

"When did you learn it was Mr. Radcliff?"

"When I picked out his picture from a group of photos at the police station."

"Is Mr. Radcliff in the courtroom today?"

"Yes, sitting in the prisoner's dock."

"Thank you, Mr. Hardcastle. Those are all the questions I have, Your Lordship."

I did not try to challenge Hardcastle's trustworthiness by reminding him of his prior inconsistent answers to police questions. Neither did I attempt to dissuade the jury from accepting as true his previous in-court testimony that it was midnight and foggy when he saw Radcliff. Although this variation in the time and the weather did weaken the strength of Hardcastle's identification, I did not want the jury to believe that I had any doubts about the truth of his identification of Radcliff.

My forbearance also posed a dilemma for Sir Roger. He could elicit Hardcastle's inconsistencies to challenge his credibility, but doing so would necessitate the jury hearing that Hardcastle had told the police it was twilight, not the "Devil's *dancen* hour," and it was not "rimy." Sir Roger opted not to cross-examine Hardcastle about his inconsistent statements.

Our case against Catesby was seriously undermined when one of our key witnesses, Cory Fox, completely changed her testimony from what she had told the police, or she had developed amnesia. In court, Fox could not remember seeing Catesby in the pub with Ratcliff and Bloodworth shortly before one of the robberies. Giles pulled out all his tricks for eliciting testimony from a supposedly friendly but reluctant witness. He did not resort to a vigorous cross-examination since that would trigger Judge Mills to ask if he was no longer offering Fox's testimony as true. As Giles put it, he examined the witness "crossly," in the hope she would be intimidated into giving him the answers he wanted. But after ten years as a barmaid, Fox was not about to be cowed by an aggressive, bewigged barrister. Giles tried using leading questions, which defense counsel could have objected to, but to no avail. Finally, he resorted to asking Fox if there was anything that would help her refresh her memory. In America, during witness prep, the witness is instructed to automatically answer "Yes" to that question, quickly followed by the request to review a prior statement or deposition—a surefire technique for attorneys to obtain the answers they want. Not only was Fox not tutored to stick to the script, but she was also stubborn. "No, there is nothing that could refresh my memory."

So, it was not entirely unexpected when we rested our case-in-chief, Judge Mills dismissed the indictment against Catesby. I know I was being cynical, but I did wonder if Giles's placid acceptance of Catesby walking free was due in part because Richard Park was a fellow member of Northgate Chambers. My more objective self had to admit that Park conducted a skilled defense for Catesby, and I also liked him personally.

In Ratcliff's defense case, Sir Roger called no witnesses. He certainly was not going to put Ratcliff on the stand. There were no alibi witnesses who would swear Ratcliff was somewhere else at the time of the home invasions. Consequently, Sir Roger had to rely on his oratorical skills to dissuade the jury from accepting our version of events. Sir Roger's strategy was to scatter an assortment of other possible explanations of the robberies, which did not include his client. The analogy of throwing undercooked spaghetti against the wall came to mind. The problem for Sir Roger was that there were no facts to support his alternative versions of reality, and he was not helped by the many incriminating comments Radcliff had given to the police and other people.

I was pleased when Giles adopted my suggestion for avoiding a long speech in which he reviewed in detail all twelve robberies. The jury would have been bored to death. Our problem, however, was that as prosecutors for the Crown, it was our burden to prove the elements of each crime Radcliff allegedly committed. We had done that with the eighty witnesses whose sworn statements were read to the jury or who had testified in the courtroom. The jury, however, did not need or desire Giles to review all that testimony in detail. Instead, we needed a thread that explained to the jurors how they could tie Ratcliff to all the robberies as soon as they found him guilty of any one of them. I proposed describing the robberies as mirror images of each other. It was like trying on a suit in a tailor's dressing room with mirrors on all the walls. Each image is exactly the same. The precise and consistent methodology of the robbers meant they could have only been carried out by the same gang of men. There was zero chance of there being three other men with Irish accents performing the same rituals Ratcliff, Catesby, and Bloodworth followed during the robberies. Ratcliff and his cronies left their "signatures" at every scene. The jury only needed to find Ratcliff guilty of one robbery to conclude he was guilty of all of them.

If Giles's final speech was short. Judge Mills's summation was interminable. In fairness to Judge Mills, he was obliged under British criminal procedure to summarize all the evidence for the jury. If he left bits and bobs out, the Criminal Court of Appeal might reverse the verdict. Therefore, inclusion of facts involved less risk of reversal than exclusion of facts. Judge Mills also had to walk a tightrope of summing up the facts of the case without giving any hint to the jury about how he assessed the evidence. Judge Mills negotiated his high-wire act by boring the jury to death. His summation took an entire day and included irrelevant and misstated facts. I found it amusing that a couple of jurors who managed not to drift off were shaking their heads when they caught a mistake. The judge's summation perhaps had one beneficial effect; any fire ignited by Sir Roger's closing remarks was smothered by Judge Mills's extinguishing words.

The judge finished his summary of the facts. The court was adjourned early and would reconvene the next day. This reprieve gave us barristers an opportunity to participate in a long-standing tradition where all the barristers in the case meet for dinner after litigating a lengthy case. The robbery trial took more than two weeks to complete. The rationale for the dinners was to foster civility among members of the Bar. The Inns of Court provided an added inducement by picking up the tab for the wine served during dinner. Giles had suggested The Swan, a restaurant he had discovered earlier in the week. Giles's reputation for his exquisite culinary tastes obviated any dissenting voices. We agreed to meet at The Swan at 8:00 pm.

When I mentioned that I would take the opportunity to explore Portsmouth before dinner, Sir Roger said he was surprised at my courage in walking around Portsmouth at night. I chuckled and explained that my family and I lived in an inner-city neighborhood in which it was not uncommon to hear the rat-a-tat-tat of an AR-15 automatic weapon during the night, adding that most of the time they were shot off by exuberant and often drunk young men.

Giles arrived at The Swan uncharacteristically early. I was there earlier, of course, abiding by my rule of never, never being late.

While we were waiting for Sir Roger and Park to arrive, I asked Giles how he had discovered The Swan since it was clearly off the beaten path. He began by saying, "We discovered it by accident when..." He was on the verge of mentioning the person who was with him when he realized the possible implications of his admission and stopped dead in his tracks. There was a long, atypical pause in the conversation. He struggled to fill in the blank with an innocuous comment. It was clear to me that the other person constituting the "We" was Francine. Although Giles and I did not yet have the kind of friendship in which he would be comfortable telling me about his relationship with Francine, his silence spoke volumes.

Giles described these post-trial dinners as a "Boys' night out." He was surprised when I told him I had not engaged in a "Boys' night out" since my college days. None of my male friends were interested in such gatherings, and I had little interest in spending an entire evening without the company of women. The conversation turned out to be much as I expected, macho male talk laced with sexual overtones and, more surprisingly, a lot of gossip about judges and other barristers. They certainly disproved the myth, told mainly by males, that men do not gossip.

I must admit that their ability to mix snide and humorous quips into their descriptions of their colleagues was entertaining during the appetizer stage of the meal. However, by the time the entrée arrived, it had become boring to me. I did not personally know most of the people they were gossiping about. It was going to be a long evening for me if it was to be spent speculating which judges and barristers were gay, sleeping with their solicitors, or closet alcoholics. The last allegation was especially ironic, given that each of us had two wine glasses constantly topped up with red or white wine by the waiter. Giles may have been suffering from cirrhosis, but he was not about to curtail his wine consumption.

In my own self-interest, and in my role as a pupil who was expected to soak up wisdom along with the alcohol from this trio of shrewd sages, I attempted to steer the conversation toward more substantive issues. I used a tactic that had worked well during this sabbatical in England, playing the role of the unenlightened provincial. It is irresistible bait for an accomplished barrister who is eager to bestow his wisdom on a naïve American lawyer.

I began by expressing my disappointment that British criminal law infringed on a defendant's right to silence by permitting barristers to comment on a defendant declining to testify in court. The diversion worked. An American's criticism of the revered British system of justice sparked a feeding frenzy among my dinner companions, with each competing to show how wrong I was. They declared it was obviously fair to pressure a defendant to take the stand once the prosecution had established credible evidence that the defendant had committed the crime. Even Sir Roger believed it was reasonable to comment on a defendant's refusal to testify.

As is my wont, I kept arguing the opposing side, even though my experience in the Isle of Wight robbery trial caused me to question what had been a revered precept for me. Sir Roger chose not to have Ratcliff testify, nor did he call any other witnesses to lend support to a defense theory of the case. Admittedly, it would have been a challenge to find those witnesses. No alternative defense was offered. During his opening speech, Sir Roger did not propose any coherent explanation of how all the uncontradicted factual evidence did not necessarily mean Radcliff was guilty. Instead, Sir Roger raised all sorts of theories and possibilities to suggest assorted hypothetical scenarios which, on their face, were inconsistent with Radcliff's guilt. Surprisingly, I had felt irritated that Ratcliff did not testify. If he had, he could have told the jury which theoretical story suggested by Sir Roger was true. I was bemused by my frustration since, as an American-trained lawyer, a defendant's right not to testify was "mother's milk" to me. At least the debate on the issue had stopped the steady stream of gossip.

The evening and the wine accomplished one of their intended side effects. It improved barrister camaraderie. I had more empathy for Sir Roger. I had wanted to slap him during the trial, but over the course of the evening, as the food courses and the wine arrived at our table, I mellowed into being bemused by Sir Roger. His personality flaws became amusing foibles. The poker was removed from his posterior, and I realized that much of his superior attitude was reflective of his own insecurities, partly caused by being shipped off to a boarding school when he was only six years old. After dinner, Sir Roger graciously drove me back to Winchester. Another lesson learned.

As the dinner was winding down, the waiter asked me if I required anything else. I told him I was not much of a dessert lover, but I had really enjoyed the dinner rolls they had served and wondered if I could have a few more. He said, "Unfortunately, all the rolls they baked for the evening had been eaten and the oven was shut down." I was mildly disappointed. I would have preferred the rolls to the custard for dessert. I had not noticed Giles saying anything to the waiter, but later, as brandy gave way to coffee, the waiter did bring out a domed cake plate with three hot dinner rolls inside. I am not sure what Giles had said or promised, but the chef had quickly fired up the oven and baked their delicious rolls.

The next day, the jury was brought in, only to be immediately sent out again to deliberate the fate of Radcliff. I thought it would take longer to select a foreperson than to find Radcliff guilty. The evidence against the defendant was overwhelming, including incriminating statements by Radcliff himself. The defense had called no witnesses. There were eleven counts to consider, but Sir Roger had helped our prosecution case by essentially admitting that the crimes were so similar they had been committed by the same three men, just not his man, Radcliff.

Twenty minutes into their deliberation, they sent the judge a note through the usher, requesting additional information. Judge Mills sent a note back to the jury room, telling them that the information they had requested was irrelevant. Was the jury being distracted by irrelevancies? They did not agree on a verdict by the noon recess. We knew they had requested a rereading of Radcliff's statements to the police. For the first time in the case, Giles was nervous. He had thought once the incriminating statement of Radcliff was admitted, it would be easy sledding from then on.

During lunch in the courthouse dining room, Giles was the butt of much ribbing about the possibility of losing an "airtight" case against a mediocre barrister. At dinner the night before, Giles was exuding much confidence, vowing to eat his wig if he lost. He told Richard Park, who would be leaving for Spain the next day, that he would call Richard in Spain if he won and, if he lost, Richard would receive a fax from the executor of his estate.

After lunch, the jury asked to replay the tape of Redcliff's statement. What were they thinking? Preparing for the worst, I began the mental process of trying to distance myself from the case. I wrote down in my copybook, "It is no skin off my nose if Radcliff walks. If this jury does not care that a dangerous man who tied up vulnerable people in the middle of the night, threatened them with a knife, and robbed them will be back on the streets, who am I to worry?"

I did sympathize with Detective Inspector Saunders, who was in charge of investigating the robberies. He had spent over a year compiling the Crown's case. All that work would be for naught, and he would have to watch a snide, sneering Ratcliff walk out of the courtroom a free man.

Giles was more agitated about the jury verdict than I had ever seen him. Usually, he would have already shifted into planning the next thing, like a trip somewhere. I sensed he felt his reputation among members of the Bar was in jeopardy. If he lost an open-

and-shut case to someone like Sir Roger, would his fellow barristers conclude his skills as a barrister were slipping? Giles's weakened condition due to the cirrhosis made him especially sensitive to the possibility that his advocacy skills were eroding, and that other members of the Bar would learn of his condition and pity him, a fate worse than death for Giles.

While waiting for the jury's verdict, we spent some time planning a trial advocacy seminar that Giles was scheduled to do for Grey's Inn. Although his energy was diminishing, and I assumed he realized he would die in the not-too-distant future, he was intent on keeping his diary full. The theme of his advocacy seminar was the similarity between trial advocacy and seduction. The irony did not escape me.

At 2:50 pm, the jury still had not reached a decision, and Judge Mills had the usher return them to the courtroom. Judge Mills gave them the "dynamite" instruction, which gave the jurors permission to return a decision if ten of the twelve jurors agreed on the verdict. Then he sent the jury back to deliberate. Thirty minutes later, they reentered the jury box and rendered their verdict. I heaved a sigh of relief when the foreman announced on count one, they found Ratcliff guilty by an 11 to 1 vote. I was more invested in the verdict than I had thought. Even poker-faced Giles could not disguise the relief on his face. On the second count, the jury returned a unanimous guilty verdict. The split was strange to me since it was so clear that all the robberies had to have been committed by the same blokes. The weirdness continued: the verdicts on the remaining ten counts were again unanimous— 12 to 0 for guilty. The verdicts demonstrated once again the unpredictability of juries. The jury spent the entire morning and half the afternoon arguing over what all the barristers in the case believed to be a non-issue. For much of the day, one rogue juror had endured the pressure of his fellow jurors on only one of the eleven counts against Radcliff. However, that same juror was quite ready to agree meekly that Radcliff was guilty in the ten similar robberies. Giles's reputation was preserved.

Once outside the courthouse, Giles said he was off to Normandy on the evening ferry to plan the upcoming weekend extravaganza for his friends, which he had announced three weeks before. I did not ask him if anyone was accompanying him. I caught the train back to Winchester.

TWENTY-ONE

Skyving On Our Own

After the three weeks of the robbery trial, I was delighted that we had no cases, conferences, pleas, or arraignments for two planned weeks. Giles had told the clerk to decline all cases for that time. Giles's two-week hiatus was partly due to his health. Still, he was mostly preoccupied with planning the gala weekend in Normandy. Our Chambers Clerk was not too pleased, since he was losing his slice of Giles's fees.

Since we had two weeks with nothing on our schedule, Susan and I decided to engage in some Sunday skiving on our own. We accepted the invitation of Sister Thomas, the headmistress of Nancy's school, Sainte Teresa Academy, to participate in a casual hike she would lead through the Hampshire countryside. Susan, Nancy, and I arrived at the school at 9:00 am. There were hints that Sister Thomas's walk was not a stroll in the park. There were no other parents or students in our group. Did they know something we didn't? The only other person in the troop of five was Sister Thomas's nephew, Alden. Sister Thomas announced the hike would be about ten miles, mostly on dedicated footpaths, with a stop midway at a pub. That part sounded good, although the 35-degree temperature with snowflakes drifting by gave us pause. It was tempting to bail out, but the dread of being thought of as wimpy Americans deterred us. Sister Thomas handed each of us a bundle of thin poles with little red flags attached, which she said would be useful for marking the footpaths.

We hadn't grasped the near-sacredness of footpaths in England until Sister Thomas explained their history over pints of Best Bitter and fish and chips at our pub stopover. Unlike the dedicated bike paths in America, the vast majority of footpaths that crisscross England like a spider's web are not owned or maintained by the local government. They are technically owned by the landowners whose property they cross. Although the landowners hold title to the footpaths, they cannot exclude the public from using them. The common people have been walking the footpaths for hundreds, if not thousands, of years. They had no choice. Public roads and byways were rare and widely separated. A few aristocratic landowners owned huge swaths of land, and unless ordinary people took shortcuts across the gentry's estates, they would have to walk dozens of extra miles to get into town. Continuous use of the paths over the centuries had transformed them into public rights-of-way, which had taken on a revered quality. When Margaret Thatcher was Prime Minister, the British Secret Service did its best to close a public footpath that ran through Mrs. Thatcher's country estate. The public was outraged when barriers were erected on the footpath. The government backed down.

Sometimes farmers try to eliminate the footpaths through their fields by plowing them under and disguising them. Footpaths that go unused for over a year are considered abandoned, and the public easement is lost. Such efforts are thwarted by the Ramblers, a tenacious group of hikers who are dedicated to preventing the abandonment of footpaths. They hike every known footpath in England once every year and mark the route with red stakes to prove they were there. Even randy bulls roaming near the footpaths do not deter ramblers. We three Americans became official ramblers by helping Sister Thomas place our red flags along some of the footpaths we traversed. She gave each of us a Rambler pin, made from enameled metal with red petals against four green leaves that point north, south, east, and west.

We earned our pins. The paths we followed were often layered with varying depths of mud. Sometimes, the worst mud could be avoided by walking on a grass berm. Mainly, we just slogged along. Giving credit where credit is due, however, I admit that I prefer English mud to Ohio mud. Ohio is rich in clay soil, which, when wet, is thick, lumpy, and sticky. It clings to boots like superglue, so that in a short time, one is hiking in heavy clumps of mud rather than boots. Southern England's soil is mostly loam or chalky, which includes a generous amount of sand and/or chalk, and which retains less water. English mud may coat one's boots with a thin glaze, but does not accumulate on them.

Over the years, Sister Thomas had hiked the length and breadth of England, so the mud we encountered was a mere inconvenience to her, if that. At one point, the path led down a slope which Nancy described as a bobsled run. We negotiated it by clinging to the trees on either side of the path. After an hour on the trail, we came to a dead end at a barbed-wire fence. There was a stile over the fence, and the field beyond the fence was covered in oats. Sister Thomas was not deterred; she led us over the stile and proceeded to march us through the young oat shoots and marked our progress by planting the little red flags every fifty yards. She told us there was a dedicated footpath through the oat field and she was not going to allow some avaricious farmer to claim rights to it.

After a while, we came to another fence and another stile. This time, instead of the field being covered in crops, it was occupied by a meandering herd of cows. Alden, who was serving as our navigator, said the dedicated footpath lay straight across the field. I had been looking at the map periodically, and I was convinced that Alden had taken us the wrong way. I faced a dilemma. Do I wrap myself in the stereotype of a pushy, bossy, carping American, or do I play the gracious visitor to a foreign country and march off through a field occupied with roaming bovines? I chose the latter, and we endured the consequences.

A person who has not trekked across a glutinous field that has been churned up and defecated on by hundreds of cows has not lived a full life. I tried to find firmer places for my feet. Nancy hit a soft spot, and the mud went over the top of her boot. There is a good reason British hikers wear Wellington boots, which stop just short of the knee. When we finally tiptoed our way across the field, Sister Thomas realized we had made a wrong turn. We had to thread our way along a fence line to avoid a deep mud hole. Susan slipped and buried her boot so deeply that she was lucky she could pull it out. With no stile in sight to climb over, we slithered under a barbed-wire fence only to be blocked by a wide brook. I was prepared to confront the indomitable nun if she suggested we remove our boots and ford the stream. It was not necessary. We walked along the stream until we reached a road that Sister Thomas recognized, which led us to the welcoming King's Arms pub. If travel is supposed to take you out of your comfort zone, Sister Thomas's hike certainly avoided any comforts. Nevertheless, we were all happy to have a hot meal and the satisfaction of surviving a Sister Thomas hike.

After the rigor of our cross-country trek, I was ready to experience what is considered one of England's most civilized activities. I cannot honestly say that seeing a live cricket match was ever on my "bucket list." Nevertheless, with time to kill and with what is considered the World Series of Cricket just a short train ride away, I thought my British immersion would be lacking if I did not attend at least one cricket match. The game was a "Test" match between New Zealand and Great Britain. It was taking place on the sacred terrain of "Lord's Cricket Ground: The Home of Cricket" in London. At first, I thought it would be impossible to get a ticket to the match, even at scalper prices, since the stadium only seats 30,000 spectators. Not so. Hundreds of thousands have an opportunity to watch parts of the match because the contest is spread out over five full days, minus breaks for lunch and tea, of course. Fans may choose to attend only one day, and often they show up for only a couple of hours, which makes their seats available for the next fan. Rarely are all 30,000 seats occupied. I decided I would go on the second day of the match.

I arrived at Lord's before the game was scheduled to start. I assumed the crowd would be spread out over the course of the day, and I would have no problem getting a seat. I was shocked to see a line of would-be ticket buyers stretching for blocks. My first instinct was to turn around, go to one of London's many museums, and forgo watching a game in which I had only marginal interest. My second thought was that this would be my only chance to see a professional cricket match. My third thought was that this was an opportunity to experience an undeniably British phenomenon—queuing up. The Brits are willing to stand patiently in long lines to attend a concert, see a play, cheer for a team, buy fresh bread, or even board a bus. The single-file queue before me, though, seemed to stretch endlessly. I began near the stadium and walked along the line. After every block, I assumed the end of the line had to be close, but instead, it would extend for another block.

I finally joined the queue, thinking I must surely be the last person in line, yet scores of people filed in behind me. I also wrongly expected that the people standing in line would be grouchy. I know I was feeling crabby. However, I was unable to sustain my crankiness when surrounded by my comrades in line. They were uncomplaining, cheerful, and exchanged witticisms about their situation. One quipped that it was a good thing it was cricket and not a football game, because one could arrive hours late and not have missed much. My line-sharing companion told me that more people wanted to see this game because Allister Cook was on the verge of breaking the record for scoring the most runs on the fewest pitches. The previous day, Allister had batted the entire day, and the Kiwis could not get him out.

As the line snaked its way toward the ticket booths, we were cheerfully greeted by a man or a woman every fifty yards who was hired by Lord's Cricket Grounds to keep the folks in line happy. They would inform the queuers how much longer it would be before they would arrive at the ticket booth. Unfortunately, they were like airline pilots assuring the passengers that the plane would be leaving the gate in just a few minutes. The greeters may have also been working at night in comedy clubs. They never missed an opportunity to tell a joke or utter a witty quip to jolly up the crowd.

When I finally arrived at the ticket booths, I was annoyed to find there were only six booths available to admit up to 30,000 fans. The line would have moved three times as fast if a few of the greeters had been employed selling tickets instead. The seating was general admission, so I chose a seat in the outfield stands. I had no choice. On a cricket pitch, the entire playing field is considered outfield. The man next to me knew somehow that I was an American and immediately struck up a conversation. He was a dairy farmer from New Zealand, and he had traveled halfway around the world to see this Test match. Having some experience on a dairy farm, I asked Eion how he could find the time to travel when cows must be milked twice a day. When he began his answer by telling me he had a herd of 1500 dairy cows, I was sure he was having me on. Eion described how the New Zealand climate is perfect for growing grass, and his cows are all grass-fed, being moved every day into a new field. The grass grows back in 10 days, so the cows can return to the first field, which had been nicely manured by 1500 cows. Nearly all his milk is converted to dry milk powder and sold to China. His cows produce enough milk powder for the Chinese market in six months, so the cows earn a six-month vacation every year.

Eion did his best to explain the game of cricket to me, which was only partially successful. The game can best be summed up by the phrase, "Protect your wicket at all costs," even if it means being hit by a ball traveling eighty miles an hour. The wicket comprises three sticks stuck in the ground six inches apart with a wooden dowel precariously perched on top of them. The bowler/pitcher tries to knock off the dowel by hitting it with the cricket ball. The task is made more difficult by the requirement that the ball must bounce first. The batsman is armed with a three-foot-long cricket bat made of willow with a handle connected to a wide, flat board. It reminded me of the paddle the nuns used on recalcitrant boys. The batsman protects his wicket by swatting away the balls hurled by the bowler. The well-padded batsman can even let the ball hit him, but risks the umpire ruling him "out" and guilty of an LBW, a "leg before wicket," meaning the pitched ball would have hit the wicket if the batsman had not blocked it with his leg.

Runs are scored depending on how well the batsman is at swatting the ball away from the wicket. A batter in baseball who hits an easy, sure-out grounder to the second baseman must try to run to first base and be thrown out. In contrast, if a batsman squibs an easy bouncer to an infielder, the batsman can choose not to run. If he does not run, he cannot be thrown out, and he gets to continue batting with the hope he might do better on the next pitch. The odds favor a batsman in hitting a ball that cannot be fielded by an opponent's infielder or outfielder. The cricket pitch is four times the size of a baseball field. There are only nine players to cover the entire pitch, so even the weakest squib will elude the fielders, enabling the batsman to get the equivalent of at least a single in baseball. If the ball is hit a bit harder, it can easily roll all the way to the surrounding wall, which is the equivalent of a home run in baseball and earns four runs. If the ball is hit over the wall, a two-run bonus is added on; it's called hitting for six. When that happens, the batsman need not run at all, which is good for him because he has so much protective gear on his body he looks like the Pillsbury Doughboy. I then understood why the programs we were handed when we entered the stadium had a large '4' on one side and a '6' on the opposite side. We were supposed to hold up the appropriate number whenever a batsman hit a four or a six.

Good batsmen try to hit grounders and not fly balls. If a

fielder catches the ball before it hits the ground, the batsman is called out. All nine members of the team take a turn at bat. Only when the umpire has called each batsman out is the inning over, and the opposing team gets its turn to bat.

Cricket might be the last professional sport in which the tradition of politeness and good sportsmanship reigns. Other than holding up a '4' or '6,' there are no rowdy cheering demonstrations from the fans. There may be polite applause for a well-hit ball with the occasional comment of "Good show" or "Well struck." As a testament to tradition, many of the fielders wear straw boater hats.

As one might expect, a team can rack up a heap of runs during an inning. Allister Cook was still batting when I got to my seat. He scored 150 runs before flying out to an outfielder who made a diving catch. Sadly, he did not break the record. Happily for England, the team was ahead by 260 runs by that point.

Then, a very strange thing happened. The last four batters for England made no attempt to protect their wickets, and the New Zealand bowler knocked off the dowel on the first pitch, getting four quick outs. I was mystified and asked my New Zealand friend why England hadn't tried to rack up more runs before New Zealand's turn to bat. Eion explained that although cricket matches seem interminable and can last for days, there is a limit. This Test match was scheduled to last five days, and it had to be completed by 6:00 pm on the fifth day. "So?" I said, "If England is ahead when time is called, England wins the match. Isn't it a good strategy for the English team to score as many runs as they can so New Zealand has almost no chance of catching up when "Time" is called?"

Eion said the rule was that if New Zealand were still batting at 6:00 pm on the fifth day of the match, the umpire would rule the game ended in a tie, regardless of how many runs England was ahead at that point in time. The New Zealand team was entitled to its full turn at bat, with each team member having a chance to bat. It would not be fair, "cricket," if New Zealand were denied the opportunity to catch up because "Time" was called. Eion proclaimed this rule as if it had been a provision of Magna Carta, signed in 1215 AD.

Now, it made sense for England not to run up the score. To do so would mean the English team would have less time to get all the New Zealand batsmen out during their turn at bat before the stadium clock struck six o'clock. The English coach was trying to strike a delicate balance: score enough runs that it was unlikely New Zealand could catch up during its turn at bat, but not so many runs that New Zealand would still be batting when time ran out, and the game declared a tie.

When I left the stadium, I speculated about whether I would ever want to attend another cricket match. The answer was, "No." It is too dull. Most of the time, nothing is happening except the bowler is walking back twenty yards, preparing for his run-up to deliver the next pitch. Then he rearranges the fielders to their best positions for the pitch he is planning to deliver. Much of the time, there is not much excitement when the bowler bowls. The batsman may just tip the ball enough to keep it from hitting the wicket and squib it to an infielder, and the batsman makes no attempt to run, knowing he will be thrown out. Then, setting the scene for the next pitch starts all over again. The subdued response of the fans when a batsman hits a four or a six may be because the game has put them into a state of somnolence.

Susan's and my next skiving excursion was a stroll on the footpath along the River Itchen. The river is fast-flowing and crystal clear because it runs over and through a vast stratum of chalk. Hundreds of years ago, it was artificially divided into multiple branches, creating acres of water meadows and waterpower for dozens of mills. The Itchen teems with brown and rainbow trout and is considered one of the best trout streams in England. We strolled around a sharp bend in the river and startled a man fly-fishing. I introduced Susan and me. He said his name was Peter, but did not tell us his surname. He seemed relieved we were Americans, which was odd. Like anglers everywhere, Peter loved to talk about fishing. He bragged about how he had taken trout as big as twenty pounds out of the Itchen and showed us a brown trout from his creel that must have weighed at least ten pounds. Susan asked why he was the only fisherman we encountered on the river when the river is an angler's paradise. There was a long pause before Peter responded to Susan's question, as if he were unsure whether he should tell us how he just happened to be the only person fishing in the Itchen that day. Peter must have decided we were trustworthy and began his tale with a history lesson.

Like many history lessons in England, the tale of the fish begins with the Magna Carta in 1215, when King John cut a deal with the rebellious barons to keep them from removing him as king. Among many other concessions, King John confirmed their ownership rights to all the streams and rivers that ran through their estates, and all the fish in them. As of 1994, our fishing friend claimed that 97% of the freshwater fishing grounds were still controlled by modern land barons who used their ancient privileges to increase their already substantial incomes. Landowners were happy to rent a small patch of their river shoreline to eager trout fishermen for £200 a day. Of course, that meant only the wealthy could afford the pleasure of catching a few trout at a cost of approximately £50 apiece. Adding a bit of gallows humor, Peter admitted penalties for poaching fish had become less draconian. A few hundred years ago, he could have been hanged for catching a baron's fish. Today, he would only be fined £1000.

Peter did not believe me when I described how, back home in Ohio, an angler could slide into his waders or climb into a boat and meander along Ohio rivers, fishing wherever he wanted. An Ohio fisherman even had the legal right to cast his fly upon the water while standing on privately owned riverbanks. It was our turn to be unbelievers when Peter said he was not sure he liked the American open fishing scheme. On the restricted Itchen, Peter did not have to compete with dozens of other fishermen, all trying to cast their flies into the best spots for finding trout. The hefty fines deterred most British anglers from "guesting," fishing on private property without a permit. Besides, he said, "Poached trout tastes better."

Another surprise awaited us around the next bend in the river. Two women were swimming downstream. One of them was towing a rubber ducky on a string. I knew the English ethos was to "keep oneself to oneself," and to ignore, or pretend to, the most eccentric behavior as long as it did not pose a danger to anyone, but in this case, I had to play the nosey American. I hailed the duo. They swam over to where we were standing on the riverbank and stood up in the four-foot shallows. We introduced ourselves, needlessly adding that we were Americans. They told us they were sisters, Heather and Miriam. The tableau was improbable and also comedic. Susan and I were perched on a riverbank in sweaters and windbreakers, chatting with two "proper" middle-aged ladies in swimsuits who stood in water up to their necks, which they said was 55 degrees Fahrenheit, almost exactly the outside temperature and over 40 degrees colder than their natural body temperatures. Susan asked how they knew the water temperature. Heather pulled over the rubber ducky and showed us the thermometer attached to it. Miriam said they tried to swim in the Itchen every day of the year, but they were not bonkers. If the ducky told them the water was 50 degrees or colder, they would have tea and scones at the St. George Tea Shop instead. My parting words were, "Keep warm and carry on."

TWENTY-TWO
Normandy Dash

The only involvement I had in organizing Giles's Normandy gala was securing his car-top carrier to the roof of his Citroën. He usually used the carrier to haul back to England a carload of food and wine from the Hypermarket in Cherbourg. This time, he wanted to convey his vintage wine in the other direction. He phoned me to lend a hand. It was obvious at the outset that he could not remember how to fasten the carrier's clamps to the roof, and Giles had lost the written instructions. As I began examining the clamps' locking mechanisms, Giles constantly interrupted my attempt to diagnose the problem with suggestions. I told Giles, "Go pack your suitcase, and don't forget your velvet dressing gown."

I enjoyed solving mechanical problems, but I couldn't do it with someone watching over my shoulder, especially when the onlooker was dropping sporadic tidbits of advice. It was doubly annoying that the helpful hints were proposed by the very same person who was incapable of solving the problem in the first place. With Giles banished, I sat down and quietly examined the four clamps. I noted they were identical, so that told me they would all fasten on the roof with the same locking mechanism. Many people at that point would place the carrier on the roof and use trial and error, hoping to discover the correct way to fasten the locks. I was not going to tinker with trying possible remedies, then assume I had found a solution, and risk Giles's wines smashing on the road to Portsmouth. I wanted to understand the theory or the principles behind the latches that made them work. Once I gained that insight, I could eliminate the solutions that were not compatible with the underlying mechanical principles. I was confident I had found the right solution when the lock latched in a way that was compatible with its design. When Giles returned with a case of expensive red wines, the carrier was ready. I did not expect praise or thanks from him, and I did not receive any. In his mind, if the problem was solvable so quickly, it must not have been that difficult. Lavishing praise would be tacky.

Giles and Dana collected Susan and me at 9:30 pm for the 11:15 pm ferry out of Portsmouth. Nancy was spending the weekend with our neighbor, Ann. Giles was actually prompt, and we had ample time to catch the ferry. This was just the first surprise in a weekend stuffed with surprises. Susan whispered to me a one-word explanation, "Dana."

The ferry was the "Normandie", a Brittany Line ferry. Although the ferry landed at Caen, and not Cherbourg, which meant an additional hour of driving, Giles said the French had nicer ships.

I could not say the accommodations were noticeably better than those on the British ferries. The room seemed smaller. When we dropped the berths down, there was not much room to move.

We took turns in the bathroom, with Dana being first. She came out after a couple of minutes and declared that the water would not drain from the sink. This led to another example of how Giles's problem-solving differed from mine. While I pulled out my trusty Swiss Army knife, Giles left to talk to the steward.

When Giles returned, I proudly declared that I had solved the problem; the sink was draining. Giles smiled and held up two sets of keys. As I was grubbing around in the sink, Giles was appealing to French chivalry. He told the steward, in French, that we could not stay in the cabin because the sink was not working, and this was an intolerable situation. "Les Dames Doivent Laver," the ladies need to wash. Suddenly, Susan and I had our own cabin, as did Giles and Dana. Giles did not bother to tell the steward I had fixed the drain.

The English Channel was unusually tranquil, and we had just enough motion to rock us to sleep. The soft rumble of the engine was as soothing as a lullaby. The Normandie docked in Caen at 8:00 am, and somehow Giles had managed to place his car in a spot that enabled us to be one of the first vehicles off the ferry. Giles's villa is located between the villages of Ravenoville and Saint Marcouf, about an hour and a half drive from Caen. The Maison Magnifique looked unchanged since our last visit. Built in 1740, the main house was framed by smaller stone buildings that enclose a large courtyard. The fireplaces in the salon and the dining room had long logs blazing away and were big enough that a man could walk into one without bumping his head.

There were six bedrooms, each with its own *salle de bain*. Ours featured a four-poster, king-sized canopy bed and had arched windows that looked out on the courtyard.

As was typical of life in the fast lane with Giles, we barely had time to deposit our suitcases in our bedroom before Giles was organizing an excursion. All the other guests had previously arrived and were eager to follow his lead. He was running on pure adrenaline and gave no hint of how ill I knew he was. I did manage to wolf down a couple of croissants before we were whisked away in a caravan of cars on the road to St. Vaast le Hougue, a small port city at the northeast corner of Normandy.

The Saturday Market in La Hougue bustled with energy and shoppers. One of Giles's guests, Graham, was more eager than most. He discovered a wine shop that sold excellent wines at half price. They had been marked down because the labels were unreadable or partially torn. Graham considered himself a connoisseur of wine and seemed to know which wines to buy without needing to consult the owner of the shop. He filled two cases with a variety of wines.

While Giles was off buying oysters, we were looking for a suitable restaurant for lunch. Susan thought the place Giles had suggested was too smoky, so the eight of us settled in at the restaurant next door, La Marina. The restaurant offered a three-course meal for only eighty-five francs, equivalent to approximately $12.00. Graham wanted to impress us, so he purchased four bottles of wine for $25 each. The food, in my mind, was excellent, and the connoisseurs in our group agreed. We spent an hour and a half at the table. The maître d' took a liking to Susan. He teased her about wanting chocolate ice cream or vanilla ice cream with chocolate sauce. He did not understand that they were equivalent. He did not know Susan. It was chocolate she craved and would settle for it no matter how it was packaged.

The maître d's appreciation of Susan was not extended to the Brits at the table. The lunch got off to a rocky start when Graham knocked over a bottle of wine. He saved most of the wine, but a glass was shattered. While the waiter was cleaning up the mess, the restaurant owner came over to our table and quipped in English, "Good beginning," which I thought rather funny. The Brits assumed it was typical French rudeness. The atmosphere around the table turned loud, ugly, and insulting toward the French. I was mortified and wanted to crawl under the table. What disappointed me most was Giles's joining in the slander. I knew, and the Brits knew, the waiters and the maître d' spoke flawless English. It was inevitable that, as the wine bottles were emptied, the Brits would resort to shouting, "We won the war!" which they considered the ultimate insult to the French. Graham loudly accused the French of being cowards for surrendering to the Germans before putting up any kind of fight. They were talking about World War II, a war that had ended fifty years before. I was the coward at the table, though. I did not speak up and point out how much the French people had suffered under Nazi occupation, and that the Americans, Canadians, and Russians could claim they had rescued Britain and won the war. The final petty insult was Giles telling everyone who had a bill from the restaurant not to leave a tip.

Rather than returning to the château, Giles drove Susan and me, along with his friends, Michael and Troi, to the D-Day Museum on Utah Beach. I am not sure if Michael was interested in the museum. He suggested to Sally, his fiancée, that they might indulge in an afternoon nap. Michael was known for his persuasive powers with juries, but Troi rebuffed the invitation. "Not today, dear, I have an urgent desire to examine German machine gun bunkers."

The museum was built on top of a German blockhouse, so we could squeeze ourselves into a machine gun post and get a Wehrmacht soldier's perspective of the D-Day invasion. It was easy to imagine the thoughts going through the machine gunner's mind as he watched thousands of troops landing in Higgins boats and crossing the beach right toward him. At the same time, shells from battleships, cruisers, and destroyers would be bursting all around the bunker, raising clouds of concrete dust and causing cracks to appear in the bunker's walls. I was surprised at the limited view of the beach the machine gunner would have had. In movies about D-Day, the scenes from the German perspective are often filmed with a wide-angle lens, capturing what was happening on a thousand yards of beach. Maybe it was less frightening for a German soldier not to have a wide-angle view of the assault. The gunner's view was limited to the part of the beach directly in front of the blockhouse, with an opening in the wall just big enough to allow the machine gunner to swivel his M-60 back and forth, spraying the GIs struggling up the beach in his line of sight with a fusillade of bullets. He was not able to see the GIs who were scrambling closer to the blockhouse where they could use their hand grenades and dreaded flamethrowers.

I tried to get inside the mind of that German machine gunner. Was he terrified? How did he cope with his terror? As a human being, he must have feared death. Was he imagining a horrible end? His intensive training may have contributed to his continued ability to aim and fire his weapon. I doubted he would feel any empathy for the American soldiers he killed. He may have been robotic, loading, shooting in short bursts, and not aiming so much at individual soldiers as having his bullets sweep about a foot above the ground, hitting any American soldiers who dared to peep over the sand dune.

In addition to the training, the machine gunner may have developed a philosophy about his death that made the prospect of his dying less terrifying, allowing him to keep his finger on the trigger. He may have lived as a soldier on the front line, thinking of himself as already dead and believing he had no hope of surviving the war. If he had no prospect of a tomorrow, today was the only thing that mattered to him. He could almost cherish that one day. His fear could be kept at bay by this psychological trick as long as hope did not creep into his subconscious. Would the worm of hope have burrowed its way into the mind of the machine gunner? Not hope that the German army had any chance of winning the war, but hope that he could surrender to the Americans and exchange an uncertain future of suffering and death for the safety and the certainty of a prisoner-of-war camp.

Such hope must have been in the minds of the *Ostlegionen* units defending the Utah and Omaha beaches. They were made up of soldiers from the Soviet Union and Ukraine who were forced to fight for the Germans. Their alternatives were a quick death by the Einsatzgruppen, Nazi death squads, or slow death by disease and starvation in a German prisoner-of-war (POW) work camp. They had no desire to die for Adolf Hitler, but surrendering is not an easy thing to do. If a machine gunner who was hoping to be taken prisoner left his M-60 too soon, he would be shot by his German sergeant. If he waited too long, he would be roasted alive by a flamethrower. Even assuming he could manage to escape the bunker and throw up his hands in surrender, there was no assurance the Americans would be in a mood for taking prisoners. Those GIs had just seen their buddies mowed down by the gunners in that bunker, and they would be in the throes of battle frenzy. Would their urge for revenge be suddenly curbed by a touch of mercy?

I was glad to escape that bunker and my somber thoughts. It was a relief when the next exhibit was a toy that I could play with. The device was not meant as a source of amusement on D-Day, though. It was a German rangefinder that was used to target American ships and soldiers as they came ashore. It was tube-shaped, ten feet long, and six inches in diameter, with lots of wires stuffed inside. At each end of the tube, there was a telescope. The instructions told me to look through the goggle-like eyepiece, aim one of the telescopes at some distant object, and then aim the second telescope at the same object. I chose a large buoy marking the shipping channel. I had no idea how far away it was from me. Each telescope was connected to a compass. Because the two telescopes were ten feet apart, each telescope had a slightly different compass bearing for the buoy. Measuring the different bearing between the two telescopes told me how far the buoy was from me—in this case, 3,234 meters. Then the penny dropped. This device was no different than the system I used when navigating a Morgan 44 sailboat in the Virgin Islands. It just had an inverted purpose. When surrounded by islands and reefs, I wanted to know my exact position on the nautical chart. I did that by pointing my compass at a known site, such as a lighthouse, and recording how many degrees it was off my starboard bow, say 15° east. I would do the same thing for a known site off my port bow, like a radio tower, maybe 25° west. I would draw a line on my nautical chart from the lighthouse at 15° east of true north and another from the radio tower at 25° west. Where the two lines crossed showed me exactly where my boat was on the chart.

In contrast, the operator of the range finder knew exactly where he was, in a concrete bunker, and the crossed lines created by the two telescopes told him the location of the intended target. The German operator also had an advantage over me on my boat because the range finder did the mathematical calculations. Of course, when I did my calculations in the Virgin Islands, I did not have shells from battleships landing all around me. The target's coordinates, spat out by the range finder, were then communicated by phone to the commander of a German battery, who adjusted his 210 millimeter cannons to drop their shells on that location.

After Giles collected us, we returned to the château, and preparations were already underway for the dinner/feast. We did not do much beyond setting out the Spode dinnerware, the silver place settings, and the crystal. Giles's friend, Ellie, was happy to do the cooking. She preferred not to have other guests trying to help in the kitchen and being in the way. Ellie had once been a chef at a Michelin restaurant and had even served members of the royal family.

I am sure someone more of a gourmand than I am could describe the numerous courses Ellie prepared in delicious detail, but I was much more interested in the people sitting around the table than the food on it. I was impressed by the amount of work Ellie put into preparing the dinner and by the sheer volume of food that was served. As for its taste, it was darn good.

We started with raw oysters, which Susan and I tried to avoid without being noticed. There is something about oyster aficionados who are disdainful of people who do not like raw oysters. They were followed by beef bouillabaisse, fish pie, potatoes, broccoli, and a dish of smashed carrots and parsnips, and finally, salad. For dessert, there were cheeses and a trifle—a brandy-soaked, layered sponge cake with fresh fruit, smothered in double cream.

The bottles of wine we had smuggled into France from Giles's vintage collection made their appearance, but four of them had their labels removed. Instead, they had been marked with white letters, "A" through "D." Giles planned to test Graham's self-proclaimed wine expertise and his ability to identify wines from tasting them. After chewing on a baguette, Graham said he was ready for the test.

The wine from bottle "A" was a red, so Graham said he would want it poured into a Bordeaux wine glass. It had a tall, broad bowl with straight, tapered sides. Showing off a bit, Graham explained why the choice of the glass was important for tasting wine. The opening of the Bordeaux glass is narrower than the bowl, allowing it to capture and enhance the wine's aroma. The wide bowl facilitates swirling, which increases aeration for better flavor. Finally, he said the elongated stem prevented body heat in his hand from artificially raising the temperature of the wine. Giles poured the wine into the glass. Graham first swirled it around and held it up to the light to check its color. He then put his nose to the glass and gave the wine an aristocratic sniff. Finally, Graham took a sip, swished it around in his mouth, and spat it out into another glass. That seemed rude to me, but I later learned that spitting out the wine made it easier to feel the wine on the palate and assess the important aftertaste.

Graham was skilled at putting on a show. He claimed he felt bad about spitting out the wine because it was an excellent vintage. He first declared the wine to be a Bordeaux from the Cabernet Sauvignon grape, aged for over forty years, since all traces of tannin had vanished. He said that was a good clue, as there are very few Bordeaux wines that could sit in the bottle for over forty years and still be as smooth as the wine he just tasted. The definitive clue for Graham, however, was the fact that Giles was a wine snob and wanted to show off owning a forty-year-old bottle of Château Lafite Rothschild. Everyone agreed Graham was spot-on about both the wine and Giles's snobbishness.

Graham did not fare as well with bottles B and C. He mistook a Dampt Frères Chablis in bottle B for a Coste Rousse Chardonnay. His guess on bottle "C" was even further off, confusing a Château Montrose with a La Fleur-Pétrus. This was surprising to Ellie, who told us the Le Fleur-Pétrus wine is primarily made from Merlot grapes, while Château Montrose is mostly made from Cabernet Sauvignon grapes.

The streaming bubbles in D clearly gave it away as a Champagne, so Graham insisted on tasting it from a Champagne flute. The larger Bordeaux glass would allow too many of the carbonated bubbles to disperse, giving what should be an effervescent wine a flat taste. Graham needed no more than a sip before declaring, "This is too easy. It is a Taittinger." He was right, making his score two for four, which struck me as impressive since I would have struggled to tell fine wine from grape juice.

There were twelve of us sitting around the table watching Graham's performance—ten adults and two teenagers. Susan and I were the only two adults who had not been divorced. If a TV producer were gathering a cast of eccentric characters for a British sitcom, our presence added a touch of boring normality. In this group, we were the equivalent of beige wallpaper.

No one seemed to notice the pervasive, haunting presence of the thirteenth being lingering in the corner of the room, the Specter of Death. Everyone around the table knew, or suspected, that Giles was very ill and that this would likely be the last banquet he would ever host. Not one word was uttered about the state of Giles's health. Even the usual pleasantries like "How are you?" and "What are you up to?" were absent from the conversations. I imagined *Death* to be amused, or at the very least, annoyed at being ignored.

The congenial atmosphere was a model for dinner parties. It was a combination of general discussion among the group on topics about which everyone at the table had an opinion, including us Americans. Giles was the perfect host, introducing interesting topics, like "Should the former Soviet Eastern European countries be admitted to the European Union?" After introducing a topic, Giles would skillfully manage the discussion by gently curbing the more loquacious folks and encouraging the more reticent diners to offer their views. Remarkably, he was even able to elicit comments from Ellie's teenage daughters. In addition to the general topics discussed, there were a multitude of Giles stories, with various guests reminding everyone of Giles's famous eccentricities and the times his less-than-prudent decisions had resulted in near disasters. It was fundamentally a "roast," and was the closest his friends came to saying he would be missed. They cleverly avoided any trace of pity in their remarks, which Giles would have loathed.

The table-wide discussions did not dominate the discourse. There were numerous opportunities for guests to have more personal conversations with their dinner companions. For me, it was the most fascinating part of the evening. The cast of characters around the table could have just walked off the set of a Merchant-Ivory production[1], and I was able to chat with most of them during the evening.

Dana, of course, was an actor by profession, and I have previously described a few episodes of her acting career and other adventures. During the dinner, she regaled me with the story of how she worked for the British Broadcasting Company and agreed to go undercover at a high-class brothel in London to create a documentary on what life was like for the women. Dana stressed that all the women she met had chosen to work in the brothel. She said before being hired, the women were vetted by the Madam running the brothel and two older courtesans. Applicants for the job were also required to undergo physical examinations by a doctor to ensure they were free of venereal diseases. Women who had previously worked as streetwalkers were automatically disqualified from the position. A part of the interview that surprised Dana was being asked about the books she had read. A woman would be rejected if she were not a reader. She said she had been quizzed about both current and historical events. The Madam explained that their clients were often high officials in government or the business world and preferred a woman with whom they could engage in intelligent conversation, in addition

---

1. A British studio that is known for producing movies and TV shows. Typical Merchant-Ivory productions are often period pieces, set in the 19th or early 20th century, and based on classic novels. They had lavish sets and elaborate costuming with some of the top British actors in the cast.

to creative copulation. At the end of the interview, the Madam emphasized that her brothel set extremely high standards, the pay was equally high, and a doctor was under contract to provide health care to all the women.

Dana was accepted, but she was in the brothel for only a month before the story was leaked. Dana was fired. The producers of the show got cold feet and canceled it. Dana admitted she enjoyed her time at the brothel and began thinking the women were more like social workers than prostitutes. She described the men who visited the brothel as ranging from a friendly neighbor to an Under Secretary of State. Although a few men were interested in kinky sex, most were just looking for uncomplicated sex. Others only wanted comfortable physical closeness and a good listener.

After the story was leaked, a tabloid newspaper offered Dana a generous sum of money to name names. She refused—another reason to admire her, and to think Giles fortunate to count her as a friend. One could say, "He didn't deserve her."

Giles's friend Sandy was one of the original shareholders of the Maison Magnifique timeshare project. Unfortunately, only Sandy's husband's name was on the timeshare agreement. When they divorced, Sandy no longer had a share of the property.

Sandy had tolerated her husband's philandering for many years. Her tolerance was spiced with a bit of revenge. When she learned of his first dalliance, she cut slits in all four tires of his car. After learning about a second affair, Sandy got even by using his toothbrush whenever she cleaned the toilet. Her forbearance, though, did not preserve their marriage. The last of the "other women" was not so easygoing. She insisted that Sandy's husband get a divorce. Susan could not understand why any man would divorce a person like Sandy. She had the kind of classic beauty that induces a little gasp in men when they first see her. Behind her loveliness was a sharp mind and wit wrapped in an engaging personality. I agreed with Susan's assessment, but suggested Sandy might suffer from extroversion excess. She talked constantly at a rapid-fire pace. Her conversation is thoughtful and her stories fascinating, but one is hard-pressed to get one's own oar in the water. I could see a husband, not me, being attracted to a quieter, less opinionated woman who was a more fawning listener.

I did not have a lengthy conversation with Ellie. She was quiet, and her Scottish accent presented a challenge. She had another good reason for her reticence. She was doing her best to hold back a flood of tears. The week before coming to Normandy, Ellie's husband left her and their two teenage girls for a younger woman. Sandy was concerned about the precarious state of Ellie's mental health. So, when a previously invited couple bowed out of Giles's party, Sandy asked Giles if Ellie and her two daughters could be included in the group. Sandy hoped that attending a Giles event would be a welcome distraction for Ellie.

Sandy's remedy seemed to work. Only a person in the depths of despair could consistently maintain a morose mood in the midst of a Giles bash. Ellie also took charge of planning and cooking the entire dinner, which meant she spent Friday night and all day Saturday in the kitchen slicing, dicing, marinating, boiling, frying, and baking.

Ellie was adamant about not allowing anyone else into the kitchen. Most of Ellie's days were in chaos, so being in total control of one aspect of her life was a welcome relief. Cooking put her on the road to restoring her self-confidence. Giles, however, did have the foresight to hire two young French women to assist Ellie in serving the food and keeping the wine glasses full.

I began my chat with Ellie, suggesting it must have required a bottomless reservoir of confidence to cook for the British royal family. Giles had told me that when Queen Elizabeth and Prince Philip were in residence at Holyroodhouse, their palace in Edinburgh, Ellie was often called in to help prepare the meals. Ellie told me she liked cooking for the royals. They were not demanding and consistently expressed their appreciation for the work of the kitchen staff.

Ellie did not think it was a state secret, but she said Prince

Philip's favorite meal was salmon coulibiac, a Russian dish consisting of salmon and seasonings wrapped in puff pastry. Since Prince Philip was an avid fly-fisher, he sometimes supplied the salmon. Ellie said that when he did provide the salmon, he sometimes liked to hang out in the kitchen to watch it being prepared. When I reminded Ellie of how she imposed a complete banishment from the kitchen for us, she laughed, which was good to see. She said the last cook who chased a reigning monarch from the kitchen had his head removed and displayed on a pike atop the castle gate. She added that she was not willing to test whether that tradition had changed.

My first impression of Graham was not favorable due to his over-the-top, boorish behavior in the St Vaast restaurant. As I got to know him better, my opinion improved. He was still loud and boisterous, but he was a large man with a natural booming voice more suited to the deck of a ship than the drawing room. Graham did go out of his way to be helpful. He frequently carried in logs from outside to keep the fire roaring. On Sunday evening, he cooked dinner. Although it was not as elaborate as Ellie's feast, it was tasty. The meat and the vegetables were well-cooked, and there was plenty of every dish to go around.

Graham told me he was fifty-five years old and the owner of five optician shops. He was also one of the few opticians in England who could craft special corrective glasses for patients with challenging sight issues. Ordinarily, he said it would have been highly unlikely that he and Giles would become good friends, or even cross paths. Many years back, however, Graham needed a good barrister. He had been charged with attempting to defraud the National Health Service (NHS), a felony that could, if convicted, result in a prison sentence and the loss of his optician's license. The law Graham allegedly violated was aimed at preventing doctors from charging the NHS for two medical procedures when one procedure should suffice. In Graham's case, he billed the NHS for two pairs of special glasses he sold to the mother of a child with severe eyesight problems. According to

NHS guidelines, an optician is not permitted to provide a second pair of glasses to a patient within six months of supplying the first pair. The child in Graham's case, however, had a general learning disability and was prone to losing or breaking his glasses. Graham's office was over a hundred miles from the child's home, and it took the ophthalmic laboratory two weeks to make the glasses. So, Graham thought it was better for the child to have a spare pair of glasses. The problem for Graham was that he did not request approval from the NHS before providing the second pair of glasses. By the letter of the law, this meant he had fraudulently overbilled the NHS.

The case was tried before a jury, and Giles did what he does so well. He provided the jury with a hook on which to base a verdict of not guilty. During cross-examination, Giles was able to get the investigator from the NHS to agree it was probable that if Graham had sought permission for the second pair of glasses, the NHS would have granted his request.

For his final speech, Giles was on top of his game. His theme was that "Sometimes it is better to ask for forgiveness than for permission." Giles reminded the jury that when Graham had testified, he admitted his failure to ask prior approval for the second set of glasses, and he hoped the NHS would forgive him for his mistake. Giles then argued that Graham not seeking permission for the second pair of glasses was the best possible solution for everyone. The young man with a learning disability received his backup pair of glasses and no longer faced the prospect of going weeks without any glasses. The mother did not need to put her life on hold to make an emergency hundred-mile trip to obtain new glasses for her son. And, the NHS did not expend any more money than they would have if Graham had jumped through the bureaucratic hoops and sought permission to order the second pair of glasses.

The jury returned a verdict of "not guilty."

It is rare for a barrister to become friends with a client. The British system and barrister culture hinder the fostering of such a relationship. Nevertheless, a close friendship did develop between Giles and Graham. Initially, it stemmed from Graham's gratitude to Giles for saving his career, and his thankfulness grew into a form of devotion. Giles was not averse to being touted as a demigod of the Bar, but such adoration could not have been the basis for a true friendship. What appealed to Giles was Graham's enthusiasm for life, his sense of humor, and, most importantly, their common interest in buying and consuming good wine.

Graham was a total wine nut. Acquiring the best wines for Graham was much more than a hobby; it was an addiction. He had built a large wine cellar under his house in Romsey and stocked it with some of the best wines he could find. He haunted estate sales in search of bargains. Once, he purchased the entire contents of a wine cellar from a stately home in Stockbridge. The dusty cellar had not been touched in twenty years. Of course, it contained the kind of vintages that only improved with age.

Learning Graham's history helped to temper my original negative feelings about him. In addition, I had to confess that his ability to identify various flavors in a wine by just tasting it had impressed me. One wine, he said, had a "grassy" taste. Whether it truly did taste a bit like grass or it was the power of suggestion, I had to agree there was a similarity between the flavor of the wine and alfalfa, the only grass I had chewed when I helped bale hay on my Uncle Larry's farm back in Ohio.

On the other hand, I can only tolerate so much wine talk. I was bored when Graham and Giles got into a debate about the detectable tastes, etc., in a bottle of Château La Mission Haut-Brion.

Graham claimed the Haut-Brion's aroma suggested a combination of black cherry, plum, and dark chocolate, while on the palate it offered a velvety smooth texture, firm tannins, and a hint of licorice. Finally, the finish or aftertaste evoked a hint of peppery spice. Giles vigorously maintained there was no chocolate or licorice taste in Haut-Brion because a strong licorice taste would mask any chocolate flavor.

I was surprised at how Graham vigorously contradicted Giles's opinion. Few people are eager to debate Giles when he resorts to his persuasive barrister manner.

The dispute dragged on for ten minutes and reminded me of academic discussions dating back to the 13th century when Thomas Aquinas and other savants argued about "how many angels can dance on the head of a pin," an argument we were still having when I was in the seventh grade. It was a waste of time since there was no way to resolve the issue. A third opinion from another person at the table would be challenged as coming from a person with an obviously flawed palate. Finally, scientific analysis of the wine would prove fruitless. There is no licorice flavoring added to the wine that could not be detected. In fact, if a bottle of an expensive wine were found to include an additive, its value would plummet so much that even the poorest wino could afford it.

Fortunately, I was able to distance myself from the ongoing debate and chat with Graham's wife, Jill. Jill made no attempt to disguise the fact that she was sixty years old and five years older than Graham. Neither did she try to mask her age using facelifts, chin tucks, or applying layers of cosmetics. Giles had opined to Susan, "She could have made more of an effort," but I thought Jill's shunning of make-up showed her inherent self-confidence. She must have been thinking about me because the first topic she touched on was the scene Graham had made in the Saint-Vaast restaurant. Jill said, "I thought you looked uncomfortable, so I wanted to assure you I had a quiet word with Graham later." With the British being masters of understatement, having a "quiet word" with someone did not mean a purred, gentle admonition. I am sure Graham had a flea in his ear when Jill finished her quiet word.

Jill was genuinely fond of Graham. She liked his boyish enthusiasm about life. Acting more maternal than spousal at times, she had to erect guardrails for Graham's fervor. Graham's wine obsession was a good example. Jill did not object to Graham building an elaborate wine cellar and stocking it with vintage wines. It distracted him from engaging in other riskier pursuits like gambling, and he could afford it. What began to test the limits of Jill's tolerance was Graham's fixation on keeping the empty bottles of the wine he consumed as a kind of inventory—reminders of both the pleasant and unpleasant wines he had tasted. Rather than having a quiet word with Graham about his fetish, Jill would simply move the empties from his stockpile to the dustbin each week. Both Jill and Graham had been divorced before finding each other, but they clearly shared many of the qualities needed for a successful marriage.

I had assumed it would be difficult to find anyone with a larger ego than Giles, but Michael, the other barrister in the group, had an ego inflated to the size of a hot-air balloon. Early in the evening, Michael proclaimed he was one of the best barristers in the country. He did not try to season his declaration with a sprinkling of modesty by inserting the word "probably" before "the best." Michael went on to tell us that he sometimes earned as much as £18,000 for a single day's work. Gilding the lily, he described all the houses he had bought, owned, or was planning to buy. His latest purchase was a home that was cantilevered on a cliff overlooking the River Fowey in Devon. The Fowey flows into the English Channel. Michael explained that because of its tidal flow, the Fowey was not comfortably sailable much of the time, so he kept his ocean-cruising Oyster 565 in the harbor of Jersey, a British Channel Island just 14 miles off the coast of France.

It was insufficient for Michael to describe not only his prowess in the courtroom, but he also felt compelled to add that he may also be one of the best-looking barristers in the country. When he made that claim, he nodded toward the beautiful Troi at the other end of the table, who was twenty years younger, and whom he planned to marry when her divorce was finalized the following week.

I assumed Giles's illness had left him too weak to challenge Michael's braggadocio since I couldn't imagine how two such monumental egos could coexist in the same room. With no push-back from anyone at the table, Michael told a story to support his Adonis claim.

Michael said he had defended one of two defendants in a fraud case at London's Old Bailey court. At the end of the case, the jury returned a not guilty verdict for Michael's client and a guilty verdict for the codefendant. Before the jury was dismissed, an attractive woman in the front row of the jury box passed a note to Michael. He wisely did not open the note and took it directly to the judge, who opened it in the presence of all the attorneys in the case. After reading it, the judge told Michael he had better read it. The note said, "Would you be interested in having a drink with me?" and included her name, address, and phone number. Michael did not tell us if he had met the woman for a drink, but I assumed he was keeping us in suspense—a lawyer's trick. The note did spark an objection from the other defending barrister and a motion for a new trial. The judge denied the motion for a new trial, and the note became a basis for an appeal. A diligent reporter for the Daily Mirror must have been keeping track of appeals filed in the Court of Criminal Appeal because the story made the second page of the Daily Mirror, along with a picture of Michael posed in front of the Old Bailey. The lead for the article asked a question: "Did Barrister get a juror's verdict which was more than he could handle?" Michael pretended he was embarrassed by the publicity, but it was clear that the attention of the media confirmed his narcissistic self-image.

During the dinner, I had the opportunity to chat with Michael. He approached me, saying he was interested in hearing about my impressions of the British criminal justice system. He used a good advocate ploy of flattery to open the conversation. "David, Giles tells me you are brilliant." The reality was that Michael had little interest in my views on anything, and it was only a prologue for him to talk about himself. He did not realize he was helping me in my quest to learn as much as possible about the British justice system and the people involved.

I asked Michael what he thought about the future of the barrister profession, given that the government was reducing fees and giving solicitors the right to appear in some courts as advocates. His answer was pure Michael, totally ego-driven. He was not concerned about all the other barristers, especially the young ones, trying to make a living as barristers. Michael said good barristers like him are not threatened by the government's cost-cutting proposals. He would still be in demand. From his lofty perspective, there would be no problem if government policies eliminated the bottom 30% of barristers, the bottom being determined by the fees they were earning. Michael speculated that the pruning would likely increase his bottom line.

I was surprised to discover how little general law a top barrister like Michael knew and how he took pride in his ignorance. He said his expertise was in understanding juries and judges. He was the master of determining what juries wanted and giving it to them. Michael did admit that judges were more difficult to manipulate. As a coda, he added that "grubbing around statutes and case law was a pedestrian occupation."

If ignorance is bliss, Michael did reside in Valhalla. His knowledge of history, philosophy, and current events was less than that of a secondary school student. He said he had expunged from his mind all the unnecessary rubbish he was obliged to learn to pass his "O Level" exams. I felt the need to explain to Michael the difference between "Natural Law" and "Positive Law," something every law student in America would know.

Giles decreed, before dessert was served, that everyone should change their seats like in musical chairs so there would be a chance to converse with new people. As luck would have it, the new person sitting on my left was Troi. Ellie and her two daughters had left the table to help with putting the finishing touches on the desserts and to begin the inevitable cleaning-up process, leaving Troi and me alone at the end of the table.

I was feeling the euphoric effect from consuming too much wine, so I was acting less than tactful when I asked Troi, "I saw you do an eye roll when Michael was telling us about his houses and his yacht." Troi may have had a surfeit of wine, too, when she chuckled and said, "I need to control that if I am to become a good trophy wife when I marry Michael. I must practice my fawning and adoring mannerisms." For me, "trophy wife" was a derogatory term, akin to being a paid escort, and the diplomatic side of me wanted to give Troi the opportunity to back away from her self-condemnation. "Surely, you do not consider yourself a trophy wife."

Troi did not backtrack and said, "I do not know what else you can call me." She then outlined the "arrangement" she planned to have with Michael after their marriage. Troi described it as a business relationship with a bit of sex on the side, which she added had been tolerable up to that point. She understood she would be just another of Michael's showy possessions, like his houses, his yacht, and his Rolex. Troi's role was to play the attentive spouse at parties and events while Michael drummed up future business with solicitors and clients. Troi added that she was good at flirting with potential sources of income, just as she was flirting with me. It was an odd, but effective, ego boost to me. Rather than engage in the game of ambiguous flirting, just tell the man you are intentionally flirting with him.

I was puzzled and could not resist asking, "Why would you choose such a life?" Troi explained the why. She said she was thirty-five years old and had four children under the age of ten. She had no education beyond secondary school and had little prospect of ever being more than an unexceptional, poorly paid dress designer. The husband she was divorcing in a week was an unemployed truck driver with a gambling habit. With Michael, Troi's children could attend the best boarding schools, such as Winchester College, and have a reasonable chance of making the jump to Oxford or Cambridge. As for herself, she would live a luxurious, pampered life with servants to do most of the chores. There would be the bonus of Michael being gone for weeks at a time, trying cases in places like Manchester, Leeds, and Edinburgh. Then Troi winked at me and whispered, "It would be okay with me if Michael had the occasional fling on those trips."

Troi was confident she could hold her own with Michael. She said his inflated ego was also his greatest weakness. By stoking and feeding it, she could get her way—a bit of the fawning, adoring wife act went a long way.

As for Troi's long-term future, she had a realistic and pragmatic perspective. She thought that with proper dieting and long gym sessions, she could maintain the "glitter" for fifteen years. By then, Michael would be 70 years old, and she would be fifty. At that point, Michael might be willing to retire and settle down for the rest of his life. On the other hand, if Michael went on the hunt for another young trophy companion, she would be happy to step aside for the new woman. The divorce settlement would ensure her a comfortable life without the need for a man. If she decided to remarry, Sally said she was confident of attracting a man. She admitted that at fifty years old, she would not be for "All Markets," but would still qualify for the High Street trade and not be forced into the discount shops.

My conversation with Troi may have been one of the best learning experiences of my sabbatical. I discovered that it may be true that "all that glitters is not gold," but sometimes things, and people, who glitter are gold.

After dessert, Calvados, and coffee, it was past midnight, and everyone was more than ready to retire to their rooms. When Susan and I were comfortably ensconced in our canopied bed, we reflected on the evening and the people we met. At the same moment, we said, "What are we doing here?"

On Sunday morning, Giles shuffled into the kitchen looking pale and haggard. The party and the wine had taken their toll. It was not a hangover. I had never seen Giles in that condition. It was his liver surrendering. Yet, everyone treated him as if he had just skipped down the stairs, greeting him with gibes and sarcasm. No one asked about his health or how he was feeling, not even when he told us he was going back to his room for a nap. No hint of pity was offered.

Susan and I were planning a morning stroll, and I had asked Giles for directions to a nearby château that had been the German headquarters until the D-Day bombing onslaught destroyed it. Giles may have been confused, as the directions he gave us were wrong. Still, it turned out to be another Douglas Adams, _Hitchhiker's Guide to the Galaxy_ experience: we did not find the château we were aiming for, but we ended up exactly where we were meant to be.

We saw a sign for the "Batteries de Crisbecq" and walked down a dirt side road. We found the remains of a German bunker that had held three 210 mm guns meant to defend Utah Beach. According to the plaque on the wall, in English, two of the guns had been knocked out by naval gunfire on D-Day, but one continued in action for six days and was credited with sinking two American ships. The battery commander, Walter Ohmsen, was a Nazi fanatic determined to fight to the last man, though the last man might have felt differently. When the Americans broke through the outer defenses and swarmed over the Crisbecq bunker, setting dynamite charges, Ohmsen radioed the nearby German Azeville battery to shell his own position to drive off the Americans. In the end, he got his wish: not one of his company survived.

When we emerged from the Crisbecq bunker, we saw Sandy waving at us from the top of one of the batteries. She had taken Ellie's two daughters on a history-focused field trip to give Ellie a much-needed break. Sandy said there was an undamaged German battery at Azeville, and she would be happy to drive us there.

When we arrived at Battery Azeville, it was closed to visitors. It was a local holiday. Fortunately, the curator for the site was just leaving, and being French, he could not resist four attractive women asking to be allowed to see the inside of the battery. He did better than that. Arnaut offered to lead us on a tour of the battery complex. We descended deep into the depths of the bunker, and many of its cell-like chambers had standing water that we avoided. I looked out the same narrow embrasures the German soldiers used to watch the approaching American GIs, knowing their bunker would soon be encircled with no possible escape. I did not need to imagine what they were thinking; I could feel their fear mixed with excitement, realizing their long, boring occupation of their cold, damp prison would be over one way or the other. The German engineers seemed to have thought of everything to strengthen the battery's defenses. It was built deep underground, covered with yards of concrete, and on the surface painted to resemble an abandoned French farmhouse. The entire landscape surrounding the battery was strewn with anti-tank and anti-personnel mines. M60 machine guns could be aimed in all directions. Should an American soldier manage to get through those obstacles, descending the steps to the bunker would be suicidal, with another M60 placed to fill the stairway with a swarm of bullets. Climbing atop the bunker would not be of any help. The GIs would be safer from the machine guns, but they could not crack open the bunker without demolition charges. Dropping grenades down the stovepipes would be useless. They were designed so that a grenade would bypass the actual flue and fall harmlessly into a pit beneath the bunker.

Another defensive advantage of the Azeville Battery was that it could not be seen from the sea. The gunners on the battleships had to guess its location, so most shells aimed at the battery missed badly. However, what the German engineers gained defensively also impaired the battery's offensive capability. The German gunners could not see the ships they wanted to sink. They were dependent on the spotters near the beach and those at Battery Crisbecq to report the coordinates of the targets, which changed every few seconds since the targeted ships were constantly moving.

Arnaut said it was unfortunate for the Azeville soldiers that the battery was not invisible to Allied spotter planes. While trying to avoid being shot down by the German anti-aircraft guns, they managed to radio the coordinates of the battery to the battleships. Of all the shells fired at Azeville, only two from the USS Iowa hit the bunker. One tore a large chunk off the corner of the structure, and the second shell did not explode. Yet, it caused the deaths of many soldiers in the bunker. The shell screamed through the firing aperture of one of the Azeville guns and blasted out the back wall of the casement. The crew inside the room were killed instantly, the rushing shell sucking all the air out of the room, including the air in human lungs. It then ricocheted around the next room, killing all the soldiers there. We could see where the shell rebounded off two walls, tore through the steel cover of the machine gun window, and bounced up the stairs to the outside. Ironically, the shell was not discovered until a few months before our visit, when it was accidentally discovered by the Azeville battery caretakers while they were digging up the ground to plant a garden.

After we climbed out of the bunker, Arnaut told us the story of the German officer in command of the Azeville battery, Hauptmann Hugo Treiber. If there is such a person as a benign invader of a country, which I doubt, Treiber may have been one. He kept the 170 men in his company on a short leash. They were disciplined if they abused or insulted the village residents. Many of the soldiers were billeted with local residents in barns and homes, and Treiber paid the owners rent. Any food or other goods obtained from the residents had to be paid for. Arnaut was sure Treiber violated army regulations when he invited the residents of the village into his bunkers during Allied bombing raids.

Treiber was not a fanatical Nazi like Ohmsen. Treiber had decided at the beginning of the D-Day invasion not to sacrifice all his men in defense of the battery. His plan was to surrender as soon as the Americans had breached the outer defenses. Treiber and his men defended the battery for days until American

Sherman tanks had skirted the minefields and were within two hundred meters of the bunker. He knew that if the tanks with the flamethrowers got within twenty-five yards, he and his men would be incinerated. Treiber ordered a soldier to wave a white sheet from the top of the blockhouse, and the Americans stopped the attack. Most of his 170 men were still alive. They were happy to surrender to the American GIs, who, immediately after taking the bunker, handed out candy bars and coveted cigarettes to the same German soldiers who, minutes before, were trying their best to kill them. All the captured soldiers survived the war and returned to Germany in 1946.

I knew there was a moral lesson I should have learned from our visit to the battery, but I was not able to decipher it. Standing outside that bunker, imagining myself in the boots of Commander Treiber, my first reaction was to admire Treiber for his generous treatment of the villagers and his humanitarian act of violating his orders and surrendering the battery to preserve the lives of his men. However, upon reflection, I questioned whether those redeeming acts could outweigh his support for the truly evil Nazi regime responsible for the slaughter of millions of people. Was his surrender less a humanitarian act and more a decision to honor his loyalty to his men over his oath to Adolf Hitler? All too often, some people do charitable deeds for individuals and yet support their government's policies, which ruin the lives of thousands of innocent people. How can they live with themselves? Another lesson learned?

When we returned to the château, Giles was much improved and insisted that after lunch, he and Dana would drive us to the château we had been unable to find. Giles would not admit to providing inaccurate directions - he was obviously feeling better. The gravel lane to the house was still bordered by tall plane trees, and the lane itself seemed blocked with weeds and small scrub, which did not deter Giles. He mowed them down in his Citroën like a Sherman tank. The remains of the château were nestled among three pleasure lakes. The large stone barn with a cone-shaped central tower was intact but abandoned. Giles was adamant we should go inside and explore the rooms, claiming it was perfectly safe. He created a game for us to play while we wandered through the château. We tried to guess what the rooms had been used for in the château's heyday.

Giles disparaged the owners of the château, which had been their family's home for several hundred years. He said the owners had been compensated for the damage to the château caused by the Allied bombing. Rather than restore the structure, however, they used the money to purchase a house in Caen, leaving the château in shambles. Giles thought they had committed a fraud. I did not know enough about the terms of the reimbursement contract to say whether the refusal to restore the building constituted fraud. Still, I appreciated their reluctance to rehabilitate the château to its former glory. Assuming the money they received would cover the cost of the restoration, which was doubtful, the cost of maintaining the structure would be a hefty ongoing expense, not to mention the cost of the staff that would be needed if the family chose to live there.

After we visited the German headquarters château, Giles decided to mimic our "Great Croissant Hunt" from my first visit to Normandy. This time, however, it was the "Great Château Hunt." We would search for and explore all the abandoned chateaus within a five-mile radius of Sainte Marcouf, and Susan and I would choose our favorite.

The whole excursion was a blur to me. We must have selected one as our favorite, but I had no recollection of which one. The château I best remember had nothing to do with its design, but instead with our embarrassment. Giles does not get embarrassed, of course. Giles glided the Citroën into the courtyard a few yards from the front door. We were a couple of steps behind Dana when she opened the door, looked in, slammed it shut, and shouted, "Run!" Her urgent tone brooked no debate. The four of us jumped back in the car, and Giles sped off with his wheels spewing a spray of gravel. Once we were back on the road, Dana explained the need for a quick exit. When she looked inside the château, she saw six men sitting around the kitchen table. They were as shocked as she was and roared, *"Qui êtes-vous?"* She knew if one of the men had been the owner, or if the men were squatters, a possible angry confrontation with them would not have ended well for us. Giles teased Dana and assured her he would have been able to diffuse any tension. Susan told me later that Dana had whispered to her in the back seat, "I have seen Giles involved in similar situations. If he adopted his superior barrister manner, it would make the quarrel worse, and those six bulky, strong men had already seemed angry."

Giles decided we had time for more "informative" sightseeing. He first took us to La Cambe, the largest German war cemetery in Normandy, where over 21,000 soldiers are buried. At the entrance gate stood a sign in German, French, and English.

"This is a graveyard for soldiers, not all of whom had chosen either the cause or the fight. They, too, have found rest in our soil of France."

Amazingly, we seemed to be the only visitors in the cemetery. Although the landscaping was well-maintained by the voluntary German War Graves Commission, I saw no flowers placed on the graves by relatives of the fallen. As we walked among the rows, Susan pointed out that there was only one headstone for six soldiers. Giles, who sometimes expressed more empathy for the Germans than he did for the French, said he wanted us to see just the tip of the iceberg of what German society had lost during World War II.

Giles then drove us to the American Cemetery on the bluffs overlooking Omaha Beach, where nearly 10,000 Americans are buried. Each grave is marked with either a cross or a Star of David.

There were hundreds of other visitors to the park, many of whom placed flowers on individual graves. It was sobering to think about all those young lives cut short. I tried to imagine what those American soldiers, as well as the German soldiers, would tell us if we could question them today about their sacrifices. Would they think the cause they fought and died for was worth it? My first instinct was to assume the German soldiers would resent dying for the evil Nazi regime, and the American soldiers would be proud to have died for freedom and democracy. That is the narrative we, the later generations of Americans who benefited from their sacrifices, would like to believe. On more reflection, though, I thought both the American and the German soldiers would say they had died for the same worthy cause, but not the glorious abstract causes which many historians like to eulogize. No, most of the dead soldiers speaking to us would say they risked their lives for the respect and love of their comrades, who were also risking their lives for them. That was a cause worth dying for. The sign over the entrance gate to the German cemetery would have been equally appropriate for the entrance to the American Cemetery.

This is a graveyard for soldiers, not all of whom had chosen either the cause or the fight. They, too, have found rest in our soil of France.

Dinner was a quiet, simple affair. There were only six of us around the table. Graham, Jill, Giles, Dana, Susan, and I. Graham did most of the cooking and, of course, supplied the wine. No one was inclined to suggest to Giles that he should consume less of it. A great deal of the conversation revolved around British history, which Brits never seem to tire of. The topic did enable me to play one of my parlor tricks. Whenever anyone made a reference to a British historical event, I added a footnote with the name of the monarch who was reigning at the time of the event. Early in my career as a law professor, I had memorized all the names of every British monarch from Æthelred the Unready (reigned 978–1016) to the sitting monarch, Queen Elizabeth II. My purpose in committing to memory a seemingly useless list of names and dates was mundane. It was a way to deal with my pesky bouts of insomnia when my brain buzzed with my "things to do list" for the next several weeks. I would start reciting the list in my mind, beginning with dear Æthelred the Unready, and I was usually asleep before I had reached James I, who ascended the throne in 1603. I did not tell my dinner companions why I knew all the monarchs of England and let them believe I knew more British history than I did. They seemed impressed, or at least politely pretended to be.

The next day started early. Giles was determined to pack in all the sightseeing possible before the Caen afternoon ferry sailed for Portsmouth. It soon became clear, however, that Dana would not be coming. The night before, she had tasted the leftover fish pie to see if it could be included with dinner. Dana gave it the okay, but Graham decided that since we had an abundance of other dishes, we did not need the fish pie. One bite was all it took for Dana to develop a disabling case of food poisoning that kept her awake all night. She was over the worst of it by the morning, but thought she should forgo the excursion to Caen.

We formed a two-car convoy with Susan and me riding with Giles in the lead and Graham and Jill following. Our first stop was Bayeux. It was still amazing to see signs in cafés and shops saying, "Welcome to our liberators." I would like to think the signs professed genuine gratitude for the sacrifices the Allied soldiers made fifty years after the event.

Giles's primary reason for stopping in Bayeux was to see the Bayeux Tapestry. Touring the Bayeux Tapestry Museum was a leisurely affair. Ordinarily, the crowds are so large that the visitors must queue up and walk steadily past the tapestry, not daring to stop and examine any interesting details. Since it wasn't the tourist season, we were practically the only visitors to the museum. We could stop and study the characters depicted on the panels and attempt to translate the Latin inscriptions, with Susan being the most adept.

The tapestry is a 280-foot-long embroidery that depicts the events leading up to the Norman Invasion of England in 1066, including the Battle of Hastings, which allowed Duke William of Normandy to claim the English throne as William I—better known as William the Conqueror. It must be the longest piece of propaganda ever produced, intended to justify William's conquest. It portrayed Harold, the Anglo-Saxon king who claimed to be the legitimate King of England, as a duplicitous oath-breaker who deserved the fatal arrow to the eye he took at the Battle of Hastings. The most intriguing question for me—and not answered in the tapestry itself or any of the museum's explanatory literature—was why such a painstaking and expensive project was undertaken in the first place. Was it meant to justify to the largely illiterate people of Normandy why their Duke declared war on a powerful kingdom like England, and more importantly, why their taxes had to rise to pay for the massive castles William was forced to build to safeguard his conquest? The Tower of London, infamous in its own right, was one of them.

After the Bayeux Museum, we drove toward Caen to catch the ferry. We were not pressed for time, but we knew we would need to have lunch somewhere, something no one willingly misses in France. Giles must have been multitasking again, looking for a place to have lunch while driving along the two-lane road at a fast clip. Long ago, I had decided not to look at the speedometer when riding with Giles. I would never dare to ask him to slow down, so knowing the speed only made me nervous. Suddenly, Giles slammed on the brakes, quickly decelerating from whatever speed he was going, and pulled off the side of the road. Graham and Jill, who were following us, were totally surprised by Giles's maneuver. Graham had to slam on his brakes, and he managed to skid onto the side of the road just ahead of the Citroën. Without explanation, Giles jogged off to what appeared to be a café. When he returned, he announced, "This is where we will have lunch." Only then did Giles explain his bizarre behavior. He told us he had seen all the trucks parked along the side of the road and knew there must be a good place to eat nearby. Truck drivers know where to find good, inexpensive meals.

As soon as we entered the café, the owner, André, and Giles began chatting away as if they were old friends. They were speaking French so fast that I was only able to distinguish a few words. I had a sense that Giles was praising the owner for running the kind of place where *camionneurs*—truck drivers—wanted to eat. I also caught the phrase *les Américains*, accompanied by a nod toward Susan and me. Giles was covering all the bases: speaking fluent French, showering the proprietor with compliments, and making sure he knew we were American tourists in Normandy.

André quickly cleared a table for the five of us. I thought it odd that he did not give us a menu. The reason soon became clear: there was only one set menu from which we could order— the Monday menu. If we ate at the café on a Tuesday, we would be offered a different menu. Soon, a four-course meal was placed on our table. We each had a half chicken on our plate, a bowl of green salad to share, and a plate of French fries piled up like the Great Pyramid of Giza. A bottle of wine was included. By American standards, the chicken was scrawny and clearly free range, but it was delicious and covered with a tart green sauce. Dessert was *Tarte Tatin*, a caramelized fruit tart. I had been feeling guilty, sponging all weekend on the generosity of others, so I tried to assuage my guilt by paying for everyone's lunch. The bill did not lessen my guilt much. The total was the equivalent of $60, not much more than if we had had lunch at a McDonald's.

Giles's fluent French and his ability to negotiate did not charm the agent at the Brittany Line ticket counter. As a VIP with the company, he was entitled to discounted tickets, so he insisted on getting us a discount on all our tickets. The agent was equally insistent that Giles was only entitled to the reduced fares if he was traveling with us on the same ferry. I was ready to concede early, but Giles claimed it was a matter of principle. He and his principle lost the round. I dug into my limited supply of cash and paid an additional £70.

We got our money's worth during the return trip to Portsmouth. The English Channel was in a cranky mood, and the ferry was buffeted by waves that sent sheets of spray cascading over the bow. I told Susan that back home at Kings Island Amusement Park, people would be queuing up to have the thrill of a ride like this. Susan was not amused. No amount of attempted humor by me would distract her from her seasickness. I thought I would be sick too, but I soon acquired my sea legs and only had to latch on to something solid once when moving around the passenger deck. After four hours, I noticed a difference in the wave motion. The waves were striking the boat from a different angle and were smaller. I assumed the ferry was in the Solent, the channel between the Isle of Wight and Portsmouth. Thirty minutes later, the ferry docked. Our whirlwind Giles adventure was over, or was it?

The troubled waters of the English Channel delayed the ferry. The weather conditions created a dilemma for the captain of the ferry. If he increased the speed, the rollicking motion of the boat would noticeably intensify, challenging the ability of even the most experienced seafarers to move around the deck, and, most importantly, get to the heads (restrooms). A ferry full of seasick passengers who cannot quickly access a restroom is a recipe for creating the pervasive smell of vomit. If the ferry arrived at the dock a few minutes late, only a few passengers, if any, would be inconvenienced. Hence, the choice was an obvious one to the captain. A thirty-minute delay for us, however, was more than an inconvenience; it meant we would miss the last train from Portsmouth to Winchester at 11:15 pm.

Fortunately, taxis were waiting outside the ferry terminal. Unfortunately, I was woefully short of cash after paying out the additional £70 for the ferry tickets in Caen. Susan and I had only £30 between us. I explained our predicament to the driver, who seemed sympathetic. He offered to drive us to Winchester for £30. He was as good as his word, but I did have a moment of panic halfway to Winchester when the taxi's meter hit £30. Would the driver stop the car and evict us? Instead, he shut off the meter, so it was stuck at £30, and he delivered us safely to our doorstep. I wished I had remembered I had a fifty Franc note in my wallet, which I could have given him as a tip.

TWENTY-THREE
The Last Trial

When Giles returned from Normandy, it was apparent his health had seriously deteriorated. He had pushed himself to the limit and beyond. I suspected he knew the stress and the wine would shorten his life, and I sensed he was okay with that. Giles was not one just to wane away like a fading photograph. He would prefer his end to be like a flash of summer lightning, gone in an instant but leaving a lasting image.

If that was Giles's wish, his last case, defending an alleged blackmailer, gave him the chance to depart the barrister stage of his life in a blaze of glory.

Our client was James Patterson, an eighteen-year-old. The Crown Prosecution Service alleged James and his best friend, Jason Pettigrew, had tried to blackmail an elderly man, Calvin Hobart. The indictment accused them of demanding £6,000 from Hobart, or else James would tell the police, and the world, that Hobart had been having sex with him since he was thirteen years old. It was a persuasive case for the prosecution. James wrote a note to Hobart demanding £6,000, and Jason handed the demand note to Hobart in person. I doubted that James had ever read <u>Treasure Island</u>, but he must have seen the movie because the note was marked with the "Black Spot." Foolishly, James made

286

the black spot with his thumb dipped in ink, creating a perfect thumbprint.

It was no defense to the crime of blackmail that the victim was a vile old man who had started grooming James when he was twelve years old. Hobart encouraged and financed James's obsession with playing arcade games. By the time James was thirteen years old, the price for Hobart giving James money for games and other things like clothes and a bicycle, was yielding himself to Hobart's predatory sexual perversion. James ended his relationship with Hobart when he was seventeen years old.

What troubled me about the case after our conference with our client was that James did not fit the image of a young, innocent lad who was exploited by a dirty old man. James was streetwise and had a hard edge. He admitted to regularly asking Hobart for spending money, which Hobart readily gave him. James was using Hobart as much as Hobart was exploiting him. He was a willing companion. I knew that, as a minor, James could not consent to being a prostitute for Hobart, but I also knew that jurors would not have much sympathy for a young, tough teenage boy who would have been a welcome member of Fagin's gang in Dickens' Oliver Twist.

Ordinarily, I would have been embarrassed when Giles made jokes about the case while the stressed defendant looked on. James, whose life was on the line, must have wondered how serious Giles was about defending him. I knew Giles would give his maximum effort to win the case to prove to himself, the judge, and his fellow barristers that, although his health had deteriorated, he still had all his advocacy skills. James, however, was not the wide-eyed innocent. So, I was not bothered when Giles, after describing the dire straits James was in, laughingly added, "It is a good thing I like uphill battles."

Giles and I discussed the case after James and his solicitor left the conference room. Giles could not represent James's friend, Jason, because of a potential conflict between their defenses. Jason's best defense might be to claim ignorance of what his friend, James, was up to and that he had no idea what was in the envelope James had him deliver to Hobart. Giles could not press that line of defense at the same time he was proclaiming James's innocence.

As soon as we were alone in the conference room, I said, "The defendants were either extraordinarily stupid or extraordinarily innocent." In retrospect, the comment was not particularly insightful, but Giles declared it "Brilliant" and wrote it down immediately.

I thought Giles's line of defense was "Brilliant." There was no way we could extricate James from being the author of the letter and the maker of the thumbprint. Neither could we spin the language of the letter as anything other than a "pay up or suffer the consequences" ultimatum.

The law required the Crown to prove:

James and Jason demanded money from Hobart in return for not revealing compromising or damaging information about Hobart. And that James and Jason knew their actions would unlawfully deprive Hobart of valuable property.

Giles proposed a line of defense: James was not trying to blackmail Hobart so much as naively seeking compensation for the physical and psychological harm he had suffered by being sexually abused by Hobart. He planned to portray James as an ill-informed teenager, molested by a nasty pedophile, who did not realize that his asking Hobart for compensation was "unlawful." The note, in James's mind, was the kind of demand letter a solic-itor would have served on Hobart if James had sought legal coun-sel. The weakness I saw in Giles's defense was that James had been demanding spending money from Hobart for years, and the £6,000 looked less like compensation for harm than, in James's mind, fees for services rendered. Giles dismissed my concern, saying Wesley York, the Crown Prosecutor, would not likely see the flaw and exploit it.

The blackmail case was one of the strangest cases I had ever encountered for several reasons. First, on paper, it was an open-

and-shut case for blackmail; the Crown only needed to prove James wrote the note to Hobart. The second oddity was not that the alleged victim, Hobart, did testify for the Crown, but that the prosecuting barrister, Wesley, was required by Judge Barth to tell the jury the Crown was not vouching for Hobart's honesty and was not asserting that anything Hobart said was true. It was like a prosecuting attorney calling a witness to a robbery and announcing to the jury, "I am not saying that this witness is telling the truth." The third wrinkle was that Giles's condition was getting worse. His energy level and his attention span waxed and waned. I did not know from one moment to the next if I would have to step in and conduct the defense. At times, he was the old Giles, full of vim and vigor with his commanding voice. At other times, he would whisper to me, "David, you have to do this."

The fourth twist in our case was the most onerous to me. Giles objected to the note-taker assigned to our case by James's solicitor. Ordinarily, the solicitor in the case does not attend the actual trial. From the solicitor's perspective, spending days in court would be a waste of time and money. Besides, most barristers, and Giles was certainly one of them, regarded solicitors as useless in the courtroom. Barristers considered solicitors helpful in finding and interviewing potential witnesses and shuffling paperwork, but any suggestions a solicitor might offer on trial tactics were inevitably ignored and were often resented by the barrister. The solicitor, however, does assign a note-taker from the solicitor's office to take copious notes summarizing the important testimony. The notes are not a verbatim transcript of the testimony, but rather a record of the significant and relevant evidence provided by the witnesses. Those notes are important to barristers. Later in the trial, a barrister may need a memory jogger about what witnesses had previously said under oath. For example, if a witness had testified that the getaway car was blue and later said it was red, they could be impeached. "Which statement is true, and which is a lie?" Having a good note-taker was an aspect of the

British trial that I appreciated. In most U.S. trials, lawyers must take their own notes while trying to question a witness. Pausing to scribble a legible note breaks up their cross-examinations, and that gives the witness more time to think of a better answer to their next question.

Our assigned note-taker seemed like he may have recently suffered a stroke. He admitted not having read the case file. Without even passing a familiarity with the case, how was he going to discern what testimony was relevant and important to our defense, and should be written down?

Giles solved the problem by telling the assigned note-taker that I would be taking notes on the case. That was an expedient solution for Giles, dreadful for me. How was I supposed to be ready to jump in and take over the conduct of the case on a moment's notice when I was distracted and concentrating on taking notes? There was an even more fundamental problem. I was an appalling note-taker. I learned in my first year of college that any notes I attempted to take in class were detrimental to my learning. I wrote too slowly. While I was trying to capture what a professor said in writing, I would miss completely the next two paragraphs of her lecture. The curse that justified the death sentence of my note-taking regime was the sad reality that my handwriting was also illegible. I was unable to read my own class notes the next day. Fortunately, on the first day of my note-taking venture, Giles did not ask me to repeat any prior testimony. By the second day, our solicitor had assigned a competent note-taker.

On the first day of trial, Prosecutor Wesley followed the usual prosecution practice of calling Detective Sergeant Wilson, the investigating officer, to testify. In an American courtroom, we are obliged to engage in a ritual dance with the investigating police officer. The Rules of Evidence require the officer to testify without referring to his notes. If, while answering a question, the officer surreptitiously glanced at his notes, defense counsel would indignantly spring to his feet and object: "Hearsay."

Technically, the objection is proper. If the officer is reading from his notebook, it is the notebook that is testifying, not the officer. When the judge sustains the objection, a *pax de deux ballet* commences. The prosecutor asks the officer if he cannot recall the information. Answer, "No." The officer is then asked if there is anything that could refresh his recollection, and the officer is well-schooled to answer, "Yes, my notebook." That response sparks the next step in the dance. The officer must describe how the notebook was created and why it is an accurate and reliable record of what the officer observed or heard. If that hurdle is scaled, the next instruction is, "Officer, please silently read the relevant information from your notebook, and when you are done, put your notebook away." The officer appears to make an intense examination of his notes, then pockets his notebook. "Officer, has your recollection been refreshed?"

The answer is always "Yes."

"Now, officer, please answer my question." The officer's answer is not hearsay because he is not reading directly from his notebook but is ostensibly testifying from memory.

The British dispense with this unnecessary and tedious tango. Immediately after the officer provides his name, rank, and a summary of his duties, the barrister asks the officer to produce his notebook. Then there are the routine questions that establish the notebook's accuracy and reliability. Once that formality is over, the officer can refresh his recollection using his notebook or even read passages from it without triggering a "Hearsay" objection.

The primary goal of Detective Wilson's testimony was to explain to the jury how he obtained the alleged blackmail note from the victim, Hobart, and then describe how the analysis of the handwriting and the fingerprint on the note determined that the author of the note was our defendant, James. Since this evidence was indisputable and confirmed by our client, we had no intention of challenging it. The kernel of our defense was that James did not "know" what he did was "unlawful."

Our line of defense was helped by James's refusal to talk with the police after he was detained. In America, the standard drill for interrogating a suspect is to advise them of their right to remain silent and the right to an attorney, and then employ every stratagem to convince them they really don't need one. A common tactic is to tell the suspect that asking for a lawyer only increases the suspicion that already surrounds him. "If you are telling the truth, why do you need a lawyer?"

British criminal procedure requires the police to inform the suspect of their right to remain silent and the right to talk with a solicitor. But then the following phrase lets the suspect know that there are consequences for insisting on silence.

"You should be aware that not mentioning something during questioning could harm your defense if you later rely on it in court."

If the suspect has evidence of innocence, such as an alibi, but withholds it from the police and later produces an alibi witness during the trial, the defendant can be accused of deceiving the police and wasting the jury's and the court's time. "If you had told the police about the alibi witness during your initial interview, no charges would have been brought, and we would not be in court today." The possibility of this scenario playing out in court is not obvious from the police caution's legal jargon. It is a potential trap for the unwary. The British criminal justice system, however, compensates for this reduction of the right to keep silent with a counterbalancing provision. Before a suspect decides whether to talk to the police, he is provided ready access to a "duty solicitor," a lawyer who, like an obstetrician, is on call, prepared to go to the police station at any time, day or night, to advise a person who has been detained by the police. The solicitor will explain the consequences of talking or not talking with the police, and the solicitor will recommend what action to take. As a usual rule of thumb, if the solicitor believes talking with the police will not help the suspect's situation, the solicitor will counsel, "Just say no."

If the solicitor advises speaking to the police, he will sit in on the interview to ensure the questions are fair and limited to the specific crime under investigation. The presence of the solicitor also prevents the police from lying to a suspect, like telling a suspect they failed a lie detector test when the suspect passed it with flying colors. As an American lawyer, I was embarrassed to tell my British colleagues that in the U.S., the police can lie to a suspect during an interrogation.

Fortunately, James was advised by his duty solicitor not to speak to the police and to refuse to answer every question posed by the detective, and verbally assert his right to remain silent. The inability of Detective Wilson to probe into James's state of mind when he sent the note to Hobart was crucial to our defense that James did not "know" what he was doing was unlawful. If James did try to explain to Detective Wilson that he did not think the demand for compensation was unlawful, he would open himself up to questions like, "I know you do not think what you did was unlawful in the eyes of the law, but did you think it was wrong?" Or, "Have you watched crime shows on the Telly involving black-mail cases?" Anything James would say could and would be spun to undermine his claim that he did not know his actions were unlawful.

Detective Wilson did interview Mr. Hobart and testified that he received the alleged blackmail note from Mr. Hobart. The hearsay rule prevented Wilson from telling the jury anything Mr. Hobart said during his interview.

Giles may have been seriously ill and weak, but he retained his sense of humor. He said, "David, why don't you handle the cross-examination of Officer Wilson," knowing the only words that would issue from my mouth were, "No questions, My Lord."

I imagine Wesley would have preferred not to call Calvin Hobart to the stand, but he was the only witness who could tell the jury why James would think he had a basis for attempting to blackmail him. Wesley needed to establish that there was a connection between James and Hobart—one that was regarded as highly improper, or a crime, and something Hobart did not want to be a topic for community gossip. Of course, Hobart testifying about his connection to James would open the door to a cross-examination that would make it clear to the jury that Hobart was a vile pedophile.

Regrettably, there was a pretrial application by Wesley, which was granted by His Lordship. Judge Barth's ruling limited our ability to question Hobart about how his relationship with James began and the graphic details of how he used James as his underage prostitute for many years. As an advocate, Giles was disappointed with the judicially imposed guardrails that restricted his ability to cast Hobart as a downright despicable villain. As a student of criminal law, however, Giles told me the ruling was probably correct. The character of the person being blackmailed is irrelevant. Trying to extort money from Satan himself, threatening to reveal his evil deeds, would still be black-mail. In fact, the more appallingly people behave, the more attractive they are as targets for blackmail. Hobart may have deserved to be blackmailed, but that did not make James any less guilty of the crime.

The sting from His Lordship's ruling was mitigated by the instruction he intended to give to the jury on how they should weigh Hobart's testimony. Judge Barth told us he would give the jury the following instruction:

"Ladies and Gentlemen of the jury, the Crown has called Calvin Hobart as a witness for the prosecution. However, the Crown is not vouching for the truthfulness of Mr. Hobart's testi-mony, which means the Crown is not asserting that any of the facts asserted by Mr. Hobart are true. Those facts may or may not be true; that is for you, the jury, to determine, and to weigh the relevance of Mr. Hobart's testimony accordingly."

I was doubtful if the jurors would fully grasp the significance of Judge Barth's instruction. Still, at the very least, the jurors knew they should take Hobart's testimony with more than a teaspoon of salt.

Before Wesley called Hobart to the stand, he made a preemptive strike. He told the jury that, as a representative of the Crown, he was not vouching for the truthfulness of Mr. Hobart and that Judge Barth would be instructing them on how to assess the credibility of Mr. Hobart. As Hobart was making his way to the witness box, I whispered to Wesley, "Kudos to you, that was a bit of first-rate lawyering." Wesley was trying to make lemonade out of a very sour lemon. He wanted to reinforce his hoped-for image of being the honest guide who was willing to acknowledge the weaknesses in his case and dispel any suggestion that Judge Barth had compelled him to admit that Hobart's testimony was not necessarily trustworthy.

When Hobart entered the witness box, Judge Barth gave his instructions to the jury. Wesley then continued to demonstrate his skills as an advocate by designing his questions to Hobart in a way that would distance himself from any inference that he was presenting Hobart as a truth-teller. His first substantive question was, "Please tell the jury, Mr. Hobart, about how you became acquainted with James Patterson and how your relationship evolved?" Ordinarily, we would have objected to that question as "Calling for a narrative."

The Rules of Evidence typically require a specific question to be followed by a specific answer, giving opposing counsel the chance to object. But asking a witness, "Tell the jury what you know about this case," means that any objection comes only after the jury has already heard the objectionable evidence. Opposing counsel would then have to resort to the ludicrous request that the judge instruct the jury to disregard and forget what they had just heard. "Ladies and gentlemen, ignore the skunk which counsel had just thrown into the jury box."

Giles did not object to Wesley's narrative question. Since His Lordship had already inferred that Hobart's testimony could not be fully trusted, we were content to let Hobart natter on. We were confident Hobart's version of events would be filled with so many blatant lies that Giles would eviscerate him during cross-examination.

Hobart tried to spin a yarn about how James was a neighborhood boy he met when James was twelve. Hobart said he felt sorry for James because he did not have a father at home, and James seemed adrift, perhaps headed for trouble. Hobart would chat with James from time to time, and he learned they both enjoyed playing arcade games. So, they began visiting arcade palaces about three times a week for several hours at a time. Hobart would purchase £30 of tokens that James would use to play the games. He also learned that James enjoyed watching horror, action, and crime movies. Sometimes in the evening, Hobart and James would watch films like "Blood Games," which depicts the plight of an all-girls baseball team stranded on a lonely road in Louisiana bayou country. Sometimes, when the movie ran late, James would spend the night in Hobart's guest bedroom. Hobart insisted James's mother would always give permission for James to stay. Hobart was adamant that he had never molested James or had sex with him.

Hobart went on, without any prompting by Wesley, to tell the jury that when James was 17 years old, he had lost interest in arcade games and horror films and that he was more attracted to girls. Hobart claimed James drifted away and that he rarely saw James except to wave to him occasionally. That was why he was so shocked when Jason handed him the blackmail note. He concluded by saying that he had immediately gone to the police to report James's attempted blackmail and gave Detective Sergeant Wilson the note.

It was Giles's opportunity to cross-examine Hobart, but he was so weak that he asked Judge Barth's permission to remain seated in his chair and not stand at the podium. As physically drained as he was, Giles could not miss the chance to crush such a vulnerable witness. Ordinarily, Giles would forgo launching a full-scale, take-no-prisoners assault on a witness, especially a victim of a crime. Giles would not want to risk that some members of the jury might feel sorry for the witness and think he was unnecessarily cruel. He would lose credibility. There was no such risk with Calvin Hobart. Notwithstanding Hobart's innocent description of his relationship with James, all the evidence confirmed Hobart was a pedophile who had begun molesting James when he was twelve years old.

Although Giles's legs were weak, his mind was firing on all cylinders. His strategy was to take Hobart through a litany of occasions when he and James were together, which supplied a mass of chronological circumstantial evidence confirming that Hobart was having sexual relations with James. Giles only asked about facts that Hobart could not deny. After getting Hobart's affirmative answer, he would ask the same question. "Was it then you began having sexual relations with James?" Of course, Hobart had to repeat his direct testimony that he never had sexual relations with James. It soon became clear to everyone in the courtroom that his denials were lies. Throughout Giles's string of questions, Hobart was forced to repeat his lies. Giles's cross-examination lasted over an hour and resembled the Chinese water torture, where cold water is slowly dripped onto the forehead of a person for a prolonged period, causing acute anxiety as the victim tries to anticipate the next drip. I am not able to recall all of Giles's cross-examination; I do remember several especially tough questions.

"Mr. Hobart, isn't it true that when James spent the night with you in June of 1990, he slept in your bedroom?"

"Yes, but I had twin beds."

"Was it then, you began having sexual relations with James?"

"I never had sex with James."

"Mr. Hobart, isn't it true that in 1991, you and James spent a weekend in Marne-la-Vallée, France, visiting Disneyland Paris?"

"Yes."

"You stayed at the Disneyland Hotel?"

"Yes."

"You shared a king-sized bed."

"Yes, but it was the only room available."

"Did you have sex with James then?"

"No, I never had sexual relations with James."

Cross-examiners tingle with excitement when a witness gives the "Yes, but" answer. It makes the witness look like a weasel. The answer also opens new lines of inquiry, such as Giles being able to introduce a sworn affidavit from the management of the Disneyland Hotel stating that, during the weekend in question, many rooms with two double beds were available.

Giles dissected Hobart with his cross-examination. If it had been purely a contest of likability between Hobart and James, the case would have ended with Giles's last question. Regrettably, Judge Barth had said he would instruct the jury that neither Hobart's character nor James Patterson's character was at issue in the case. The only issue was whether James, knowing his actions were unlawful, demanded money from Hobart in exchange for silence. I teased Giles that the irony was his success in painting Hobart as a despicable pedophile might actually have strengthened the Crown's case against James. I said that if I were representing the Crown, I would agree that Hobart was indeed loathsome and then argue his very vileness made him a tempting target for blackmail, a target James could not resist. Giles, as usual, got the last word. "Luckily, Wesley is not as smart as you are."

We knew that James's state of mind was the critical issue in our defense. Did James know his demand note was really blackmail and unlawful? Or, as we maintained, did he genuinely believe he was only asking to be compensated for the harm Hobart did to him? The nature of our defense compelled us to do what criminal defense lawyers loathe doing: putting the defendant on the witness stand. James would have to convince the jury that his note was only meant to seek compensation from Hobart, which, in James's mind, was not unlawful. As I had seen in our previous trials, the British rule, which limited a barrister's ability to prepare a witness, added an element of extra risk to having James testify.

That potential risk increased when Jackie Simpson, the barrister for James's codefendant, informed us that if we did put James in the witness box, she intended to cross-examine him, as was her right. Giles was furious. He pointed out to Simpson that by cross-examining James, she would be playing straight into the prosecution's hands, getting co-defendants to point fingers at each other. I tried to explain in a more measured tone how James and Jason's cases were so closely tied together that weakening James's defense would only weaken her own defense of Jason. In fact, if James were convicted, Jason would go down too. Giles resorted to more bullying tactics by saying Jackie would be flirting with malpractice if she challenged James's testimony. Simpson was not to be bullied. She stormed out of the conference room, saying that she did not take instructions from Giles, only from her client.

Giles was not deterred. He told me that if Simpson would not listen to reason, perhaps she would listen to her client. I had no idea how he could make that happen, since he was forbidden to talk to Jason without Simpson's approval. Giles then did something I thought was borderline unethical. He explained the situation to James and told him how bad it would be for his defense if his best friend's barrister cross-examined him when he took the stand. Giles added, "Of course, if Jason instructs his barrister not to cross you, she will probably abide by his request." Giles did not urge James to pass on his seemingly spontaneous comments to Jason, but he was confident James would discuss Giles's advice with his friend.

Giles was right again. Before the trial resumed the next day, Simpson requested an in-chambers meeting with Judge Barth. She had obviously followed the breadcrumbs, and they led directly back to Giles. When Jason had asked Simpson not to cross-examine James because it might hurt their case, she knew that neither James nor Jason would have come to such a conclusion without the behind-the-scenes manipulation by Giles Adams-Smyth.

The meeting with Judge Barth was short. After Simpson described what she thought had happened, Judge Barth did not bother to ask Giles to respond. Judge Barth told us he did not want to get involved in that kind of problem, and it was up to Simpson and Giles to work things out. Giles looked rather smug when he left the judge's chambers.

That afternoon, after the close of the Crown's case, Giles told me that since he was in for a shilling, he might as well be in for a pound. He casually mentioned to James that if a barrister, like Simpson, did not follow their client's advice, the barrister could be sacked. We would not know until the next day, of course, whether Jason would take Giles's not-so-subtle hint and sack Simpson.

Giles told me the night before we were to begin our defense case that, due to his near exhaustion, I would have to make the opening speech and conduct the direct examination of James. The main difficulty for me with the opening defense speech was that Giles had written it. I had never developed an actor's ability to deliver lines written by someone else persuasively. Mercifully, it is not unusual for barristers to read their opening speeches. And since barristers are tethered to their podiums, it does not appear to be a lack of advocacy skill if they occasionally refer to notes lying there. By contrast, in an American courtroom, a lawyer who stays rooted to the podium instead of moving about the well of the court is seen as lacking confidence. When I tried a case, it was vital for me to have the ability to move closer to the jury or further away, all the while adjusting my tone and volume to emphasize important points and foster intimacy with the jurors. I was sure the effect of my opening speech would be much diminished if I stopped every few moments to read my notes from the yellow notepad I held in my hand.

I was gratified that I gave Giles's speech without embarrassing myself. I described to the jury the kind of pedophilic relationship Hobart had created with James from the time James was twelve years old. A relationship that continued for five years. I told them that James would explain how Hobart's predatory behavior had caused him physical and emotional trauma. Finally, I indicated that James would characterize his note to Hobart, not as a black-mail threat, but as an unsophisticated attempt to obtain compensation from Hobart for the personal harm he had caused James.

James was our only witness. Everything depended on his testimony and his ability to persuade the jury that he was no black-mailer. Giles provided me with a broad outline of his plan for the direct examination of James. Since its structure was chronological, the task was simpler. I began by asking James to describe his initial contact with Hobart when he was twelve years old and how Hobart groomed him. James told the jury that at first. Hobart assumed the role of a friendly uncle. He acted as if they had many interests in common, such as arcade games and horror movies. James said he was often at Hobart's house watching films and eating pizza. The first time there was any sexual activity was the first night James slept at Hobart's house. The only bed available for James was one of the two beds in Hobart's bedroom. While James was undressing, Hobart masturbated in front of him. James admitted he was not disturbed by Hobart's action and did not object when Hobart asked him to masturbate while Hobart watched.

From that point on, the sexual aspect of James and Hobart's relationship became much more intimate. I did not ask James to provide graphic details of what happened between him and Hobart, but he did testify to how they engaged in sexual acts at least twice a week. To reinforce Giles's cross-examination of Hobart about the trip to Disneyland Paris, I asked James to confirm they slept in the same bed. I thought it important that James tell the jury about the money and other things Hobart gave him, including additional "fun" money.

Finally, I inquired about the sequence of events leading up to James severing his relationship with Hobart when James was seventeen years old. James then described how he decided to demand £6,000 from Hobart. He turned to the jury and told them that he did not realize at first how damaged he was from Hobart's long exploitation. The first indication was when he started dating girls. They were more than willing to have sex with him, but he could not perform. Some of the girls laughed at him and called him a poof. James said he and Jason talked about what Hobart had done to him, and they decided Hobart should pay for his messed-up life. James said the £6,000 was a guesstimate. James then drafted the note, and Jason delivered it.

All these questions were the build-up to the next and final question I would ask.

"James, if Clavin Hobart had given you £6,000, would you have been satisfied?"

James's answer was a harpoon in my chest.

"No, the £6,000 was only the beginning, and I would take from Hobart all I could get."

James had just admitted to adopting the classic modus operandi of the blackmailer: accept the first payment, wait a while to let the victim think they are home free, then ask for another installment. If the blackmailer does not get too greedy, the victim may supply a steady source of income for years. I glanced at the prosecutor, who could not suppress a smile. Wesley's challenge of trying to prove James knew his actions were unlawful had vanished.

I concluded James was not so naïve as he was extraordinarily stupid. Had he been sleeping during my opening speech when I laid out our defense—that James was only seeking just compensation for the damage Hobart had caused, and that he would have been content once he received the money? Surely, James was smart enough to know how to answer the critical question. Once again, I lamented our inability under British criminal procedure to prep our witnesses.

I was at a loss for what to do, other than to pretend James's answer hadn't sunk his defense. I sat down, hoping the jury might somehow miss the obvious.

Things got worse. As Giles predicted, Wesley did not miss the flaw in our "just seeking compensation" defense. Wesley got James to admit that from time to time he asked Hobart for spending money, sometimes as much as £50. James refused to agree with Wesley's description of the requests as demands. Nevertheless, James's appeals for money intimated that he knew he had power over Hobart and demonstrated that he did not hesitate to use that power to get cash, which was more extortion than compensation. Wesley could argue that the demand for £6,000 was just more of the same—blackmail.

The final nail in what I regarded as our client's coffin was driven in by Barrister Simpson. She was clearly not cowed by Giles's bullying, and she had not been sacked by Jason. The first set of questions Simpson asked James were clever and careful questions that aligned with the nature of our defense strategy. She could use leading questions, so she asked: "Isn't it true, Mr. Patterson, that your intent was to seek compensation from Mr. Hobart and that Jason was helping you out as a friend?" The easing of the tension in my stomach lasted only a moment because the next question was: "Isn't it also true that Jason was to receive £1000 for his help?" With one question, Simpson managed to blast a hole below the waterline of both of our cases. She had linked Jason to a blackmail scheme in which he was one of the intended beneficiaries. She also helped the Crown's case to prove that James knew his demand for money was unlawful. James had to pay Jason for the risk he was taking. Therefore, James and Jason were co-conspirators.

Not content with the damage she had already done to both our defense and her own client's defense, Simpson attempted to paint James as a liar. James admitted he had lied to Jason's mother about Jason's involvement in his attempt to get money from

Hobart. James told his mom not to worry; Jason was not involved, and he would assume total responsibility for his actions. Giles whispered just loud enough for Simpson to hear, "She is a prater." I had to agree: she was an idiot.

At the end of the day, Giles assigned me the unhappy task of meeting with James and apprising him of the state of the case. I did not mince my words. I told him when he came to court on Monday morning that he should have packed his toothbrush and his undies because he would be led from the dock directly to the cells. James looked shocked, which convinced me beyond a shadow of a doubt that our client was extraordinarily dense. Rather than yell, I lowered my voice a notch, moved in closer to James, and in a stage whisper, I said, "You gave the classic black-mailer's line—you would squeeze every penny you could from Hobart. You made it patently clear to the jury you were black-mailing Hobart." I did not feel uncomfortable about my harsh-ness. I believed James was guilty.

On Monday morning, Giles must have been drawing on his last reservoir of strength. His blue eyes had regained their sparkle. He made his confident entrance into the courtroom after the judge and the jury were already seated. He was clutching in his left hand a bunch of what appeared to be pamphlets. Giles performed his obligatory bow to Judge Barth and apologized for being late. He explained he had stopped at the kiosk in the courthouse atrium, which was displaying dozens of public service pamphlets, and now he was prepared to make his closing address to the jury. His final speech revealed Giles at his finest. He constructed his speech on the fly, using the Social Services brochures as his props. From his first words, it was clear he was jettisoning our "only seeking compensation" defense. "Ladies and Gentlemen of the jury, we as a community, and especially James's mother, have failed James Patterson. We failed to protect him from a vile pedophile." Giles described how the Social Services pamphlets described multiple ways to safeguard children like James. Giles read from one pamphlet. "Sexual abuse thrives in secrecy. Children find it very difficult to tell anyone that they are being abused. Talking to and listening to your child, your student, and your neighbor's child is the best prevention. Monitor the children for signs that they are not happy. Be alert to the warning signs that they may be being abused. Be aware of who is paying attention to the children and who their friends are. Don't ignore any unease you feel about older people showing interest in a particular child."

Giles told the jury these warning signs were ignored by James's mother, his teachers, the visiting social worker, and his neighbors. Now, he said, because we failed to protect James, we want to punish him by putting him in a prison where he is in danger of being sexually abused again. James is there in the dock instead of the real criminal who abused him.

It dawned on me that Giles was attempting to make a case for jury nullification. This questionable advocacy tactic is detested by judges everywhere, who consider it a rejection of the rule of law. Jury nullification occurs when it is clear beyond a reasonable doubt that the accused is guilty, yet the jury nevertheless returns a verdict of not guilty. The jury may have concluded the defendant committed the offense, but did not believe the defendant deserved punishment for it; the possible sentences ordered by the judge would be excessive. The jury has no say in the punishment the judge imposes, so the jury's only option to achieve what it believes is a just result is to find the defendant not guilty. The jury ignores the judge's instruction that they are not to consider possible sentences in reaching their verdict, only whether they are sure the defendant committed the offense. It is a slap in the face of the judicial system, and the judge is powerless to overturn a jury's not-guilty verdict.

Giles was not so subtly urging the jury to acquit James

because, between Hobart and James, James was the more innocent of the two. James only resorted to his scheme of extracting money from Hobart to obtain some financial compensation for the harm he had suffered. Whereas Hobart was a dangerous pedophile.

While Giles was speaking, I kept glancing up at Judge Barth to see when he would stop Giles from making an improper final argument for jury nullification. Was Judge Barth nodding off, or was he feeling sorry for him, knowing it was probably the last time Giles would appear in court, and was maybe reluctant to interrupt his final, final speech?

Finally, Judge Barth said, "Mr. Adams-Smyth, you know the argument you are making is improper, and I will be instructing the jury not to consider possible sentences I may impose when assessing the guilt or innocence of the defendant."

Giles apologized to Judge Barth and, without missing a beat, transitioned to our original line of defense. He explained to the jury that James was so traumatized by what Hobart had done to him that he wrongly believed the note demanding money from Hobart was a legitimate way to obtain just compensation. "James did not intend to be a blackmailer." He then reminded the jury of James's testimony about whether he would be satisfied with the £6,000. I quickly raised my pencil, our signal for Giles to stop and consult me. I suspected he was having one of his mental lapses. Why would he want to remind the jury of James's most incriminating testimony? James had flaunted the classic blackmailer's mindset and said, "I would take from Hobart all I can get."

Giles ignored my waving pencil and calmly repeated James's most damning statement, punctuated by holding up two fingers in each hand to emphasize to the jury it was a direct quote. "No, the £6,000 was only the beginning, and I would take from Hobart all I could get." Giles's comments were a bold attempt to turn a very bitter lemon into lemonade. Giles began by describing James as a confused, emotionally damaged, not very bright teenager who muddled the difference between extorting money and seeking money as a recompense for the harm he had suffered. Giles said James's testimony on the stand showed two things: his honesty and that he lacks the criminal mentality of a blackmailer.

Giles argued, "No blackmailer would ever testify the way James did, boasting he would continue to squeeze the victim for more and more money. In brief, ladies and gentlemen of the jury, James did not know what he was doing and was clueless as to whether his actions were unlawful or not."

The penny dropped for me, and I grasped Giles's strategy. It was his Quixotic attempt to show James did not know the unlawfulness of what he and Jason were doing. It was window dressing for Judge Barth. Giles was attempting to camouflage his appeal for jury nullification. Giles hoped the jurors just could not bring themselves to send James to prison.

Everyone in the courtroom, except perhaps the jury, knew that Giles was attempting to persuade the jury to act contrary to the law and ignore Judge Barth's instruction. Judge Barth attempted to keep the jury on the right track by instructing them that, in deciding the guilt or innocence of James and Jason, they were not to consider the possible sentences he might impose, nor were they to consider the character of Mr. Hobart. For good measure, Judge Barth added, "No matter how despicable you think Mr. Hobart is, he can still be a victim under the law even if the person trying to extort money from him is Prince Charming himself."

Other than that instruction to the jury, Judge Barth delivered a relatively unbiased summing up of the evidence. However, it seemed clear to Giles and me that the judge believed James and Jason were guilty of blackmail. When the jury returned two hours later, however, they disagreed. They found both James and Jason not guilty. Giles had pulled off a miracle with his final speech.

My stomach was performing backflips, but Giles and I donned our blasé expressions as if the verdict were nothing more than what we expected.

Giles could not resist needling Judge Barth before the jury was excused. "My Lord, I request that costs be awarded to the defendant." The awarding of costs to a defendant who had been found not guilty is a splendid British practice and was not available anywhere in America. An accused person can incur many thousands of pounds of expenses to secure exoneration—money they can never recover. In England, the judge has the discretion to reimburse defendants their costs when they are acquitted of the charges. Judge Barth was not pleased with Giles's request. Judge Barth leaned forward and looked over the top of his glasses and said, "Mr. Adams-Smyth, you should count yourself fortunate to have won an acquittal in this case. Do not push your luck. The defendants brought this on themselves. No costs."

Sadly, the blackmail case was the last Giles and I would try together. In fact, it turned out to be the last case Giles would ever try. I had hoped that his triumph would allow him to leave the advocacy stage happy. He had managed to win what James's solicitor thought was an impossible case—one he had wanted James to plead guilty to.

Looking back, I had the satisfaction of realizing that of all the cases Giles and I tried, whether prosecuting or defending, we never lost. Somehow, we had forged a team made up of opposite personalities.

TWENTY-FOUR

Saying Good-By

I did not see Giles for several days. During that time, he was
admitted to Royal Hampshire County Hospital when his liver
stopped filtering out the toxins in his body. Before I visited him, I
tried to prepare myself for what I would encounter, determined
not to let shock or pity show on my face. I knew if Giles were
conscious, such behavior would only annoy him. I tried to plan
our meeting as a lawyer would plan a final speech to a jury. I
created a hoped-for scenario in my mind and then devised tactics
to make that scene happen. I wanted to create an atmosphere of
camaraderie, similar to the one we had over the past year. The
challenge was how to avoid discussing his terminal condition
while maintaining an upbeat conversation.

Dana told me Giles had been diagnosed with hepatic
encephalopathy. His liver had ceased to function and was no
longer filtering neurotoxins from his blood, causing
encephalopathy that would ultimately result in a coma, permanent brain damage, and death. A strictly temporary treatment was
hooking him up to a diachysis machine that removes the toxins
from the blood and then recirculates the toxin-free blood back
into his body. Unlike kidney dialysis treatment, however, which
requires one or two dialysis sessions a week, Giles could not live

beyond a few hours without being connected to the diachysis device. Dana also forewarned me that Giles was very jaundiced and seeing him in that condition might come as a bit of a shock.

I knew I had to come on strong, on the attack, like nothing had changed. Giles would detect any hint of pity, sympathy, or regret. I planned to sprinkle our conversation with humor and the good-natured teasing that was the hallmark of our time together. I thought about calling him a milksop for delegating me to give our client the bad news in the blackmail case, telling James he was probably going to prison. As soon as I entered the room, though, I saw another approach for keeping the dialogue light. I told him he looked like a yellow canary caught in a spider's web. The diachysis machine must have been doing its work. Giles was mentally sharp and quickly responded, "Like the canary you looked like you had swallowed when James confessed during your direct examination that he planned to squeeze every pound he could out of Hobart?"

Game-on! I told him I was pleased to see his perfectly coiffed hair, with that silly bang drooping over his forehead, but it was sad that the oxygen tubes in his nose would not let him perform his head flip. He agreed, "Sadly, David, that is true, but there are compensations. Every half-hour, an attractive nurse comes in to comb my hair."

After the opening sallies, we began to reminisce about our cases and other adventures, including the gastronomical ones. Giles's only allusion to his medical condition was when he quipped, "I probably ate too much foie gras." My response was not meant as repartee; it was driven by my curiosity. "Giles, if you could live your life over, would you do anything differently, like drink less wine and eat less goose liver?"

I thought I knew what he would say and hoped he would say it. Giles did not disappoint. "I would not change a thing." He could not resist some embellishment and quoted the last lines of Shakespeare's Richard III: "I have set my life upon a cast, and I will stand the hazard of the die."

Maintaining the conversation while avoiding the elephant in the room was exhausting for me, if not for Giles. Before leaving, I told him that we were scheduled to fly back to Dayton in three days, but I was considering asking for a leave of absence to remain in Winchester for three more months. Giles's last words to me were, "Go home, David."

Epilogue

I took Giles's last piece of advice and flew out of Heathrow three days later with my family. I never saw or spoke to him again. Less than a week after we left, Giles told his doctor to turn off the diachysis machine.

Acknowledgments

First and foremost, I must thank my wife, Kathy. Without her encouragement this book would never have been written. It was Kathy who suggested that the several hundred pages of journal I kept during two of my sabbaticals in England would be a good basis for a book.

During those sabbaticals, I was taking a deep dive into the British Criminal Justice system and worked closely with barristers trying criminal cases. I was not only given the opportunity to observe trials, but I was able to attend interviews of witnesses and defendants, sit with barristers in the well of the courtroom, and I was often consulted by barristers on trial strategies and tactics. I was also given extensive access to the behind-the-scenes activities of the courts, judges and barristers. So, I would be amiss if I did not acknowledge all the cooperation, support and kindness extended to me by so many judges, barristers, solicitors, bailiffs and ushers of the Western Circuit.

Finally, kudos to the folks at The Book Whisperer whose advice and superb editing was invaluable.

About the Author

Dennis Turner graduated from Georgetown University in 1967, with a degree in History. He received his Juris Doctorate degree from Georgetown University Law School in 1970. Since 1974, he has been a Professor of Law at the University Of Dayton School Of Law. During his tenure at the University of Dayton he has served as Assistant Dean, Acting Dean, Director of the Law Clinic and Director of the Legal Profession Program. The University of Dayton has awarded him its highest award for teaching, The Faculty Teaching Award. He has served as a visiting professor for the University of Notre Dame London Law Program. During two six months sabbaticals he gained extensive experience with the British criminal justice system when he collaborated with British barristers trying criminal cases in England.

Dennis Turner is the author of many law review articles and a law textbook, *Steele v. Kitchener Case File*. For two years, he also wrote a bi-weekly column for the Dayton Daily News entitled, *On the River*. His latest publication is a book of historical fiction entitled, *What Did You do in the War, Sister?*, which told the story of how Catholic nuns in Belgium defied and deceived the Nazis in World War II.

Dennis Turner lives in Dayton, Ohio, with his wife Kathy, and spends summers in Michigan sailing, rowing a scull, playing tennis and Pickleball. They have been married for over 56 years and have three children and three grandsons.

Also by Dennis Turner

What Did You Do In The War, Sister?

An American Yankee in King Alfred's Court

www.ingramcontent.com/pod-product-compliance
Lightning Source LLC
Chambersburg PA
CBHW021027130626
46552CB00005B/1715